Cambrensis Giraldus, Frederick James Furnivall

**The English Conquest of Ireland, A.D. 1166-1185**

Mainly from the Expugnatio hibernica of Giraldus Cambrensis: a parallel text from

1. Ms. Trinity College, Dublin, E.2.31, about 425 A.D. 2. Ms. Rawlinson, B. 490,

Bodleian Library, about 1440 A.D.

Cambrensis Giraldus, Frederick James Furnivall

**The English Conquest of Ireland, A.D. 1166-1185**
*Mainly from the Expugnatio hibernica of Giraldus Cambrensis: a parallel text from 1. Ms.
Trinity College, Dublin, E.2.31, about 425 A.D. 2. Ms. Rawlinson, B. 490, Bodleian Library,
about 1440 A.D.*

ISBN/EAN: 9783337322243

Printed in Europe, USA, Canada, Australia, Japan

Cover: Foto ©ninafisch / pixelio.de

More available books at **www.hansebooks.com**

# The
# English Conquest of Ireland.

### A. D. 1166–1185.

*MAINLY FROM THE 'EXPUGNATIO HIBERNICA'*
*OF GIRALDUS CAMBRENSIS.*

## A Parallel Text

**FROM**

1. MS. Trinity College, Dublin, E. 2. 31, about 1425 A.D.
2. MS. Rawlinson, B. 490, Bodleian Library, about 1440 A.D.

## PART I.  THE TEXT.

EDITED BY

## FREDERICK J. FURNIVALL, M.A.,

TRINITY HALL, CAMBRIDGE, HON. DR. PHIL. BERLIN.

## LONDON:

PUBLISHT FOR THE EARLY ENGLISH TEXT SOCIETY,

BY KEGAN PAUL, TRENCH, TRÜBNER & CO., LIMITED

PATERNOSTER HOUSE, CHARING CROSS ROAD, W.C.

M DCCC XCVI.

*See opposite.* Mr. Thomas Austin sends me some more forms worth notice in the Dublin MS. :—bethwen, between, 10/12 ; bolthenys, boldness, 75/15 ; ather, either, 100/3; ayse, ease, 148/1 ; behoud (? th), behoof, benefit, 112/30 ; culuertnesse, falseness, 126/31 ; cytteyns, citizens, 122/27 ; durr, door, 42/22 ; ense, ends, 80/29 ; fale (fele), many, 74/10 ; fobler, feebler, 68/6 ; forume, form, 39/12 ; ? heuedes (as in note), 14/17 ; hym þriddesum, Greek αὐτος τρίτος, 14/1, 32/20 ; I-shwerne, sworn, 24/26 ; mich yuell, leprosy (comp. great pox), 32/7 ; neyght, nigh, 74/16 ; pynsynge (pinching), affliction, 88/6 ; rechest, reckest, 108/9 ; ruthlynge, ? rattling, 16/13 ; schavnge, change, 51/6 ; senne, synod, 120/15 ; senthe (? senthe), seventh, 58/30 ; scnfte, 59/30; soine, soon, 60/11 ; soldrys, shoulders, 89/11 ; sortely, shortly, 149/22 ; shechynge, seeking, 147/19.

# FOREWORDS.

THE first manuscript of this interesting story of "oure knyghten gestes yn Irlnnde" (92/15), and of Henry II's Conquest of our sister Isle, was sent over to me from the Library of Trinity College, Dublin, by Dr. John K. Ingram, to be copied, printed, and edited by him for the Early English Text Society. He hoped to do his work at it during his July–September holiday (1893) in Scotland, on Loch Lomond, I having read his proofs with the MS. for him. But illness prevented him; and so I (as the Society's man-of-all-work) had to take the book up. Both the story told—mainly, though freely, from the *Expugnacio Hibernica* of Giraldus Cambrensis,—and the forms of the words, interested me. For the copier of the englisht text has often slipt into his own Irish dialect, specially in the use of *d* and *t* for *th*, and has written *dynge*[1] and *tynge*[2] for *thing*; *drogh*[3] and *trogh*[4] for *through*; *day* for *they*[5]; *idrow* (18/1) for *thrown*; *tanked* for *thanked* (14/19); *tynke* for *think* (6/26); *toght* for *thought* (16/25, 18/7); *tough* (as once in *The Three King's Sons*) for *though* (22/14); &c. At the same time he has used *th* for *t* and *d*: *thedynge* (10/7) and *tythynge* (6/15) for *tidings*; *onther* (6/31) for *under*; *reut* (8/1) for *ruth*; *bethwen* (10/12) for *between*; *thwey* (12/35) for *two*; *herth* (2/8, 13, 22/28) for *heart*; *ibansheth* (24/1) for *banisht*; *Iendeth* (22/16) for *ended*; *smyth* (24/12) for *smile*, &c. The copier has other peculiarities, both in the use of other consonants and vowels[6], which the reader will note as he goes along, and which will be collected for him in the Introduction by Dr. Douglas Bruce, of the Ladies College at Bryn Mawr, Philadelphia, that will form

[1] 88/27; 134/13.    [2] 24/14; 28/8; (no)tynge 8/12; 16/5; 20/9; &c. [3] 14/8.    [4] 22/6, 7; 26/1, &c.    [5] 10/19; 12/21; 24/10, 11. [6] *Both har'* 128/20 doesn't at first look like *But ere*: still, you soon get accustomed to the scribe's little weaknesses. *Harym*, harm, is in the Rawlinson MS. 143/12: cp. *sarrif* serve, in Misyn. E. E. T. Soc. The Southern infinitive in -*y* or -*ye* occurs in both MSS. 58/27, &c. For other odd spellings, see opposite.

Part II. of this book, when complete, and will no doubt be finisht in 1894, or '95.

As it was now and then hard to understand the Dublin text, and one nearer the standard tongue turnd up in the Rawlinson MS. B. 490—the MS. that contains one of Mr. Steele's text of the prose *Secreta*—I got Mrs. Parker to copy this Bodleian MS.[1], and the Clarendon Press to set it opposite the Dublin one. The comparison of the two versions is full of interesting points, as the Rawlinson is generally less archaic than the Dublin[2], while each helps to fill up the other's occasional leavings-out. There is at least one other MS. of the *Conquest*, the later one in Trinity College, Dublin, F. 4. 4, which is said to be a 16th century transcript of E. 2. 31. From it, an extract is given below, pp. xiv–xvi as a specimen. Doubtless, other MSS. of the text exist elsewhere. Luckily for us, the late Rev. Jas. F. Dimock re-edited the *Expugnatio Hibernica* in vol. v. (1867) *Giraldi Cambrensis Opera* in the Rolls Series of *Chronicles and Memorials*; and his notes, dates, and Preface have been of the greatest use to me. He says (p. xxix) that there are two editions, and perhaps a third, of the *Expugnacio*: (1) that in an early 13th century MS. at Lambeth, No. 371, "probably penned during Giraldus's lifetime" (p. xxxi), and in (R.) and (B.), MSS. Bibl. Reg. 13 B. viii in the British Museum, and Rawlinson B. 188 in the Bodleian. In treating the two latter MSS. as of the first cast of the work, Mr. Dimock neglects the marginal additions of the Royal MS. These additions make (2) the second version of the *Expugnacio* (pp. xxxii, xxxiv), shown in (R.), and MS. Ff. 1. 27, in the University Library, Cambridge, in which "there is one whole chapter, (also in our English, p. 38–40 below) the eighteenth of the first book—giving the account of the synod at Armagh in 1170, of which no other mention is known besides this,

---

[1] Mr. George Parker has collated the proofs with the MS. Mr. Thomas Austin has made the Glossary and Indexes to both Texts. Dr. Ingram wrote the English side-notes to the even pages 10–32, tho I've alterd 2 or 3 of em.

[2] I suppose the first englishing now represented by the Dublin MS. was made in the 14th century.

in this chapter of Giraldus—which is not in Lambeth 371,
but is in Bibl. Reg. 13 B. viii and Rawlinson B. 188."

We now come to the MS. of most interest to us, Harleian 177,
for in it only (as I gather from Mr. Dimock's note 3, p. 236)
is the original of one of our English bits on pp. 16, 18 below :—

| Trin. Coll. Dublin, E. 2. 31. | Harl. 117, lf. 14, bk. 15. |
|---|---|
| A wonder was of that fanta-syo : A-morowe, whan it was day, the place ther this folk iseyo smyten vpon ham, the wedes and the grase that stoden al euen vpright, thay lay alle idrow adouno, and icast to grond. | Mirum *autem* fantasmate tali, quod *in* crastino die clarescente, *in* loco ubi uidebatur exercitus ille *in* ipsos irruisso, herbe & vrtice, que prius alte fuerant, & erecte, solotenus prostrate iacebant, & complauate. |

For this, the other MSS., R. and B., have "primus hic
miles, qui in hac insula niso mansueto et domesticato Nisi
filiam infestavit."

On this Harleian 177, Mr. Dimock says, at p. xxxv of his
Preface :

(it) "furnishes a copy of the *Expugnatio* which, so far as it
goes,—it has many and large omissions—generally agrees closely
with the text of this second edition. . . . The omissions are more
especially of the extraneous matter, not relating to Ireland ; but
there is much curtailing also of Irish matter, when not directly
historical. In the descriptions of the heroes, for instance, much
often is left out ; and in the orations which Giraldus puts into
their mouths, still more. The compiler of it never condenses, but
simply omits. In an oration . . . he will retain two or three
sentences of the beginning, and two or three more of the end, with
perhaps another or two out of the middle, if not very much less
than all this, word for word as in the complete oration, without
much care about connection or sense . . . it certainly is only an
abbreviation, such as I describe it."

This is just the case with our English text[1], though here
and there it has bits not in Harl. 177. As to that MS.,
Mr. Dimock continues, pp. xxxv-vi :

"It generally agrees closely, as I have said, with the second

[1] It stops at chapter 34 of Book II (75 of our pages go to 171 of the Rolls
*Giraldus*).

edition, as in (R.) and (F.); but it exhibits a somewhat more advanced text. For instance, the word *Stadia* of (L)ambeth MS. occurs only twice instead of four times, out of eight as in (R)awlinson MS.; and instead of *Arcarii* always, as in the early manuscripts, it has the *Satellites equestres* of the later ones, in about half the instances where the words occur. And, moreover, in a few instances, it has a word or two that are not in the early manuscripts, but are in the later ones.

This manuscript has no note whatever as to its history; but it, or its original perhaps, would seem to have been written by one of the English settlers in Ireland, as it attempts occasionally, instead of Giraldus's Latin of all the other manuscripts, to give an English rendering of the Irish names. Thus, instead of *Murchardi filius*, or *Dermitius*, or *Murchardides*, it has 'Macmorthit' or 'Macmorhith'; instead of *Ororicius*, 'Oroch.' In one instance the writer appears to make a blunder in his Englishing: he renders *Otuelhelis* 'Oneyl' instead of O'Toole. . . . It is not the work of a very correct scribe."

As a sample of the cutting-down, by Harl. 177, of Giraldus's descriptions of men, take the most trenchant instance, that of Henry II. In the Rolls edition, this description takes nearly six big octavo pages, *Op.* v. 301–6, the whole of Chapter 46, Book I. Leaving out the first page, Harl. 177 and the englisher start with the second, p. 302:

*Expugn. Hibern.* lib. i. cap. xlvi.
Harl. MS. 177, lf. 44, bk. 45.
**Descripsio anglor*um* regis**
**Henrici secu*n*di.**

E rat *igitur* anglor*um* rex, henr*icus* secundus, uir sub-ruffus, cesius ; amplo capite & rotundo; oc*u*lis glausis; ad iram toruis, & rubore suffus*is*; facie ignea; uoce quassa; collo ab hum*er*is aliq*u*antulum demisso; pect*ore* quadrato; brachiis ualidis ; corp*ore* carnoso; Et nature magis, qu*am* gule

Dubl. MS. E. 2. 31.
Page 88 below.

T he kynge henry the othe*r*, was a ma*n* saunrede, roune heed, & round grey eghe*n*; roghly lokynge, & rede yn wreth; vysage rede bernynge, grete speche, neke somdel logh of þe sholdres, brest thyk, armes

uicio, citra timorem [*read* tumorem] enormem & torporem omnem; moderata quadam immoderancia uentre peramplo. Erat *enim* cibo potu*que* mo-destu*s* ac sobrius, & p*ar*simonie quo-ad principi licuit, p*er omniu*datu*s*.

[*Here a page and a quarter of the full text, Op.* v. 302–3, *is left out by Harl.* 177, *though our englisher gives a little of it* [1].]

Vrgentibu*s* incomodis, nemo benignior: resumpta securitate, nemo rigidior. Acer i*n* [in]-domitos; clemens i*n* subactos; Duru*s* i*n* domesticos; diffusus i*n* extraneos; largu*s* i*n* publico; parcu*s* i*n* priuato.

[1] Et ut hanc naturae injuriam iudustria reprimeret ac mitigaret .... immoderata corpus vexatione torquebat .... sibi nec pacem ullam nec requiem indulgebat. Venationi namque trans modestiam deditus, summo diluculo equo cursore transvectus, nunc saltus lustrans, nunc silvas penetrans, nunc montium juga transcendens, dies ducebat inquietos: vespere vero domi receptum, vel ante coenam vel post, rarissime sedentem conspexeris. Post tantas namque fatigationes, totam statione continua curiam lassare consueverat.

staluarthe, of flesshy body; &, more of kynde than of glotony, grete of wombe; for he was, as to prynce belongeth, [of] mete, & of drynke ful meen & for-berynge; ....

Whan any vnhappes hym be-felle, noman mcker; efte whan he was yn sckernesse, no man sterner͛. Suert ayeyn the bold, meke wyth ham that werenͩ vnder͛ y-broght, hard amonge hys owne, & priuely large amonge vnkouth.

&, for to a-quenche that gretnesse, he put hymself to ful mych trauaylle, that wnneth he lete hys body haue eny reste, ether͛ by day other͛ by nyght; ffor, wynter & somer, he arose euer more yn the dawnynge, & herd fyrst hys seruyce of holy chyrch; ther͛-aftyr, most what al þe day he wold ben out, other͛ wyth houndes other͛ wyth hawkes, for yn thay two thynges he delyted hym swyth mych wythal; & vnnethe he wold ryde any amblynge hors, bot myche trottynge hors, for to trauaylle hys body the more. Aftyr al hys trauaylle a-day, vnnethe he lete hys body haue a lytell reste for to syte to hys mete the whyle that he eete; & anoon aftyr mete, & namely aftyr soppe͛, anoon he wold aryse & stonde, & so dryue forth al þe meste p*ar*te of the nyght, so that al þe court was oft ennyede ther͛-of.

Quem semel exosum habuerat,   þe man that he ones hated,
                         vnnethe he wold *euer* eft loue;
uix in amorem; Quem semel   & man that he oues loued,
amauerat, uix in odium reuocabat.   vnneth he wold *euer* eft hate.

[*Two-thirds of a page of the full text is here left out, on Henry's "extreme delight in falconry and hunting; his open violation of his marriage-vow; his untruthfulness; his dilatoriness in matters of justice; his simoniacal practises; his love of peace; his almsgiving, humility, &c."*]

Humilitatis amator; nobilitatis oppressor, & superbie calcator.

    & openly mekenesse & debonerte he louede; pryde & hauteynesse he hated, & wold brynge vnder fote.

[*Nearly two pages of the full text are here left out, on Henry's "usurpations in things of God; his inattention to divine service; his seizures of the revenues of vacant churches; his treatment of his sons; his wonderful memory," &c., &c.—and Harl. 177 begins again with the final paragraph, of which it gives the first sentence, and the last six words.*]

   sed haec [h]actenus, nec preter rem tamen, cursim & breuiter hic delibasse sufficiat. [*11 words of print left out.*] ad nostram de cetero hiberniam reuertamur.

    [*not english.*]

   It is not my business to follow up this question of our

englisher's original.   Dr. Bruce will, I hope, do that.   I note only what I have just seen, that Mr. Dimock printed part of our Dublin MS., E. 2. 31, in five pages (on six) of his vol. v., pp. xciii–xcviii [1], our pp. 2–10, to line 14, ' prince of wales '; and that from this part, he said (p. lxxvii) our MS. " seems rather a paraphrase of such portions of the treatise [*Expugnacio*] as the writer, no doubt an Anglo-Hibernian [2], deemed most worthy the notice of Anglo-Hibernian readers "; while Prof. Earle held it " a truly interesting specimen of fifteenth century English " well worthy of publication.

Why didn't one of these excellent folk write to me about it at the time?

F. J. FURNIVALL.

MS. ROOM, BRITISH MUSEUM,
    28 *September*, 1893.

On the authority of Giraldus, Mr. Dimock comments on pages lxxx–lxxxii of his Preface, and thus concludes:

" Recent Irish scholars have quietly received Giraldus for what he is worth, as an impetuous, strongly biassed writer, whose statements have generally more or less of truth in them, but with much unfair one-sidedness.   They have seen that his abuse is not confined to Ireland and the Irish, but is almost equally as fully lavished upon his own Wales and the Welsh; that, in fact, he has praise for scarcely any thing or body except himself and his near friends and relations.   Some late Irish writers, under the reaction perhaps of his having been found too much fault with, seem to me to put more faith in Giraldus's history than it really deserves."

---

[1] His 'blethcher,' xcvi/13, is the MS. 'blethelier,' 6/14 below; his 'foden,' xcvii/7 from foot, is the MS. 'fondene,' 8/28; his 'with,' xciv/19, is the MS. 'swith' very, 4/3 below; his 'onenth' (half), xcv/2, is the MS. 'euerich,' 4/16; his 'ichaushed,' xcv/23, is the MS. 'ibanshed,' 4/34 below; his 'inewed,' xcviii/17, is the MS. 'ineued' moved, 10/12 below; and so on.   The copier, Mr. J. P. Prendergast, didn't know his MS.

[2] And evidently a strong Churchman.   See how he makes Henry II attend church-service daily 86/27, when Giraldus complains of his neglect of services. Other instances occur of like bits not in Giraldus.

F. 4. 4, Trinity College, Dublin, p. 7 (middle of page).

*For comparison with Chapter XIII of the other MSS.*
*pp. 30–35 below.*

When the kinge did knowe his entent, and whether he would goe, he gave him fully leve, and warned him not. but with such leave as he hadde, he dighte and made him ready the wynter, till the begininge of may, he sente before him into Irelande a knighte that was called Reymonde le gras;—with him, tenn knights, and fortye Squiers, and fourescore bowemen;—a man full hardy, and well proved in weapon; Roberts nephewe, and Morices Eldeste brothers sone. They arryved at a place called Dondoneuile, foure myle besouthe the hawen of Waterforde; and there they arrearede a diche, and a feble castell upon, of yards and turues [? MS. iureus]. The men of Waterforde, and with them Malaughlyne Ofolane, they did understande that they had such Neighbourehede which them lothed: they concluded that they would upon them, or enny more weare to them come. they assembled them together, well thre thowsande men, and wente over the water of sure, that partethe the twoe counties of leynester and of Mounester, and sett them in thre hosts, bouldely for to assaile the Englyshmen within there Castell. Reymounde and his men, thoughe they weare but fewe, they weare not fainte to fighte with uneven hoste, they assemblede them together; But, as noe wonder was, soe fewe men mighte nat fighte againste soe many; theic turned them againe to there receipte. the other, thinkinge that they departed in discom-feture, they brake there sheldrun, and followed them: and they weare not fully within the gate, but some of them weare rather in [than] thenglyshe men. Reymonde sawe that he and his weare in greate perill, and upon pointe to losse there lyves. he cried to his fellowes, and turned worthely upon there foemen. and the firste that came in, he clave his hedde, and throwly killed him: all thoste

weare dyscomfitted, and toke them to flighte.  The others them
followed into all the plaine, and layde them one soe, that in litle
while they slowe of them fyve hundreth and moe; and the moste
parte of thother fell downe into the see from the hie roke, and drowne
themselves.  in this fighte, was a knighte that heighte William
fferande, that did over well, and above all other.  he was a man
that hade semblante as thoughe he weare one the much yuell; and
therfore he put him-selfe whear the moste perill was; for [he]
raughte not whether death came betwen him and his yuell, or it
weare overmuch smitte [? MS. suirtte] upon him.  here the pride
of Waterforde fell; all there mighte went to noughte : herof came
the Englyshe hoppe and comforte; and to the Iryshe, dredd and
wanhop ; for it was never therbefore harde, that, of soe fewe men,
soe greate a slaughter was done.  but unwise counsaile they did
thereafter, that turned them to much crueltie ; ffor when the
Maystry was all thers, and all there foemen overcom, In the fighte
weare taken well threscore men and tenn, that them had yelded,
and weare the higheste and the richeste men of all the Cytty, such
that theye mighte have had the Citty deliuered for them, or els
asmuch Catell as they woulde desire.  Henry of mountad, that to
them was come, and Reymounde, upon diuerse domes stroven whate
they shoulde doe with there prisoners; ffor Reymounde travailede
aboute for to deliuer them, as a man of Rewthefull mode, and thus
saide to his fellowes : " Lordings, whate is us beste to doe with oure
wrechid prisoners ?  I saye nat that one anny manner one shoulde
spare his foemen ; but they be nat nowe oure foemene, but be men
nat rebells, but in Battaile for to defende there county, overcome.
me thinke they are nowe in such state, that we oughte better to
have mercye of them, and gyve them lyfe,—for to gyve others
example to be boxom,—then cruely to doe them to deathe, wheare-
throughe others, ffor feare of mystruste, the lesse will yeld them to
us."  When Reymonde had theise wourds saide, in all the folke
was amoste none to graunte them lyfe ; Arose up Henry amonge

them all, and this them saide: "I-noughe Remounde openlý to us
hathe spoken of mercý and almosedede, [1]how vnked[1] landes are
wonne; and not with slaughter and burneinge.  whether Alixandr
and Julius Cesar, that weare lords of all the wourde, wonne lands
bý such waý, I woulde Reýmounde woulde me answere.  when theý
came to us well arrayed for to fighte, yf theie had wone the over-
hande and overcome us, woulde theý, for almose and for rewth,
haue had mercý one us? noe, I trowe not.  therfore, but those one of
twoe waýes : eyther doe manly that thinge whea[re]fore we benc
come, and the folke that rebell againste us, with [out] any noyse,
with weapone heartely bringe owt of dawes; otherwise, yf we shall
doe almose-dede one them, and spare them, as Reýmounde hath
saide, lett us wend to oure shippes, and turne agaýne ; and lett we
the wreched men houlde there lande, and Brouke it, without any
challendge."  Henries dome licked them better then Reymonds ;
and the Cittizens weare demed to death.  They had noe wonte of
waritrees; and therfore They ladd them to the clyffe of the see, and
putt them downe, and drowned them.

of the firste goode adventure that him befell, they that beste
weare worthýe should haue there parte, and the hoste.  all the
towne of wexforde, with the twoe nexte countýes, he gave to
Roberte Stephensson and to Morýce fitz Geraude, as forwarde was
to-for made.  other twoe nexte counties, he gaue to Henrý of Mount-
morthie,—nexte thay twoe, one the sýde towarde waterforde,—
a knighte that came in that same flote, hým þridsome of knights,
and came throughe thearle Richarde, more for to spýe the land,
then for to fighte.

[1]-[1] Afterwards written above the line in MS.

CORRECTIONS BY HENRY BRADLEY, M.A. ·

FOR

# THE ENGLISH CONQUEST OF IRELAND.

EARLY ENGLISH TEXT SOCIETY. NO. 107.

*Original Series,* 1896.

**Boxom-fastines** 62/18 : this should be two words, buxom fastness, an obsequious covenant, meant to render L. *fucato foedere.*

**Costes** : part of far-costes below.

**Ense** 80/29 : read Euse, eaves, edge, border : 'the wode evese (*ms.* hevese) voc. 159.'—Bradley's Stratmann.

**Far-costes** 80/5 : 'O.N. farkostr ; means of conveyance, boat, ship, *Engl. Metr. Hom.* xix.'—*ib.*

**Fawes** 96/2 : perhaps the Irish fogha (O'Reilly), a dart, O.Ir. fogae (Lat. jacula).

**Folk place** 50/15 : the folk (for febyll in the Rawlinson MS.) was caught from the 'lond-folk ' in the next line.

**Herrer** 116/30 : the Latin is ' et citra majoris auctoritatem urbem obtenturum.'—Gir. *Cambr. Op.* v. 342.

**I-quenyted** 36/35 : miswritten for Iquemed, pleased.

**I-suywed** 116/9 : read I-snywed, 'snowed ' their arrows ; the Latin is ' sagittarum . . . grandine perfuso.'

**Lygne** 102/17 : as fayre & lygne translates 'procerus et pulcher,' the word must mean ' tall ' ; perhaps it is a misreading for hyghe, high.

**Lyme** 62/18 : the Latin has *amorem* ; the scribe must have misread luue (love) as *lime,* and transcribed it *lyme.*

**Ost** 50/2 : cannot mean 'burnt.' The word is superfluous ; perhaps the translator at first wrote lytell ost (little host), and then altered *ost* into *stonwal,* but did not clearly enough expunge the rejected word.

**Priuisant** 80/28 : cannot mean ' foreseeing ' ; it is probably a mistake for pursiuant, pursuivant (the Latin is *satelles*).

**Ryuely** 128/12 : rifely, abundantly.

**Sheldrun** 31/29 (R) : company-formation, O.E. scild-truma (whence *shelter*) ; the Rawlinson MS. here preserves the right reading, that of the Dublin MS. being unmeaning.

**Spourges** 112/3 : ? for spronges, shoots, sprouts.

**þorwe** 28/12 : ? through ; wel þorwe ' well through,' urgently (the Latin is ' omnibus modis ').

**Trukked** 48/9 : ran short, trukien, O.E. trucian, fail, be lacking.

**Wecchene** 36/31 : cwecchen, to twitch, shake.

**Wenttene** 106/8 : for weten, know (þat is to weten = that is to say) ; the scribe was misled by seeing wentten (went) in the line above.

**Yonre** 104/10 : **Youre** 114/27 : yovre, ʒeofre, O. E. ʒīfre, greedy.

# THE ENGLISH CONQUEST
# OF IRELAND

## FOUNDED ON THE *EXPUGNACIO HIBERNICA* OF GIRALDUS CAMBRENSIS

———————

## A PARALLEL TEXT

FROM TWO MSS., I. AB. 1425 A.D.   MS. TRIN. COLL., DUBLIN, E. 2. 31 ;
II. AB. 1440 A.D.   MS. RAWLINSON B. 490, BODLEIAN LIBRARY, OXFORD

B

# THE ENGLISH CONQUEST OF IRELAND

FOUNDED ON

## GIRALDUS CAMBRENSIS.

(*MS. Trin. Coll., Dublin*, E. 2. 31.)

[CHAPTER I.]

[Fol. 1 a.]
When Henry II reigned in England,
Dermot Macmurgh ruled over Leinster, A. D. 1135-71.
His folk hated him;
[¹ &, an, a].
[² heart].

but the wife of King Rory of Meath loved him,

and sent for him when Rory was away.

He took her to Leinster, A. D. 1152,

YN the tym that the kynge henry, þat was the kynges fadyr Richard & the kynges fadyr Iohn, regned in englaund well, &¹ heighe man in Irland, þat het dermod Macmorgh, *princes* of leynyster, that is I-told þe fifte *parte* of Irland. That dermod, 4 from the tym that he was lord of lond, & foll shold *gouerne*, he went amonge his heighe men, and so hard ham biladde þat þay casten grete hat to hym, and myche thay wax hym ageyn in herth², þegh þey ne durst nat oppenly shewe. Whan he hade 8 longe whill þus bilad hym amonge his men, bettidde an aduenture that turnede hym þer-aftyr to mych harme; ffor in mythe was a kynge that hegth Rowry, & a well fayr womman to wif; and as men tellede oft, and soth it is I-found, that som of heme ben 12 to vnstable of herth², wher-throgh many harmes ben oþer-whill, þat ne ben nat now al to rekne. This Rouryes wif worthen to þe loue of Macmurgh mor þan hyr own lord; and he hir also, & this was longe; bot to-giddre ne myghtyn þei nat com as 16 the wold; for hit betid a tym þat hir lord went owt of his contrey in-to fer londes, for grete nedes þat he hade to don. his wif a-waitede full well, & aspied þat hir lord most longe be owt of lond, send to Macmurgh, & bade hym, þat if he euer wold his 20 will hawe of hir, that he shold com to hyr, for sho was redy to do all þat hym likede. ⁌ Macmorgh name power with hym, and went thar this lady was; & as hit be-spoke was, he name hir, & broght hir out of myth into leynestr, and hell hir that to 24

# OF THE CONQUESTE OF IRLAND
## BY ENGLYSH MEÑ.

(*MS. Rawl.* B. 490, *Bodl. Libr.*)

[CHAPTER I.]

IN the tyme that Kynge Henry, that was the kynges Fadyr [Fol. 1 a.]
Rychard and the kynges Fadyr Ihoñ, regned in England, was an hey man in Irland, whos name was callyd Dermot Macmurgh, Prince of leynystre, that is y-toldo the fyfte Parte of Irlande. That Dermot, from the tyme that he was lorde of lond, *and* folke sholde goverñ, he werret cruely amonge his hey men, *and* so harde hame lade, that thay castyn grete hate to hym, *and* muche they were ayennes hym in herte, theght they ne dvrste nat opynly shewe. Whan he hadd thus longe tyme lade hym amonge hys men, be-felle an aduenture that turned hym ther-aftyr to mych harme; For in myth was a kynge, whos name was Roury, *and* hadd a wel fayre woman to wyffe; and as men tellyth ofte, and sith hit is y-found, that some of them ben vnstabill of hert, wherfore many harmys ben ofte-tymes, that ben nat now all to reherse //

Capitulum 1m.

Leinster is a fifth part of Ireland.

Tiernan O'Rourke, king of Breifny.

This Rouries wyfe lowyd more Macmurgh than hyr owyn lorde; and he hyr also, and this was longe; but to-giddyr ne myght they not come as they wolde ; for hit be-felle in a tyme, that hyr lord went out of his contrey into fere londys, for grete neddes that he hadde to done. His wyfe be-thoght hyr ful well, and, Supposynge that hyr lord moste longe be out of londe, Sche sente to Macmurgh, and sayde to hym, that yf he euer wolde his wille haue of hyr, that he sholde cvme to hyr, for she was redy to do al that hym lykyd //

'Varium et mutabile semper femina' (Virg.Aen. iv. 569).

Macmurgh toke wyth hym many men, and went there this lady was. and as hit was be-for spoke be-tweñ them both, he toke hyr wyth hym out of myth into leynestere, and helde hyr there to hys

A.D. 1152. O'Rourke's wife carried off.

B 2

A.D. 1152. his will. Nat for-þaið sho grad and cried, as thogh he naið hiP
**and kept her there.** agaynes hiP will, as hit nas nat so. Than hir lord hit herde, he
was theP-of tened swith stronge, and mych moP of the shamme
**Rory and his ally, the King of Con-naught,** þat to hyið was doð, þan of the harme; all that he mygth do, 4
he didde, for to awreke hyið; he sent after his owið poweP,
ande eke all þat he myght of other; and the kynge of Connagth,
þat was that tyið lorde of Irlanď, coið to hyið with his poweP:
**march into Leinster.** he gadrede so moch folke (?) þat noið end' nas, and coið into 8
leynestP for to wreke hyið of his shame. Tho Macmorgh this
herd', he sent to his meið þat þay sholde hyið helppe aycyið his
fomeið þat þus wereið commyng toward hyið. They bethoghten
**Mac-murgh's men refuse to help him;** hamð of the teið & the traysoið þat they haið hade ydoið þer- 12
to-fore | and' forsoke, al out of dout, þat þay nogth woll hyið
helpe; and' many of haið openly turneď to his fomeið ayeyns hyið,
ffor to wreke haið of the iniurie þat he haið had' doð. Macmorgh
saw þat poweP hyið failleď, & euerich half he was amyde his 16
fomeið beset. he was maið of hegh hert; and with þe litill poweP
þat he had', he werrede as long as he myght; bot he ne myght
nat all-way all-oið ayeyns all the lande folke | he was so narowe
bilaď þat nedes he most tholl deth, otheP þe lonď leue; he saw 20
þat noið oþer remedy was: he went to the see, and' fonď shippe
**so he sails to Eng-land, A.D. 1166,** redy, and' wynde at will, & passede oure into englanď, with well
few with hyið; and' on this maner he sawit his lif, & lefte lonď
& lede & all his otheP gooď. Hereby þat meið may witte, þat 24
be a maið of neuer so mych power, bettre hym is þat hys men hym
loue þane hate. ℭ Whane Macmorgh was thus icome in-to
england, al hys thoght was how he myght hym best worck of the
schame þat hyme was done, & of þat þat he was so vilich out of 28
hys kynd lond I-dryue, he nyst of whom he myght bettre besech
**[*Fol.1b.]** help þane of þe kynge. And þe kynge was þane fer in the
**and then to France, to ask Henry II's aid.** realme of fraunce for grete nedes þat he hade to done. Macmorgh
passed ouer to hym. þe kynge fayr hym vndrefynge, *& with mych 32
mane shipe. and whan had he tolde hyme the enchesoun of hys
comynge to hym, and whar-for he was out of hys londe ibanshed,
þe kynge was swyth wo therfor, & good hert hadde hym to helpe,
naP oþer grete nedes þat he hade to done. Whane he ne myght 36

wylle. And ther-fore she Cryed, and mad moche sorow and lemen-   A.D. 1152.
tacioñ, as thogh he toke hyr ayeynnes hir wyll: As hit was not So /

Than hyr lorde hit herd, he was ther-of full stronge a-greued, and   O'Rourke
mych more of the shame that to hym was don, than for the harme.   is wroth at
Al that he myght do, he dyd, forto be wroke on hym.  he Sente   the shame
aftyr his owyn men, and eke al that he myght of othyr; and the   and
kynge of Connaght, that In that tyme was lorde of Irlande, come to
hym wyth his Power.  And he gaderid so myche Pepyll, that they   invades
were vnnvmerable, Comynge Into leynystre, forto be vengyd of his   Leinster.
shame //

Tho Macmurgh her[de ther]of, he Sent to his men, that thay   Mac-
sholde hym helpe ayeynes his foe-men, that thus weryn comynge   murgh's
to-warde hym.

Thay bethoghten them of cruelte and the traysouñ that to ham
he hadd done therto-fore, And forsoke al out of dowte that thay
wolde noght hym helpe.  And many of them opynly turned to his
Ennemys ayeynes hym, ffor to wroke tham of the Iniury that he
to them hadd done //

Macmurgh sawe that his men failled hym; and on Euche halwe   men fail
he was amyd his ennemys besegyd.  He was a man of hey herte;   him,
and wyth the fewe Pepill that he hadd, he werrid as longe as he
myght; but he ne * myght not alway dure ayennes the Londe folke.   [*Fol. 1 b.]
He was so narow bylade, that nedys he mvste suffyr deth, or the
londe leue.  he saw that non othyr remedy was.  He went to the
see, and fovnde shippe redy, and wynde at wyll, *and* passyd owyr   so he
into England, with wel fewe with hym; *and* on this maner he sauyd   crosses to
                                                                       England,
his lyfe, *and* lefte lond and lede, and al othyr good //  Here-by men   A.D. 1166,
may witte that, be a mañ neuer of so mych Powere, bettyr hit is to
hym, that his men hym loue, than hate //  Whan Macmurgh was
thus y-come Into England, al his thoght was, how he myght hym
best wreke of the shame that hym was y-doñ, and of that that he
was so shamfully out of his kynde londe I-dryue.  He wyst not of
whoñ he myght bettyr beseke helpe *and* sokovre, than of the
kynge.  And the kynge was then fer in the reame of Fraunce, for   and then
gret nedys that he hadd to doñ.  Macmurgh passyd ouer to hym.   to France,
                                                                       where
the kynge fayre hym vndyrfonge, *and* with mych vyrchipp.  And   Hen. II
when he hadde tolde hym the cause of hys comynge to hym, *and*   welcomes
                                                                       him.
the cause where-for he was out of his Land y-baneshyd, the kynge
was sory therfor, *and* good-will hym hadd to helpe, nere othyr grete
nedys that he hadde to don.  Whan he ne myght nat ellis do, he

A. D.
1165–7.

nat elles do, he name of hym homage, & othes, & lete hyme mak
hys lettres, that thus mych ben to vndrestond : 'Henry, throgħ
gode-is grace kynge of englond, duc of normandy & of Acquitayne,

Henry
appeals to
his sub-
jects to
help Mac-
murgh,

& erl of angoy, to al hys liegemen, englyssħ, normannes, Walshe, 4
Scottes, and to al oþer that to hym ben subiect, sendeth gretynge.
Whan þese lettres to yow ben i-com̅, witte ye þat we, dermot,
prince of leynester, in ouꝛ grace and in ouꝛ goode wiłł hawe
receyuet ; wharfore þat ałł þay that hym as ouꝛ lawfułł man̅ 8
hełł[pe] willeth, into his lond̅ hym to restore, ouꝛ grace and ouꝛ goode
leue haue þay þer-to.' Whan̅ Macmorgħ hade the kynges lettres
thus y-purchasede—þe kynge hym yaf also richely þat hym̅ nedet

who
returns to
Bristol,

of his tresouꝛ—he nam̅ leue of the kynge, & wentt in-to englond 12
& com̅ to Bristow, & soiourned̅ thaꝛ a whiłł ; & so mycħ the
blethelieꝛ, for þer com̅ oft shippes theder out of Irland̅, & men̅,
þat he myght hiꝛ tythynge of the lond̅ & of his folkis, for his hert
was mycħ there-to. The whiłł þat he theꝛ was, wełł oft he let rede 16
þe kynges wrytte to-for the peple ; & largely he beheght londes and̅
rentes, & Rich yiftes, if any wer that hym helpe wold. Bot he ne
fond̅ noon̅ with-ałł, that sucħ tynge wolde ne durst vndirtake,

and agrees
to give
his
daughter
and Lein-
ster to
Earl
Strugoill,
in return
for aid.
Macmurgħ
goes to
South
Wales,

tiłł þat the erle of Strugoiłł, Richard þe Erles son̅ Gilbert, com̅ 20
to hym̅. Ther was þe parlement so longe y-dryue betwen̅ ham̅,
& sekiritesse y-makyd, þat the Erle shold̅ hym̅ helpe with ałł
his poweꝛ þe next somer þer-after, and he shold yeue þe Erle
his doghtre, with ałł þe lond̅ of leynestre. ⁕ Whane this was on 24
this maner ypu[rueied, for the grete] talent þat Macmorogħ had̅
to ben̅ neeꝛ his lond̅—as man̅ tynke [no place so [1]] mery lyghtly, as
in his kynd̅ stidde,—he went hym thennes in-to south walys, to
seynt dauyes toun, vp-on̅ þe see ; & mycħ hit gladet his hert, 28

A. D. 1167,

thogħ he stronghly mourned̅, þat he myght in fayꝛ weder haue
somdełł sygħt of his lond̅.

where Rys
is prince.

⁕ In that tym̅ was prince in wales, Rys, Gryffyues son̅, onþer [2]
the kyng of england ; & a swith good man̅ bisshoppe of seynt 32
dauy, and was his nam̅, 'ahon dauy' ; & both þe prince & eke þe

---

[1] Dermitius, desiderio visendae patriae plurimum accensus, eaque dulcedine,
qua natale solum cunctos ducere solet, amplius allectus.—Gir. Camb., Expugnacio Hibernica, cap. ii, Op. v. 228, Rolls Series.          [2] under.

toke of hym homage *and* othis, *and* lette hym make his letter*es*, that thus myche bene to vndyrstond' // 'Henry, throw goddys grace, kynge of England, Duke of Normandy and of acquytanyc, *and* Erle of angoy, to al his lege men, Englyssh, normannes, Walshe, Scotes, and to al othyr that to hym ben subiecte / Sendyth gretynge. Whan this *lettr*es ben to yow y-come, witte ye that we, Dermot Prince of Leynystre, in oure grace *and* in oure goode-wyll, haue receouet; wherfor that al thay that hym / as oure laufull man he[l]pe will, Into his londe hym to restore, oure grace and oure good'-wyll haue they therto ' // ' When Macmurgh hadd' the kynges Letter*es* thus y-Purchasyd', (the kyng hym yafe also rychely, that hym nedyd' of his tresoure,) He toke Leue at the kynge, *and* went into England', *and* come to Brystow, *and* soyorned' ther awhyle ; *and* myche radyr, for ther come oft shippis thedyr out of Irland'; *and* men, that he myght hyr thythynge of the Londe *and* of his Pepyll ; for his hert was mych therto // The whyle that he there was, well oft he made to be redd' the kynges *lettr*es to-for the Pepyll ; and largely he promysyd' londys, and rentis, *and* othyr ryche yeftys, to them that hym wolde he[l]pe. But he ne found' none, wyth al that, that Suche thyng wolde ne druste vndyrtake, tyll that the Erle of Strugoill, Richarde, the Erlis Sonne Gylbert [1], come to hym.   Ther was the Parlement [2] so longe y-dryue be-twen ham, and' sekyrnesse y-makyd', that the Erle sholde hym helpe wit*h* al his Powere the nexte somere ther-aftyr, And he sholde yeue the Erle his doghtyr, wit*h* al the lond' of leynystre // Whan this was on this maner purueyed' [3], For grete affeccion that Macmurgh hud' to ben neere his londe, (as man thynkyth no Place so Myrry lyghtly as in his Kynd' [*] Place,) [*Fol. 2 a.] he went fro thens Into Suthe Walis, to Seynt Dauyes toun vp-on the see; *and* mych hit gladdyd' his herte, thegh he strongly mornyd', that he myght in fayre weddyr haue somdel Syght of his lond / In that tyme was prynce in walis, Rys, Gryfynes Sonne, vndyr the kynge of England', And a wyrshipphul man, Bishope of Seynte Dauy, *and* also his name was dauy [4]. And' both the Prince *and* also

A.D. 1166-7.
The Kyngys letteres
in favour of Murrough,
who comes back to England,
and is promist help by Richard, Earl of Striguil.

---

[1] Camden adds 'dictus Strengbow, *fortis arcus*.'—D.        [2] Colloquium.
[3] Hiis itaque seriatim hoc ordine completis.        [4] Davidque secundo Menoviae praesidente.

A.D. 1167. bisshop well wýrshipfully vndrefýnge Macmorgh, & mych reut
had of his enemyte, & of his mych lostes, & of þe mych shammo
þat hym was i-doñe.

### [CHAPTER II.]

**Rys has in prison a Sir Robert Fitz-stephen, once Constable of South Wales.**

In the týme þat this was so, was in prisoñ with þe prince of wales, a knyght þat heght Robert Stefenes-soñ, þat soñ tyñ had y-be constable of all south walys, & many il turnes had idoñe vpoñ þe princes meñ whañ þay any thýnge mysdedeñ; & þrogh traisoñ of his owñe meñ he was I-take & delyuered to the prince; & þre yeñ he was I-hold in prisonne ar Macmorgh theder cañ. Oft þe prince hyñ profred to delyuer hyñ out of prisoñ, so þat he wold be his helppe to werry vp-oñ þe kynge; bot Robert was a trew mañ, & for no tynge wold do thynge wher-of he myght be þer-after I-wyted of wntrowth. Thañ—þrogh

[*Fol. 2 a.]

**He sets Robert free, on condition that he and his half-brother Maurice Fitz-gerald help Mac-murgh.**

[¹ MS. kyng.]

besechýnge of * þe bisshope & of Moryce fitz-Geraud, þat wereñ Robertes two brethereñ on his moþer half,—he was delyuered owt of prisoñ on this manere: þat he & Morice his brother shold, þe next somer, wend in-to Irland, with ar poweñ to helppe Macmorgh; & he shold hym yeue þe toñ of weysford, with þe twey next cantredes; & of this was good sekernes Imaked on etheñ half. ❡ Whañ this thyng¹ was all thus bespokene, Macmorgh ne myght no lengere suffre þat he ne most to his land wend, thegh he ne fond nat þe aduentures þat he soght, such as hýme lif weñ, ne nou

**Macmurgh sails to Ireland, and winters at Ferns.**

other poweñ he ne broght with hyñ than he out ladde. He had shippe redy, and good wynd, and passed ouer in-to Irland, & boldly arýued in lond þer he had many fomeñ and fewe frendes. froñ þe see he went to fernes; and well simply he lyued þer all þe wynttyñ with the Clergie of þe chirch, wiche well sayñ hyñ vndrefýnge, and by hare poweñ to hyñ & to his, fondeñ þat hame was nede.

### [CHAPTER III.]

A.D. 1169.

**Fitz-stephen collects 30 knights, 60 squires, and 300 foot-men**

Vnder that tyme, Robert Steunes-soñ hyñ dyght to wend in-to Irland, as a mañ þat on all maner wold hold lawfully his trowthe and his behest . he hade purueied hyñ of xxxti knyghtes and lx skyers, & ccc of foot-meñ with bowes and arowes; and knyghtes and þe skyers well I-horsed and well y-wepened, all of his owñ kyne and of his owne nurtuñ. Thay

the Byshope wel wyrchipphully vndyrfonge Macmurgh, and myche A.D. 1167.
Pite hadd of his Enemyte and of his mych Lostys, And of the mych
shame that hym was done.

[CHAPTER II.]

IN the tyme that this was so, was in Prisonne wyth the Prince Capitulum
of Walys, a knyght, whos Name was Robert Steues-Sonne, 2ᵐ.
that sometyme hadd y-be constabill of al Suthe Walis, and many Ea tempes-
yll tvrnys hadd y-done vp-on the Princes men, when thay eny tate Rober-
thyng mysdedyn; and throgh traysoun of his owyn men, he was qui apud
y-take and delyuerid to the Prince. And thre yere he was holde Aberteivi,
in prison, are Macmurgh thedyr come. Oft the Prince hym regionis
proferyd to delyuer hym out of pryson, So that he wolde be his caput, &c.
helpe to wer vp-on the kynge; but Robert was a trew man, and for
nothyng wold do thynge wher-of he myght be ther-aftyr reprovid
of vntrowth //

Than,—throgh be-sechynge of the Byshope and of Moryce fiz- Interveni-
Geraud, that weryn Robertys two bretheryn on his Modyr syde,—he entibus
was delyueryd out of Pryson on this manere: That he and Morice uterinis
his brodyr sholde, the nexte Somyr, wende Into Irland, with har ejusdem
Powere, to helpe Macmurgh; and he sholde hym yeue the toun of &c.
weysford, with the twey nexte cantredes: and of this was good
swrte y-fondyd on euery syde. / Whan this was al thus Spokyn,
Macmurgh myght not lengyr Suffyr that he ne mvste to his Lond
wende, thegh he ne found nat the aduentures that he Soght, suche
as hym lykyd, ne none othyr Powere he ne broght wyth hym, than
he out-ladd. / he had shipe redy, and good wynd, and Passyd ouer A clero
into Irland, and boldely arryued in londe ther-as he hadd many loci illius
Enemys and few frendys. / From tho see he went to Fernys; and juxta
wel sympylly he lyued there al the wyntyr, with the Clergy of the modulum
chyrche, whych wel fayre hym vndyrfonge, and by har Power to hym exhibitus,
and to his, foundyn that ham was nede.

[CHAPTER III.]     A.D. 1169.

VNder that tyme, Robert Steues-Sonne hym dyght to wende Capitulum
Into Irland, as a man that on al maner wolde holde lawfully 3ᵐ.
his throuth, and his beheste. He had Purveyed hym of xxxti Nec pro-
knyghtes and lx Squyeris, and ccc of fote-men with bowes and immemor,
arowes; And the knyghtis and the Squyris wel y-horsyd and wel nec fidei
wepenyd, al of his owyn kyn and his owyn nurture. Thay dyddyn tor, &c.

and lands at Banow, c. May 1, 1169.

A prophecy of Merlin was thus fulfild.

Macmurgh and Fitz-stephen unite their forces,

and march to Wexford, about twelve miles from Banow.

The towns-men at first resolve to meet them in the field, but, on seeing their array, retire within the city.

[*Fol. 2 b.]

The assault on Wexford is success-fully resisted.

Robert de Barri has a

didden hame to saill att send dauyes, and aryuedeñ at Banow in Irlaund, well vnsikere on euery halfe. thay vncharged hare shippes, & made haṁ loges on lond. Thane was fulfilled a *prophecie* þat *merlyñ* seid of this commynge: "A knyght *with* party armes 4 shall formost breke þe clos of Irland." Such armes bare þat Robert. he send soñ to *Dermod* Macmorgh, and didde hyṁ to witt of his commynge; and þe thedynge spronge fort soñ into all þe lond, what folke was to hyṁ Icoṁ. and of þo that to-for hyṁ 8 hade I-left, and litill told by hyṁ, commyn soñ to hyṁ, so þat he had I-gadered fywe hundred meñ. he wentt witt this folk to þe Englysse-meñ; and [when] þay coṁ to-geddr, euery of haṁ was the gladder for other. Ther was the forward meued bethweñ haṁ, 12 and othes y-swor, and sekernesse I-made to conferme all þe forward, as hit there-by-for was puruecied by-for the *prince* of wales.

[CHAPTER IV.]

Whan this sekernesse was thus y-maked, þese twey *maner* folkes, with ooñ will, and *with* ooñ hert, *with* Baners 16 i-lacet, nam the wey toward weysford. The meñ of þe self toñ wereñ ywar of har commyng, and tok haṁ to rede—for þe tother wereñ so few, & day so many—that þay wold figth *with* haṁ in þe pleyne felde. They caṁ owt of the toñ arraied on har *maner*; bot 20 whan þay sawe the Englismeñ, *with* hors I-helled *with* yreñ harnes, haṁ-self well I-wepned *with* haubergeons, and Bright helmes and sheldes, wich the sawe *neuer* þer-to-for, they toke a-nother rede, and turned ayeyñ to toñ; & all þat was *with*-owt þe 24 walles, thay sett a-fyr and brent, & redied haṁ to hold haṁ *with*-yne the wallys *with* streynthe. Robert *with* his meñ went strongly for to assayll to toñ, & sette the bowmeñ for to wer the fight of the kernels, and turned the wepned meñ to fill þe *diches. 28 thay *with*-yn defendet haṁ stalwarthly *with* stonnes and stakes, wher-of they wer I-warned, and wer many I-hurt whit-yn and eke *with*-out, so that thay *with*-out mosten nedes leue of the assaut, & withdraw haṁ. Among haṁ was a yong knyght þat het 32 Robert de Barry, þat drogh yong blodes hete, and for hys stalwardnes, reght nat of his lif: as he wold *with* þe formoste passe ouer the wall, he hent a dynt *with* a greth stone vpon þe

ham to sayle at Seynt Dauyes, and londyd at the Banow in Irland, A.D. 1169.
wel vnsykyr on euery syde.   thay vnchargid har shippis, *and* made
ham logis on londe *.   Than was fulfillid a prophesy that Merlyn [*Fol.2b.]
seyde of this comynge : 'A knygħ[t] *with* Party armys shall formyst Party per
breke the clos of Irland.'   Such armys bare that Robert.   He sent pale gules
sone to Dermot Macmurgħ, and didde hym to vndyrstand of his & ermyn
comynge; And thythyngis spronge forth sone Into al the londe, what a saltyer
Pepill was to hym come.   And many of them that to-forin hym chaunged.
hadd forsake and lefte, *and* lytill seett by hym, comen sone to hym, bipartitus
So that he hadd gaderid v. C. men. / He went *with* this pepyll to armis,
the Englysħ men; And when thay come to-geddre, eu*er*y of them claustra
was the gladdyr for othyr / Ther were the for-sayde conontis primus
rehersyd *and* mevid betwen tham, and othis sworn, *and* sekyrnesse irrumpet.
made, to conferme all the forsayde, as hit was ther-to-fore Purveyed
be-fore the Prince of Walys.

[CHAPTER IV.]

WHan this sekyrnysse was thus madd, this two maner Capitulum
Pepyll, wyth on wyll, and *with* ooin herte, *with* baners 4ᵐ.
lacyd, toke ther wey towarde*s* weysford.   The men of the toune
weryn y-ware of thare comynge, *and* toke them to consayll,—for the
othyr weryn so few, and thay so many,—that thay wolde figħ[t] *with*
ham in the Playn felde.   Thay come out of the tou*n* arrayed
on ther mane*r*; but when they sawe the Englysħ men, *with* hors equestrem
y-hellyd *with* Iryn harneys, ham-Selfe wel wepenyd *with* hauber- turmam
geons, and brygħt Salletis and sheldys, whych thay sawe neue*r* clipeis
there-to-forin, thay toke anothyr consayll, *and* turned ayayn to fulgenti-
toun; and al that was *with*-out the wallis, thay sette afyre *and* bus in-
brente; *and* arrayed tham to kepe ham *with*-In the wallis *with* signem...
Streynth.   Robert, wyth his men, went Strongly to assaylle the
toun, *and* sette the bowmen forto were the fygħt of the propugna-
cornelis, *and* turned the wepenyd men to fill the dichis.   thay sagittariis
wythin defendyd ham boldely *with* Stones and Stakys, wher-of eminus
they were y-warnyd, [.....] and mosten nedis lewe the assaute, and bus...
wythdrawe ham / Amonge ham was a yong knygħt / whos name
was Robert de barry, that, throgh yonge blodis hette, *and* for his juvenili
boldnys, rogħt not to lesse the lyfe / As he wolde wyth the fryst calore...
Passe ouer the walle, he hadd a stroke *with* a grette stoñe vp-on

A.D. 1169.
narrow
escape.

heued' al wit͡h the helme, þat he fel doun yn the ground' of þe dich; & vnnethes he was I-draw vp throgh his felowes, þat mych put har lyf in aduentuꝛ for to saw his lif. The cry was well gret on euery syde, for this knyght þat thus was I-hurt. Thay 4 wit͡h-drow ham͡ fro the wallys and' wenten ham͡ to þe strond'; and'

The assail-
ants of the
town burn
the ships
they find
on the
strand.

all þe shippes þat þay þer fond', thay settene a-fyre. And . O . shippe þer was, that was I-com͡ owt of Brittayne aftyr cheffaꝛ, and' was y-charget wit͡h whet & wit͡h wynes, and' lay I-ancred in the 8 hauene: the best parte of the englismen͡ wenten͡ wit͡h bottes and' toke his shippe. þe shippmen͡ werne many, and' saw that þer weren bot a few englys in the shippe, & the wynd' was of þe lond'; thay cutte the cable of the ankre, and' þe wynd' bare the shippe 12 in toward' the see: her fellowes saw this, and' wenten͡ after wit͡h bottys; and' vnnethe wit͡h rowyng, and' wit͡h gret peril of all har lyues, þay come ayeyn to lond. Macmorgh saw this, & weren͡ sore amaied, for thay wend' neuer more þat on [of] ham shold' haw 16 com͡ to lond' a-lyue. The assaut was I-left all þat day. A-morowe, whan masse was I-herd', al þe host þay wentene to the assaut wislyere and' warliere þan thay didden the day befor, and strusten

Next day,
the
townsmen
surrender.

as well to sleght as to streynt͡h. The men͡ of the ton͡ sawe ham 20 commyng, and wer right soꝛ aferd' that day shold nat withstond the assaute, and vndrestonden al-so that wit͡h wrong day holden ayàyn her lord'; thay tok ham to red, and besoghten pees; & drogh be-sechynge of twe bissoppes, that þat tym weren wit͡h-yn 24 the toun, and other possible men al-so wit͡h ham, thay yolden ham͡ al to Macmor[gh]; and fouꝛ hostages, the best þat he wold' chese, delyuered to hym͡ for the pees, and trywly wit͡h hym for to hold' frome þat tym forward, as har kyndly lord. Macmorgh, 28 as wise & waꝛ, ffor-thy that he wold' that þe out-commyn men shold' haw the bettre hert, and will, hym͡ for to serue, he bethoght

Macmurgh
gives
grants
of land to
Maurice
Fitzgerald
and
Hervey of
Mount-
maurice.

þat, of the fyrst good aduentuꝛ þat hym͡ was befall, þay that best weren worthy shold' hawe haꝛ parte, and þe host. Al þe 32 ton of weysford, wit͡h twey cantredes aller-next, he yaf to Robert, steuenes sone, and to Morice fitz-Geraud', as forward' was to-foꝛ maked; othere thwey cantredes he yaf heruy of Mountmorthy,— neghest thay twcyn on the syd toward Waterford,—a knyght þat 36

the hedde al with the Sallet, that he fell doun to the grovnde of the dyche ; and vnnethis he was vp-rerid˜ throgh his fellovys, that myche Put har lyfe in aduenture forto sawe his lyfe. The cry was well grette on euery syde, for this knyght that thus was y-hurte. Thay wythdrow ham all from the wallis, and wenten to the stronde ; and al the Chippis that they ther found˜, thay setten afyre. And oo shippe ther was, that was y-come out of Brytayn aftyr cheffare, and was y-chargid˜ with whete and with wynes, and lay y-ancred˜ in the Havyn. The beste Parte of the Englysh men wenten wyth botis, and toke this shippe : the Chippmen weryn many, and saw that ther weryn but a fewe Englysh men in the shippe, and the wynd was on the londe syde ; thay cvtte the Cabilys of the ancre, and the wynd bare the Chippe to-ward the see. Her Fellouys sawe this, and wentyn [1] aftyr wyth botis ; and vnnethe with rowyng, and wyth gretto Perill of al there lyues, they come ayeyn to lond˜. Macmurgh saw this, and was sore aferde, for they wende neuer * more that one of Ham sholde haue come to Londe a-Lyue. The assaute Was Lefte al that day. A-morrow, whan masse was herd˜, al the Oste the[n] wenten to the assaute wyslyer and waryr than thay diddyn the day to-fore, and trusten as well to sleght as to streynth. The men of the toun saw ham comynge, and were ryght sore aferde that thay no sholde not wythstonde the assaut, and vndyrstodyū also that with wronge thay heldyn ayeyñ her lorde. thay toke ham to consayll, and besoghten Pees ; and, throgh besechynge of two Bisshopis that that tyme weryn wythin the toune, and othir Pesibbill men also with ham, thay yoldyn ham al to Macmurgh ; and foure Hostagis, the beste that he wolde chese, delyuerid˜ to hym for the Pees, and trewely wyth hym forto holde from that tyme forward˜, for har trew Lorde / Macmurgh, as wysse and ware, For cause that he wolde that the strangeres sholde haue the bettyr hert and will, hym forto serwe, he bethoght hym that, of the fryste good˜ aduenture that to hym was fall, thay that best weryn worthy, they sholde haue there Parte, and the heghesto. All the toun of weysford˜, with twey cantredes alther-nexte, he yafe to Robert Steuenes-sone and to Moryce fiz-Geraud˜, as the Promes to-for was made / othyr twey cantredes he yafe Heruey of Montmvrthy,—nexte to thay two on the

*Marginal notes:*

A.D. 1169.

A Breton ship with wheat and wine is taken by English sailors.

The French cut their cables and set sail ; but the English are rescued.

[1 wentyntyn, MS.]

[*Fol. 3 a.]

The allies march to assault Wexford again ;

but it is yielded to them.

It is given to Fitz-Stephen and Fitz-Gerald.

A.D. 1169. com̃ in that same * flote, hym þriddesum of knyghtes, and com̃
[*Fol.3 a.] þrogħ the Erle Ric*hard*, more for to spýe the lond' than to fight.

[CHAPTER V.]

The united [1] Vħan this was thus I-don al aft*er* haꝛ will, they tok wit*h* hame
forces
invade            the folk of weysford', and' wenten ham̃ toward' Ossory, with 4
Ossory, to   ferd' as mýght by tre thousant men̄; and was than pri*n*ce of
the prince
of which      Ossory, Macdonenild', a man̄ þat was Macmorogħ swith lotħ and
country
Macmurgh     all his men̄, for mýcħ shame that thay had hym i-do. At þe
was a        begýnynge, as thay com̃ in-to the contrey, in narrow weys drogħ 8
bitter
enemy.       woddes and' mores, thay fonden the men̄ of the contrey stalwartħ
             for to defend' haꝛ lond'; & mýcħ tene ham̃ didde, ar that daý mýght
             [take] the pleyne; and' eke into the pleýn thay folwed' ham̃ full
             freslý. the horsman̄ saw this, and' turned manly vp-on ham, & 12
             anoon slowen right many of ham̃, & discomfited' ham̃ eu*er*ychone.

They         And' thay þat þe horsmen̄ kest to ground' wit*h* speres and' wit*h*
defeat him,  swerdes, þe yrisshe fotemen̄ smotene of the heddes. Whan þo
             slagħt was all I-do, and' har enýmýes all ou*er*-comen, thay 16
             broghten well ccc heudes[2], and kesten at Macmorgh feet. he
             be-held' ham̃, & tried eu*er*ý of ham̃ bý ham̃-self, for to know hame,
             & hild' vp his handes and' tanked' god almýghtý ful Inwardly.

and          Oon hede ther was, a-monge þe otheꝛ, of a man that he ou*er*-dede 20
Macmurgh
triumphs     and' mýcħ hated; he name hit be the heeꝛ and' by the eers, and'
in a brutal  wit*h* girslicħ bit, as no man̄ ne oweth to done; wit*h* his teetħ
way.
             he karue of his nose and' botħ lippes. There-after þeý wenten̄
             forther into the contrey, slowen, robeden, and branden full manly 24
             al þat hame withstonden, in-to the tým the pri*n*ce of Ossory, by
             consaill of his men̄, send' to ham̃, & be-soght pees: the pees was
             graunted' whan he hit býsoght, vp-on good ostages, and' othes
Peace is     I-sweꝛ, þat he, to his lord' Macmorgħ, shold' be trew, and' trowth 28
made with
the prince   hold', trýwly serue fro that týme forward'. in these fightes as in
of Ossory.   many othere, thogħ that in the englishe host noon weꝛ bot good
Robert de    and stalward', Robert þe Barꝛ and Meiler fiz-henrý weren thaý
Barri and
Meiler       that best deden. Thaý weren both ýong knýghtes, and Robert 32
Fitzhenry    Steuenes-sonnes neues; the oon his brotheꝛ sone, the otheꝛ his
fight best.
             susteres sone; of diuerse man*er*s, both [3] of hardnes & of stalworthnes

────────────

[1] a small w is inside the V.        [2] heuedes, heads.        [3] but.

syde toward watyrford [1],—a knyght that come in that same flitte, A.D. 1169.
hym thyrdesum of knyghtes, and come throgh the Erle Rychard,   [1] mari con-
more forto spy the londe than to fyght.                       terminos.

[CHAPTER V.]

Whan this was thus don al aftyr har will, thay toke with  Capitulum
      tham the Pepill of weysford, and wenten ham to-ward Ossory,  v<sup>m</sup>.
with osto as myght be by thre Mł. men [2]. And was than Prince of  [2 cum
Ossory, Macdononylde, a man that was myche be-hatyd of Mac-  exercitu
                                       virorum
murgh, for myche shame that thay hadd hym donne. At the  quasi
                                       trium
begynnynge, as thay come into the contrey, in narrow weyes throgh  milium.]
woddis and mores, thay foundyn the men of the contrey bolde forto
defende har londe; and mych sorrow ham didd, ar thay mygh[t]
take the Playne: and when thay come to the Playne, thay folwid
ham ful fresly. the hors-men saw this, and turned boldely vp-on
ham, and anoone slowyn rygh[t] many of ham, and dys-comfited
ham euerychon. And thay that the hors-men keste to ground
wyth Sperys and wyth Swerdis, the Iryssh footte-men Smoten of  300 heads
                                      of foes are
the hedis. Whan the slaght was al y-do, and har ennemys al  brought to
                                      Mac-
ouer-come, thay broghten wel ccc. hedis, and kesten at Macmurgh  murgh.
is fete. he behylde ham, and tvrned euery of tham [3] by hym-Selfe  [3 than,
forto know tham, and hilde vp his handis, and thankyd almyghty  MS.]
god ful Inwardly. Oone hede ther was, amonge the othyr, of a man
that he gretly dreddid and myche hatid; he toke hit by the heeres  He bites
and by the Ers, and grymly hit bitte, as no man sholde haue doun;  off the
                                      nose and
wyth his tethe he kutte of his nose and bothe lippis. Ther-aftyr  lips of one.
they wenten fourdyr Into the contrey, kildyn, robedyn and brandyn  His men
ful boldely al that ham wythstodyn, into the tyme the Prynce of  kill, rob,
                                      and slay,
ossory, by consaylle of his men, sent to ham, and besoght Pees. the  till Mac-
                                      donough
Pees was graunted whan he hit be-soght, vp-on good Ostagis, and  sues for
                                      peace.
othis y-Sworne, * that he, to His Lord Macmurgh, shold be trewe,  [*Fol.3 b.]
and trowth Hold, and trewely Serwe fro that tyme forth. In this
fyghtes as in many othyr, thoght that in the Englysh hoste noone
were but good and bolde, Robert de barry and Meyler fiz-henry
weryn thay that best diddyn: they wer both yong knyghtes, and
Robert Steuenes-sones emys [4] both, the one his brodyr sonne, the  [4 neveus,
othyr his Systyr Sonne; Of dyuers maners, but of hardynes and  nepotes.

A. D. 1169. mostdele al I-lýcĥ; ffor Meyler was a maiᴅ that ouer mycĥ
desyred̃ to be I-preisede, and þat meiᴅ sholden mýcĥ speke of
his stalwardnes, and preisen hym.  Robert was kýndlýc, hardy,

[*Fol.3 b.] & stalwarde, * and euer witĥ the forthmost in euerý fight and 4
in euerý peril, bot he hatede notynge so mycĥ as that me
sshold̃ spek of his stalwardnes, ne hyme preiese.  The whill the
host was thus in Ossory, befel þat þay wereiᴅ a nýght I-loget

A phantom  in an old̃ castell, & aboute; and̃ these tweýn, as haᴊ wone was, 8
army at
night       weren botĥ I-hosted to-gedderes: ffeᴊ witĥ-yn nyght come an
creates     host vp-on ham, of so mycĥ folk as thegĥ hit were fele thousand̃,
terror
among the  on euerý side smýtynge vp the host as they wolden in wode
English;    raas ferly ouersaiħ hame, al, witĥ wepne rýngýnge, speres and̃ 12
sparthes ruthlynge to-geddre, witĥ cryynge so gryslý that noon

['¹ MS.     ende was of helf faᴊ, as ¹hoft-sithes was wonet to be-faħ in ostynges
host.]      in Irland̃; of whiċhe frightnes the most parte of the oste was so

['² MS.     aferd̃, that þay flowe ² and hidden haᴆ, some in wodnes, som in 16
slowe.]     mores.  These twey stalward̃ meᴍ henten haᴊ wepene, & lep to
but Meiler  hors, and wenten a-noon to Robertes tentes, (Steuenes sonᴇ,) and̃
and
de Barri    cryed vp-on haᴊ felowes þat day sholden withstond̃, and̃ tak hert
manfully
withstand   to hame, and̃ defend̃ ham-self; bot few theᴊ weᴊ that so diden, 20
the panic.  til they saw that this crie and̃ þe noise was all I-left, & nas
bot fantasy.  Whan the host hem gaddred ayaýn to-geddre, thaý
weᴊ full soᴊ ashamet that thay so arglý put ham to f[l]ight, and̃
mycĥ speche was amonge ham, and̃ maný, hadden gret enuý, and̃ 24
mých wonder toght of Robert de barᴊ, that whan the host was

Character  in so gret frightnes, he was that maiᴅ þat stydfastlý most hým
of Robert
de Barri.   held, and̃ most hým entised for to witĥstond̃ and̃ fight; and̃
amonge all the goode thewes that in hym weren, þis inamliċhe is 28
i-told̃ of hým, that for no violence ne ferlý aduentuᴊ þat hym
mýght betid, he was neuer whan-hopefully argh, ne aferd̃, ne
amayed̃ of hert, ne shamefully ne didde hym to flight, bot euer
moᴊ he was I-liċĥ redy to weppen and̃ to defend̃ hym-self, and̃ 32
to helpen all oþer; he the formost knýght that in this conqueste
of Irland̃ first receyued̃ dýnt and̃ hurtýng in battaill.  A wondeᴊ
was of that fantasye: A-morowe whaiᴅ hit was daý, I the place,
ther this folk I-scýe smýten vp-on hame, the wedes and̃ the grase 36

boldnys mostdele al y-lyke.  For Meyler was a mañ that gretly A.D. 1169.
desyryd' to be Praysid', and that men sholde myche Speke of his
boldnys, and Preysyn hym. / Robert was kyndly, hardy and bold,
and euer with the fryst in euery fyght / and in euery Perill ; but *nec*
he hatyd' nothynge so myche as that a man sholde speke of his *laudis*
*eractor,*
boldnys, ne hym Preyse. / The whyll the hoste was thus in Ossory, *nec aurae*
*popularis*
befell that thay weryn a-nyght y-logid' in an olde castell, and aboute. *aucupator.*
And thus two, as they wer wonyd', weryn in one Plase to-gedderis.
Fer with-in nyght, come an hoste vp-on ham of so mych Pepill, as A phantom
host
they were many thowsandis, on euery syde Smytynge vp the hoste, [*tanquam*
*in impetu*
as they woldyn, in wode raas, fersly ouersayle hame al, wyth wepyñ *furoris*
ryngynge, Speris and sparris rutlynge to-giddyr, wyth cryynge so *sui cuncta*
*derorau-*
grymly, that none ende was Of elf fare, as ofte-tymes was wonet to *tium*]
befall in hostyngis in Irland'[1].  Of whych ferde, the moste Parte of frightens
the
the Oste was so a-dred', that they flow and hiddyn ham ; somme in English-
woddis, some in mores / This two bolde men token har wepyn, and men, who
run and
lepe to hors, and wentyn anone to Robert Steuenes-sonne, and cried hide ;
on har fellowis that ' they sholdyn wytstond', and take herte to hame,
and defende ham-Selfe ;' but fewe were that so diddyñ, tyll they saw
that this cry and this noyse was al cessid', and nas but a fantasy. but are
much
whan the host them gaderid' ayeyn to-giddyr, they wer ful sore ashamed
asshamyd' that thay so fently Put ham to flyght ; and mych Speche when they
find it was
was amonge hame ; and many haddyn gret enuy, and mych wondyr all fancy.
thoght of Robert du Barry, that Whan the host was in so gret ferde,
he was that man that moste stidfastly hym helde, and moste them
styrrid' to wythstond' and' fyght. / And amonge al the good' dedis
that in hym weryn, this Pryncipaly is of hym tolde, that for no
vyolence ne ferly aduenture that to hym chaussyd', he was neuer in
wanhope sette, ne agaste, ne aferd', ne abassid' of herte, ne shamefully did hym to flyght ; but euer-more he was lyke redy to wepyn,
and' to defend' hym-Selfe, And to helpyn al othyr.  he was the
formyst knyght that, in this conqueste of Irland', fryst receyued' *in hac*
*Hiberniae*
stroke and hurte in bataill // A wondyr was of that fantasy *expugna-*
a-morrow, whan hit was day : In the Playn ther this Pepill y-seye *tione.*

---

[1] Cujusmodi phantasma in Hibernia circa expeditiones frequens esse solebat.
—*Op.* v. 235.

c

A.D. 1169. that stoden al euen vp-right, thay lay all I-drow a-doune and I-cast to grond. [*This grass, &c. only in Harl. MS. 177.  Op. v. 236.*]

[CHAPTER VI.]

[*Fol. 4 a.]

As this was on this maner I-don, the tythynges sprongen in-to al Irland hwow Macmorgh conquered his lond * vpon 4 his men, and that no man myght hym withstond for out-comen men that he lade with hym.  Roryk O'Concowr of Connaght, that was that tym kynge of al Irland, vndrestod hym, and toght in his hert the gret peril that myght be-fall hym and al the 8 lond folk, drogh the owt-comen folk þat was thus in-to the land I-com; he sent his messagers to al the gret men of the lond, and in a lityll whill gaddred ham to-geddre to a parlement, and tok ham to rede that euery on his half shold gaddre al the 12 power þat they myght, for to wer vpon Macmorgh.  And as hit was purueied, so hit was don; Thay assemblet so many hostes and so mych folk on euery half, that noon end was, and comen to Okensely for to weren vpon Macmorgh.  Whan this hostes 16 weren thus assemblet, the most parte of Macmorghis men, ayeyne har trowth and ayeyn har othes, some priuely whithdrow hem that day, nold nat to hym com, some al openly leften hym, and wenten to his fomen ayeyn hym; so that, in his most nede, trew 20 frendes ne fonde he non, sawe Robert, steuenes son, and his. With the lityll folk that thay hadden, thay wenten in-to a place nat fer frome ffernes, a pleyn place bisette about with montaignes and woddes, watres and mores, on euery side il to com [to].  the 24 entrees that ther weren, by Robert-is deuice thay setten men for to stopen, in some place with trees I-cast don, and in other places depe diches I-cast.  thegh the place wer stronge of kynde, thay maden hit mych stronge[r] with engyn, so that hit was 28 I-now seker recet to ham, and [to] her enemyes ful strong to com to, and with litill folke hit myght be I-kept; & derne weies thay hadden purueied to ham-self, owt to goo, ayeyn In to com, whan ham liked.  Whane the kynge of Connaght, with so many 32 hostes, was to ham I-com, he send to Robert by Messangers, and present hym with rych yiftes, and many mo he hym be-het, and fast hym be-soght that, owt of þe Contray, wyche no Right

Roderic O'Conor tries to raise the whole country against Macmurgh and the English.

Many of Macmurgh's followers desert him, but Fitz-stephen and his men stand by him.

They occupy a strong position not far from Ferns.

smytyn vp-on ham, the wedis and the grasse that stodyn al euyn A D. 1169.
vp-ryght, thay lay al y-throw dovñe *and* cast to ground.

### [CHAPTER VI.]

As this was thus donñe, the thythyngis Spronge Into al Irland, how Macmurgh conquerid his londe vpon his men, *and* that no man myght hym wythstond, for strange men that he ladd wyth * Hym.  Roryke Oconghoure, of Connaght, that was that tyme Kynge of al Irland, vndyrstode hym, and thoght in his herte the grete Perel that myght be-fall hym *and* al the londe-Pepill, throgh the strangeres that was thus in-to the lande coñe. He sende his messangeris to al the Lordis of the Londe, *and* in a lytyll whylle gaddred ham to-gedre to a parlement, *and* toke ham to consayll, that eu*er*y on his Syde sholde gaddyr al the Pepill that thay myght, forto werre vpon Macmurgh.  And as hit was Purueyed, so hit was doun.  Thay assemblid so many Hostis, *and* so mych Pepill on eu*er*y syde, that were vnnowmmerabill, and comyn [1] to Okenseley forto werre vp-on Macmurgh / Whan this hostis weryn thus assemblet, the moste parte of Macmurgh-ismen, ayeyn hare trowthe and here othis, Some priuely with-drow ham, that they nolde not to hym come.  Some al opynly leften hym, *and* wenten to his ennemys ayeyñ hym ; so that, in his moste nede, trewe frendis ne sownde he noñe, Sawe Robert Steuenes-Sone *and* his. wyth the Lytill Pepill that they haddyn, thay wentyn into a place not fare fromo Fernys, a pleyne place be-sette aboute with monttanys and woddis, watris and moris [2], on euery Syde il to come to.  The entrees that ther weryn, by Robert-is deuyce thay setten meñ forto stopyn ; in some Place with trees y-caste douñe, and in othir Placis depe dichis y-caste.  thegh the Place were stronge of kynd, thay maddyñ hit mych strongir with Engyn, So that hit was sure recette to tham, and to ther ennemys stronge to come to, and with lytill pepill hit myght be kepte.  And Erthe-weyes thay huddyn madd to tham-Selfe, out to goo, and ayeyñ In to come, when them Plesyd.  Whan the kynge of connaght, with so many hostis, was to tham come, he sende to Robert by Messangers, *and* presentid hym with rych yeftys, *and* mych more hym Promysyd, and gretly hym besoght that, out of the contery, whych no ryght

*Capitulum vj.*

[*Fol. 4 a.]

*tam sibi quam patriae tott.*

[1 comyn, MS.]

*in necessitatis articulo*

[2 paludibus.]

*naturalem difficultatem industria plurimum et arte munirit.*

C 2

he ne hadde to, ne no chalange ne myght setten vp-on, he and
his, with pees and lou[e] shold departe. Mich they spek of this,

Roderic
urges Fitz-
stephen to
retire from
the
country,
and litell thay sped. Ther-aftyr, the messagers turned to Macmorgh, and be-soghten hym on the kynges half, OConghour, 4
that he forth, with ham, shold turne vp-on the owt-comen folk,
ham to slee and vndo. And if he so wold, thay wold delyuer

[*Fol.4 b.]
and, failing
in this,
tries in
vain to
induce
Macmurgh
to turn
against the
English.
hym al leynestr, and stidfast pees and freud- *shippe mak hym
haue of the kynge and of all other. Many reisons thay shewed, 8
both for the land & for the land folk; bot notynge thay ne spedde,
ne noon answar ne hadden, that ham liket. Oconghour saw and
herd of his Messagers that he myght nat in such maner spede,
and that he most with streynth do, that he myght nat with fair 12
speche: he tok his wepne grymly, and stod vp a-monge his folk,

O'Conor
addresses
his
followers,
and thus sayd to ham; "Mighty men, and stalward in fight for
to defende your lond and your franchise! vndrestondeth, ayeyn
whice folk, and for what encheson, ye sholl this battaill tak an 16
hond: al oure enemy, that afor thus was owt of lond I-dryw
for his wykkednesse, In commune confusion of vs all, al be-tak
with owt-comen & wepned folk, is ayayn commen for enuy and
harme of vs, & hath I-broght vnked folk vp-on vs, that the harme 20
wich he had no power to don vs hym-self, throgh helpe of ham &

and de-
nounces
the
poisonous
Mac-
murgh.
mayntenaunce, the better myght brynge to end; and hath dight
hem to sheden his attyr so wide, that he rechet nat of his own
deth, bot that al mowen hawe our bale troghe hym, and for 24
noon shold be I-spared, and he ne spared hym-self. Ther-for we
willen withstond the begynynge, and þe yuel whil hit is comyn,
ar hit be Iroted; ffor harme wexet euer with longe abiddynge.

Patriam
itaque
tuentes, et
libertatem
Our lond & our fredom defended we manly; so that the slaght 28
of þese fewe be ferdnesse to many; & be ensample of these, al
other out-lond men to be adrede, such folies to begyn, and the

[' MS.
best.]
mynd of vs, with-out end to rest ¹."

[CHAPTER VII.]

Macmurgh
harangues
the men of
Leinster.
Macmorgh, on his halue, be-held his men, and saw ham 32
sor amayed: with wordes that he myght, he conforted
ham on this maner: "Men of leynester, which, sothfast trowth
& stidfaste kynd in al aduentures, vs hath felawes I-maked,

he hadd therto, ne no calange ne myght setten vpon, he *and* A.D. 116).
his, wyth Pees and loue, sholde deperte.  Mych[1] they spoke of  [¹ Myth,
this, and lytyll thay Spede / There-aftyr, the messangers turned  MS.]
to Macmurgh, and be-soghten hym on the kyngis be-halfe, Oconnoghoure, that he forth, wyth tham, sholde turne vpon the strangeres, *ut in*
hame to kyll and vndo.  And yf he so wolde, thay wolde delyuyr *exterae nationes*
hym all leynystere, *and* stydfaste Pees *and* frendshippe make hym *delendas*
haue of the kynge and of al othyr.  Many reysonys thay shewid; *simul cum ipsis arma*
both for the londe and for the lond-pepill ; but nothynge thay ne *conrer-*
spede, ne noone answere hadde, that ham Plesyd.  Oconnoghoure *teret.*
saw and herde of his messyngers, that he myght nat in suche
maner spede, and that he moste with streynth do that, that he
myght not with fayre speche.  He toke his wepyn grymly, and
stode vp amonge his pepill, and thus sayde to tham :—" Myghty
men, and bolde in fyght forto defende youre londe and youre *patriae*
fredome !  Vndyrstondyth, ayeyn whych * Pepill, and for whate [*Fol.4 b.]
cause, ye sholde this Bataill take on Honde.  Al oure ennemy, *tutores, et libertatis.*
that afor this was out of londe ydrywe for his wickidues, In
comynne confusion of vs all, all be-take wyth strangeres and
wepened Pepyll, is ayeyn comyn, for Enuy and harme of vs, and *quod,*
hath broght strange Pepill vp-on vs, that the harme whych he *cunctis communi*
hadde no Powere to don vs hym-selfe, throgh helpe of them and *labe in-*
mayntenavnce, the bettyr myght brynge to ende ; and hath dyght *fectis, ut nemini*
hym to shedyn his wenym so wyde, that he takyth no fors to dye, *purcatur,*
but that we al mow haue oure [e]will throgh hym, and for none *nec ipse sibi*
sholde be Sparid, and he ne Sparyth hym-Selfe.  There-for we will *pepercit.*
wy[th]stonde the begynnynge, and the Perel whyle hit is comyn, are *exterae nationes*
hit be rotyd.  For harme wexeth euer wyth longe abydynge.  Oure *ab ausu*
londe and oure fredome, defende we manly ; So that the slaght *tam nefario*
of this fewe be ferde to many ; and by Ensampill of thes, al othyr *imper-*
strangers sholde be aferde, suche folies to begynne, And the mynde *petuum abstru-*
of vs, wyth-oute ende to abyde."  *antur.*

### [CHAPTER VII.]

MAcmurgh / on his syde, be-held his men, *and* Sawe hame *Capitulum*
sore a-bassyd. with wordis that he myght, he confortid *vij^m.*
ham on this manere : " Men of leynyster, wych, trusty trouth and *comites*
stydfaste kynde in al aduentures, vs hath fellowis y-made, wyth- *indivisos*

A.D. 1169. wit*h*out any partyng, a-rer we our hertes, styfly vs-self to defend.
The maistre of wreth and of Coueytise, that wit*h* streynth wold

Let us defend ourselves !

vs brynge vnderfoot, and ows ayeyn dryue out of lond, other, that
wors is, in the same lond, vs tynken vndo: that god shild'! loo, her 4
is I-com vpon our hed, of his myčh gaderynge of folke prowt &
hauteyn. be ye well vndrestond, þat nat trogh gret tale of men

[*Fol.5a.]
Right, not numbers, win battles.

ne trogh greth streynth, both drogh *right and trowth that man
hath wit*h* hym, battailles doth ouercom. We haue for vs, ayeyn 8
har pryd, mekenes ; ayayns har vnryght, right and trouth ; ayeyn
har boldenesse and ouer-truste, mekenesse and maner. Thay
fighten for coueytise, for to get good ; and we, for to flee harme.
with al this we bene in strong place and wel I-warned. The mor 12
that her commeth, the more encombrement we shall do hame, by
lityll folk ham to ouercom, so that we be of on hert, and stifly

Be of one heart, and fight !

withstond.'

[CHAPTER VIII.]

Fitz-stephen makes a speech to the English-men.

Whan Macmorghe had his tale I-endeth in his speche, 16
Robert Steuenes-son, spake to his felaws and to his
meigne on this wise: "ffightyng fors, & yongelynges I-corne,
that so many perilles hawe to-geddre I-soffred, and euer in al
aduentures, and of heigh hert ibe! If we inly vndrestonde wiche 20
men we ben, wit*h* what lodes-man, and for what thynge we this perille vndre-tok wit*h* stalwardnesse, as our [wone]ys, we shullen ouercome ; & the grace that ye I-haue i-hadde ar this of god, ne shal vs
nat forlete. Of the folke of Troy we ben kyndlych y-come, on þat 24

From Troy we get bold-ness ; from France, skill in fight.

oon half, fro þe first begynnyge ; of ffraunce, we haue kynde on
other half. Throgh kynd of Troy, we owe to be hardy ; throgh
kynd of ffraunce, we ben vsed in wepene ; & so as we bene of double
mane kyndly, of good herth & well y-wepned, & well y-lernet yn 28
wepne, ne dout no man, þat such vnwepned rascayll any power

We come not for hire, or as pirates, but to help a noble man unjustly treated.

haw ows to wythstond: on that other halue, we come nat yn-to
thys land as hyryng men, ne for no couetyse of gold, ne of syluyr,
ne galyotʒ ne robbers ; bott for to helpe thys heyth man that ys so 32
noble & so fre, &, þrogh hys owne men, lodderly was of lond
y-dryue. we hawe reuth of hys harm ; & helpeth vp þat adoun was
ẏ-broʒthe ; to hys kynd sted, bryngeth hym þat vnkyndly was

out eny partynge, arrere we vp oure her*tes*, boldely vs to defende. A.D. 1169.
The maystyr of wreth *and* of couetyse, that wyth streynth wolde <sup>the</sup> oration
vs brynge vndyrfote, and vs ayeyn dryue out of londe, Othir, that [in a later hand].
wors is, in the same londe Purposyth vs to vndo / that god <sup>quod</sup>
forbedde / be-holde, here is come vp-on oure hedd, of his mych <sup>absit</sup>
gadrynge of pepill Proute and hauteyn.  be ye wel vndyrstond,
that not wyth many men, ne wyth grete Streynth, bot by ryght
*and* trouth that man hath wyth hym, batalis doth ouercome.  We
haue for vs, ayeyñ har pryde, mekenys; ayeynes hare vnryght, ryght
*and* trouth; ayeyñ har boldnys *and* ouer-truste, mekenesse *and* *modus et*
maner. thay fyghtyn for couetyse, forto gete good; And we, to *modestia.*
shonne myschefe. wyth all this, we byth in stronge Place, and well *tam arte*
warnyd.  The more that here comyth, the more encombrement *quam natura*
we shal do ham, by lytill folke ham to ouercome, So that we be of *munitissi-mum.*
one herte, *and* styfly wystonde."

### [CHAPTER VIII.]

WHen *Macmurgh* hadd his tale y-endyd in his speche, *Capi*tulum
Roberte Steuenes-Soñe spake to his fellowys, *and* to them *viij*<sup>m</sup>.
in this maner Sayde : " Fyghten feris, *and* yonglynges y-know, that *Bellorum*
so many Perelis haue to-geddyr Sofferid, and *cuer* in al aduentures, *socii,* *adole-*
and of hey hert ben ! If we Inwardly wndyrstonde what men we *scentes electi.*
ben ; wyth what lodes-man, *and* for what thynge, we this Perel
vndirtoke ; wi*th* boldnys, as we were wonyd, we shall ouercome ; and
the grace that we haue hadd ar this of god, ne shall vs not forsake.
// Of * the folke of Troy we Ben Kynly come, on that one syde, fro [*Fol. 5 a.]
the fryste begyn[i]nge; of Fraunce, we haue kynde on the othyr
halfe.  Throgh the kynde of troy, we sholde be bolde ; throgh
kynde of Fraunce, we ben wsyd in wepyñ; and so as we ben of
doubil maner kyndly, of good herte *and* wel wepenyd, and wel
lernyd in wepyñ,—ne dout no man, that Suche vnwepenyd rascaill *populum*
any Powere haue to vs to wyth-stonde.  One that ouer syde, we *inermem.*
come not into this londe as wagid men, ne for no couetyse of
golde, ne of Syluyr, ne of galiotz, ne robbers ; but forto helpe *Nos ergo*
this goodo man that is so nobill and so fre, and, wyth his owyn *piratae, non prae-*
men, wickydly was out of his londe drywe.  We haue Pite of his *dones huc adrenimus.*
harme ; and helpyth vp that adouñ was caste / to his kynde state,

A.D. 1169. ther-of I-bansheth. And he, as largh man & good prynce, hat
He has
given us  vs yeuen wyde londes & ryche townes, & owr lond folke wyll
land.  setten & planten stydfastly yn þys lond, nowe & euer¹.  Therfor,
['MS.
ouer.]  men, full [of] streynth & stalwarthnes, such thyng y-magyneth 4
to-day hartly to do, that owr kynred ne go nat out of kynd,
We'll win  & yn thys, lyuynge oþer dey, we manly wyn the pryce, that
the battle
and glory.  euer more torne to whyrshyppe vs & al our that aftyr ws shullen
come."                                                                 8

[CHAPTER IX.]

Wythe these wordes, & other suche, these heghe men
comforted har folk, for day schulden hawe the bettyr wyll
O'Conor,  well for to fyght.   And whan day were on euery half redy for to
doubtful of  smyth to-geddre, OConoȝwyr, be-thoȝghthyng that the aduentur 12
the issue,
makes  of battaylle ben ofte doutouse & myche vncerteyne, And as the
terms with  whysman seythe 'all tynge me shall assay, rather than fyȝth,'
Mac-
murgh,  & all-so he & hys doutenden well sore to assemble with folke
[*Fol.5 b.]  I-wepned, On al maner that he myȝght, * He was abowte thame 16
sholde make peas.   thane, throgh besechyng of goode men
that went betwene, & throgh grace of the holy goste, was
the peas y-made, on þis maner ; that thay sholde leve leynester
who, it is  to Maccmorghowe, & he sholde hitt holde of Oconoghour, & 20
agreed,
shall hold  hym knowlech, & suget be to hym as to a kynge & prynce
from
Roderic,  of Irland.   And þat thys shold be stydfastly I-hold, Macmorgh
and give  bytok hym hys sone to astage, by so, þat yf he good pees hold,
him his
son as a  & trewly hym helde, Oconghur shold hym yeue hys doghter to 24
hostage.  wyff.  Whan thys was comynly I-shewed & I-knowe, & othes
I-shwerne on euery half, all thys trewly to hold, Another thyng
was bespoke bytwen ham, bott þat preuely, that Macmorgh ne
shold nomore brynge vnked mon yn-to the lond, & thay that 28
he hade y-broght, as rathe as he had leynestre yn good pees,
he shold anoon send ayenne home, & delyueryd þe lond of ham.

[CHAPTER X.]

Maurice
Fitzgerald  Aftyr that þe pees was thys Imaket, þe host departed,
now
arrives,  euery on hys half.  Sone þer-after come Moryce, Geraudes 32
with a fol-
lowing, at  son, Robertes brother, of whom we spoken ar thys, wyth .x. knyghtes
Wexford.  & .xxx. Squyres & ij houndred footmen, & ar[y]ued at weysford ;

bryngyth hym that vnkyndely was therof y-banshet. And he,   A.D. 1169.
as large man and good Prince, hath vs yevyꝺ wyde landis and *gentem hic nostram in*
ryche townes; *and* oure londe-pepill will setten and Plantenꝺ *insula plantare.*
stydfastly in this londe, nowe and euer. Therfor, men full of *seu rin-*
streynth and of boldnes, Suche thynge ymagyneth to-day hertely *cculo seu morienclo*
to do, that oure kynred ne go not oute of kynde; and in this, *perpetuam*
lywe or dye, we manly wynn the Pryce, that euer-more shall *nobis gloriam*
tour[n]e to oure wyrchippe, and to al oure that aftyr vs schalle *strenuitate compa-*
come." *remus.*

[CHAPTER IX.]

Wyth this wordis, and othyr Suche, thes good men confortyd *Capitulum*
hare Pepill, for thay sholdyn haue the bettyr wyll, well *ix^m.*
forto fyght. And when thay were on euery halfe redy forto smyte
to-geddre, Oconghoure bethoght hym that the aduenture of bataill
ben ofte doutfull *and* mych vncertayn. An[d], as the Wysman *Ter. Eun.*
Seyth, "Althynge we oghte to assay, radyr than fyght" / And also *IV. vii. 19.*
he and his douteden well sore to fyght wyth Pepill wepenyd. On al
maner that he myght, he was besy to haue Pees. Then, by the
besechynge of goodꞋ men that wente betwene, and throgh grace of
the holy goste, was the Pees mad on this maner; that thay sholde
leue leynystere to Macmurgh, and he sholde bite holde of Oconghoure, and hym knowlech, and Subiecte be to hym as to a kynge
and Prynce of IrlandꞋ. And that this sholde be stydfastly holde,
Macmurgh toke hym his sone to hostage, by So, yf he good Pees *filium*
helde, and trewely hym helde, Oconghoure sholde hym yeue his *suum*
doghter to wyfe. whan this was comynly shewyd *and* know, and *Cnuchurum.*
othis sworꝺ on euery Syde, al this trewely to kepe, Anothyr thynge
was spokyn be-twen them, bothe that Pryuely, that Macmurgh ne
sholde no more strangeres brynge into the londe; And thay that
he hadd broght, as Sone as he hadd leynystere in goodꞋ Pees, he *statim*
shold Sende them home, and delyuere the londe of hame. *remitteret.*

[CHAPTER X.]

Aftyr that the Pees was thus made, the hoste departydꞋ on *Capitulum*
his halue. Sone there-aftyr come Morice, Geraudis Sonne *, *x^m.*
Robert-is Brodyr, of whom we Spokyn ar this, Wyth x Knyghtis [*Fol.5 b.]
and xxx^ti Squyeris, and two hundredꞋ fotemen, and londidꞋ at

A.D. 1169. A man full queynt, trow trogh al thynge, & stalwarth, & stydfast of word, & of hert symple, & shamffast as a mayd. Wañ Macmorgh & Robert hyt wysten, thay weren ful glad, & boldeř þan thay before were : thay come to ham sone wyth þe oste þat thay had. 4

Macmurgh determines to attack Dublin; and goes, accompanied by Fitzstephen.

Macmorgh be-thoght hym̄ of the mych vnryght that þe men of deuelyng̃ hym hadden done, & hys fadeř all-so, many sithe : he assembled hýs hostes, & redied hym to wend thedere. Boot Robert byleft with somdell of þe meýne, fore to rere hym a castell 8 at a place that me clepeth þe karryke, & ys twey myle out of weysford ; & Moryce went wyth hým. Macmorgh, as mayster & leder of the host, & cheuetayn of al. In lytell whyle, all þe contreys about dyuelyn, wyth robynge & bernyng & sleýng, 12

[¹ MS. wepen.]

weren ¹ neght I-broght to noght. The siteჳeyns of dyuylyn, whan thay thys wysten, thay sentten to ham, & besoghten pees, & yaue

The citizens submit and acknowledge Macmurgh as their lord.

ham so mych gold & syluer that non end was at har wylle, & good ostages, & othes I-[s]wore that þay sholden to Macmorgh 16 trew be, & hým knowleche þan-forward as lord & prynce.   Fro that tyme that thys was y-do, ther was noon Iryshman yn leynnesteř, of hey kyne ne of low, that for seruesse ² of englysse-

[² for ferdnesse?]

men ne yeldet hym to Macmorgh, so þat þer was noght of þe 20 londřfolke þat all nas subyett to hym, & redy to hys wylle.

[CHAPTER XI.]

O'Conor makes war on O'Brien of Limerick

IN thys whyle, wax a grett wreth & a grete stryfe betwyx þe kyng̃ of Connaght, & donoll Obreyñ, þe kyng [of] lymeryke, & of thomond.   the kyng of connaght, Oconoghuř, gaddereď hys 24

[*Fol.6a.]

hostes for to werř vpoñ Obreen.   Obreen sent * to mamorrowჳ, for

and sends Fitzstephen and Maurice to oppose him.

allyaunce that was betwen ham, that he shold hym helpe.   he spake þer-of to Robert & to Moryce, & bad ham that þay sholď go theder for to helpe Obreen.   Thay name har meñ wyth ham, & wenten 28 ynto thomonď, and ffondeñ Oconoghuř, that stryffly stode ayeyñ ham, & many fyghtes ham yaue.   Bot the dysconfituř turned vpoñ

O'Conor is defeated, and O'Brien becomes independent of him.

Oconoghuř, & many of hys meñ wer I-sleyñ, so that wythe shame he most turne ayeyñ ynto Connaght.   And fro that tym, Obreen 32 wythdrow hym from̄ Oconoghuř, & neuer after was subyect to hyñ as he was thař-by-fore ; & the englysh hoste, wyth grett gettynges & with rych yiftes, turned ayeyne yñ-to leynestre.

weysford.  A man full quent, trew throw al thynge, bolde, and A.D. 1169.
stydfaste of word, *and* of hert sympil, and shamefaste as a mayd //
Whan Macmurgh *and* Robert hadd' wyttynge of Morice-is comynge,
they weryn full glad, and boldyr than thay before were.  thay
came to thaim Sone wyth the hoste that thay hadde / Macmurgh
bethoght hym of the mych wronge that the men of Deuelyn to hym *graves*
hawydyn done, and his fadyr also, many tymys : he assemblid' his *Dubli-nensium*
hostes, *and* made hym redy thedyr forto goo.  But Robert lefte *injurias.*
wyth some of the meyngne forto rere hym a castel at a Place that
is callid' the Karryke, and is two myle out of weysford'; And
Morice went wyth hym.  Macmurgh as gouernoure and ledere
of the hoste and capytan of all.  In lytell Processe of tyme, al
the contreis about deuelyn, wyth Robynge and brennynge *and*
kyllynge of pepill, weryn al-meste broght to noght //  The Citseynys *ad exter-minium*
of deuelyn, whan thay of this had wyttynge, thay Sendyn *and* *fere*
besoght Pees, and yaue hame so myche golde and Siluyr that none *redacto.*
ende was at har will, and good hostagis, *and* othis Sworne that thay
Sholdyn to Macmurgh be trewe, *and* hym knowlege as lord and'
Prynce.  Fro that tyme that this was done / ther was none
Irysh-man in leynystre, of hey kyn ne of low, but that, for fere
of Englysh-men, thay yaue hame to Macmurgh, So that ther was
none of the londe-pepill, that al nas subiecte to hym, and redy
to his wille /

### [CHAPTER XI.]

IN this tyme, rose grete debate and' wrete be-twyxe the *Capitulum*
kynge of Connaght, and Donalde Obreyn, the kynge of *xj^m.* [Fol. 6 a.]
lymerike, and of thomonde.  the kynge of Connaght, Oconghoure,
gaderid' his hostes forto werre vp-on obreyn.  Obreyn Sende to
Macmurgh, for allyaunce that was betwen ham, that he sholde hym
helpe.  He Spake therof to Robert *and* to Morice, *and* bade them
that th[a]y sholde go thedyr forto helpe obreyn.  Thay, and har men
wyth hame, *and* wentyn Into thomonde, and' foundyn oconghoure,
that styfly stode a-yennes hame, *and* many fightes hame yaue. *post*
But the dis-comfyture turned' vp-on oconghoure; *and* many cf his *varios conflictus*
men were sleyn, So that wyth shame he mvste tvrne into *vbique*
connaght. / And fro that tyme, Obreyn wythdrowe hym from *victoria potitus.*
oconghoure, and neuer aftyr was subiecte to hym as he was
ther-to-forn.  And the Englysh hoste, wyth grete gettynges *and*
wyth ryche yftis, turned' ayen Into Leynystre.

[CHAPTER XII.]

A. D. 1169.
Macmurgh
aspires to
be king of
all Ireland.

Macmoroȝwȝch sawe the englysshe-men so stalwarth that no power myght ham wythstond: he bethoght hym̄ of thynge that was passed, & that sume of hys eldre to-fore hym̄ hadden̄ somtyme the kynge-dome of all Irland, & that al the 4 lond was subyet to hym : he wold, by hýs myght, by ryght of hys eldren̄, brynge hyt yn-to the self state, that al þe lond shold be vnder̄ hys lordshyppe, as hyt was wndre hys eldren̄ to-fore hýs tým. Of þys týngẽ he spak preuely wýth Robert, & wyth 8 Moryce, & besoght har consaýll therof ; And þay hym̄ answerd, & seiden̄, that 'lýghtly that mýght be done, yf he wold make come more plente of englyssh men̄ ynto þe lond.' he bad ham well

Fitz-
stephen
and
Maurice,
whom he
consults,
advise him
to bring
over more
English-
men.

þorwe, that thay sholden yn al manere senden after more of har 12 kyn̄ & frendshype. & for thay shold̄ the bettyre wyll haue ther̄-to, he profred̄ ham̄ to yeue hys eldest doghtre to on of ham, whych hyre so wold, wyth all hys lond aftyr hýs daý. bot, fore euery of ham had wyf & I-spoused that tyme, after mych spech, & 16 many dalyaunce ther-of at thys consaylle, thay thoght þat he, to the erle Rychard, (of whom we haue ar thys I-spoke, & to whom he behete the same doghter ther-to-fore at Brystowe,) hys lettres

He sends a
letter to
Earl
Richard
urging him
to come
over.

shold send on thys maner : " ❦ Dermot Macmorgh, priynce of 20 leynestre, to Rychard, Gylbertes son̄, erle of strugoýl, sendeth grettynge. If þou rekenest the tyme that ys Igoo, as well as we that nede haue, our̄ mone nys ycome to þe no rather than̄ hys tyme. Storkes & swalewes, & oþer somer foules, we haue 24 aftýre I-loked : thay comen̄, & wyth þe cold north-westre wýnd þay ben awey ywent. Bot thy comynge, that we so mych haue desyred & so longe I-loked after, nether estren wyn[d]e, ne noon other, vs ne hath I-send, as thou vs be-hete. þerfor, that thou ne 28 hast y-dene troght some grete lette, hastylý be about to do; for that wer̄ al our̄ gladnes, that thou hast swyth. If þou stalwardlý comest, & wyth good myght, the four̄ partyes of Irland shal sone be turned to þe fyft." Whan the erle had thys I-hard, he was 32

[*Fol.6b.] yn many thoghtes; & aftyr many selcouth * & dyuers redes, at the last he bethoght hym, that so fewe men̄ as weren̄ yn-to the lond I-come ther̄-to-fore, hadden̄ yn̄ so lytyll whýll so well I-sped of har aduentures : he name to hym the better herte, & thynge 36

[CHAPTER XII.]                                    A.D. 1169.

MAcmurgh sawe the Englysh-men so bolde, that no man *Capitulum* he myght ham wythstoud. he be-thoght hym of thynge *xij<sup>m</sup>.* that was passyd, and that some of his eldryn to-fore hym haddyn some tyme the kyngedome of al Irland, and that al the land was subiecte to hym.  he wolde, by his myght / by ryght of eldryn, *ad arita et* brynge hit Into the same state, that al the londe sholde be vndyr *antiqua jura.* his lordshipe, as hit was * Vndyr His eldryn to-fore His tyme.  Of [*Fol.6b.] this thynge He Spake wyth Robert *and* wyth Moryce, and be-soghte har consayle vp-on this.  And thay hym answerid, *and* sayd, that 'lyghtly that myght be done, yf he wolde make come more Plente *hoc facile* of Englysh-men into the londe.'  He Prayed ham, that in al haste *fieri posse.* thay sholde sende aftyr more of hare kyn *and* hare frendis.  and for thay sholde haue the bettyr will therto, he profered hame to yeue his eldyst doghtyr to one of ham, whych hyr so wolde, wi*th* al the londe aftyr his day.  but, for euery of hame hadd wyfe, and *legitime* spoused that tyme, Aftyr mych spech, *and* many delyaunce therof *copula gaudebat* at this consayle, thay thoght that he, to the erle richard (of whom *uterque.* wo haue ar this spoke, and to whom he promysyd the same doghtyr there-to-for at Brystowe,) his lette*res* sholde sende on this manere // " Dermot Macmurgh, Prince of leynystere, to Richard, Gylbertes sone, Erle of strugoil, sendyth gretynge.  If ye haue *Ovid, Ep.* rekenyd the tyme that is I-goo, as wel as we that nede haue, oure *Her.* ii. 7. compleynte is not come to yow no radyr than this tyme.  Storkys and swalewes, and othyr Somyr fowlis, we haue aftyr a-waytid: thay comyn; and wi*th* the colde north weste wynde thay ben *circio jam* away I-went.  But youre comynge, that we so mych haue desyrid *flante nec* and so longe lokid aftyr, nethyr estryn wynd, ne none othyr, vs ne *favonius* hath sende, as ye vs promysid.  Ther-for [as] ye ne haue this done *nec eurus.* but throgh some grete lette, hastely be a-but to do ; for that were al oure gladnys, that ye haste blywe.  Yf ye boldely come, and wyth good streynth, the foure Parties of Irland shal sone be turned to *de facili* the fyfte " // Whan the Erle hadd this hard, he was in many *conver- tentur* thoghtis ; and aftyr many and dyuers thoghtes, at the laste he be-thoght hym, that so few men as weryn into the londe y-come ther-to-fore, haddyn in so lytill tyme so wel y-spede of har aduentures : he hade the bettyr herte, and thynge that he dowtted

A. D.
1169-70.
The Earl
resolves
on the
enterprise.

that he douted myche ther-by-fore to begyne, he wax tho the
bolder to tak an hond. Fro that tyme, al hȳs thoght & all hys
wylle was, nyghte & day, wyth all hys myȝth to wend in-to Irland.
He went hym to þe kyng henry, & hym swith be-soght þat he shold 4
delyuer hym hys londes þat sholden be hys by ryght of herytage,
other yeue hym leue to do hym yn adventur, lond to purchace yn
vnked land.

A. D. 1170.

[CHAPTER XIII.]

Whan the Kynge wyst hys entent, wheder he wold go, 8
      he ne yaue hym fully leue, ne fully hym ne warned ; bot
wyth such leue as he had, he dight hym þe wynter tyll the
begynny[n]ge of Maye. He sent to-for hym ynto Irland A knyght

He sends
Reymond
le Gros to
Ireland,
who lands
near
Waterford,
ab. May 1,
1170.

that was I-called Reymond le gras ;—wyth hym, x knytghtes, & 12
fourty Squyers, & four score bowmen ;—A man ful hardy & stalwarde, & well proued yn wepne, Robertis neueu, & Moryces, har
eldest brother, sone. Thay arryued at a place i-called dun-
doneuile, four myle a south halfe Waterford ; & ther thay arered 16
a dyche, & a feble castel vpon, of yardes and turues[1]. The men
of Watterford, & wyth ham Malaghelyn of olan, thys waren
I-ware that thay y-hadden such neghborhede ful loth, & toke
ham to rede, þat þay wolden vpon ham, ar mo com to ham. Thay 20
assembled ham togeddre, well thre thousand men, & wenten ouer

He is
attackt
by the
Waterford
men and
O'Phelan,

the wattyr of sur, that parteth the twey contres of leynestre
& of mounestre, & setten ham yn thre hostes, ful boldely for to
assaylle the englysshe-men with-In har castell. Reymond & hys 24
men—thogh they fewe wer, they wer nat feynt—with vneuenly
host wenten out & assembled wyth ham. Bot, as no wonder was,
so few men ne myght nat all priuely fyghten ayeyn so many,
thay turned ham aye to har recet. the other weneden that thay 28
departed yn dyscomfyte ; thay braken har sheld. In, & wentten

and is
forced to
retreat to
his camp.

aftyr : & thay war nat fully wythyn þe yate, that some of ham
ner rather In than þe englyssh. Reymond saw that he & hys
weren yn gret perylle, & vpon poynt to lese the lyfe. he be-cryed 32
hys felewes, & turned stalwarthly vpon her formen[2] ; & þe fyrste
that come yn, he claue hym the heed, & throgh slaght of that

---

[1] MS. iurues, or inrues.             [2] men in front.

mych ther-be-for to begyn, he .wax than ~~the holdyr to take~~ an
honde.  Fro that tyme, al his thoght and al his will was, nyght
and day, wyth al his myght to wende into Irland.  He went then
to the kynge, and besoght hym that he shold delyuere hym his
londis that sholdyn be his by ryght of heritage, othyr yeue hym
leue to do hym in aduenture, londe for to Purchase in vnkyd
land.

A.D.
1169-70.
rel in
exteris
regionibus
se satis et
fortunae
commit-
tendi
licentiam
daret.

### [CHAPTER XIII.]

A.D. 1170.

When the kynge vndyrstode his entente, whedyr he wolde
goo, he yaue hym not full leue, ne fully be-namo hym not ;
but with suche leue as he hadd, he dight hym tho wyntyr till the
begynnynge of may / he Sende to-for hym into Irland a knyght that
was callid[1] Reymond Legras ;—wyth hym, x knyghtis and fourty
Squyeris, and foure score bowmen ;—A man ful hardy and bolde
and wel proued in wepyn, Robert-is eme [2], and Morices, hare eldyts
brodyr, sone.  Thay londyd at a place that is y-callid Dundonenyld,
foure Mile on the Sowth syde of watyrford; and there they rerid a
dyche, and a febill castel vpon, of Iardis and turues [*].  The men of
Watyrford, and wyth ham Malaghelyn Of olan, this waryn y-ware
that thay haddyn such neghboris, that ham were loth [3]; and toke
ham to consayle, that thay wolde vp-on ham, ar mo come to hame.
Thay gaderid ham to-gaddyr, wel iij⁰. Ml. men, and wentyn ouer
the watyr of Sure, that partyth the two contreis, that is to Say
leynystre and mounestre, And settyn ham in thre hostis, ful
boldely forto assayle the Englysh-men with-In har castel.  Reymond
and his men (thegh thay fewe were, they were not feynte) with few
pepill wentyn out, and mete with hame.  But, as no woundyr hit
was, so few men myght not al plenary fyghten ayeyn so many, that
turned ham to thare recette. the othyr wende that thay depertid
in descomfite; thay brakyn har sheldrun, and wentyn aftyr. and
thay were not fully wythin the gate, that some of hamo nere
radyr In than the English.  Reymond saw that he and his were
in grete Pereil, and on Poynte to lese here lyfe.  he cried on his
fellowis, and tvrned boldely vp-on here enemys. and the fryst that
come In, he clewe his hede. and throgh deth of that o man, al tho

Capitulum
xiij^m.
quasi
licentia,
ironica
namque
magis
quam
vera.
[2 eme,
uncle, is
'nephew'
in this
MS.]
[*Fol.6b.]
ex virgis
et cerpite.
de plano
resistere
non potuit.
intra
valvas
vix plene
suspensas
certatim
intrando
succe-
perunt.

---

[1] R. Legras.          [2] Exterorum viciniam suspectam habentes, v. 248.

A. D. 1170.  maiɴ, all the ost was dyscomfyte, & tok haɴ to flyght. The
oþer ham folwed yɴ-to all þe pleyɴ, & leyd haɴ oɴ so, þat yɴ

He turns
on his
assailants,
and repels
them with
heavy loss.

lytell whýll thay slowe of· haɴ fyfe[1] hundred & mo; & þe most
parte of þe otheȓ felleɴ adoɴ yɴ-to þe see, of þe heye rokes, & 4
drent haɴ-selfe.  In thys fyght, was a knyght that hete Wyllyaɴ
ferand, that dydde ouer-well & aboue all otheȓ: he was a maɴ
that hade semblant as thoght he weȓ oɴ the mich yuell, & þer-foȓ

[* Leaf 7.]  he put hyɴ-selue[2] alwey theȓ *the most perille was; ffor he ne 8

William
Ferand
shows
special
bravery.

raght thegh deth come betwene hyɴ & hýs ýuell, ar hyt waȓ to
mých I-smýt vpoɴ hyɴ.  Heȓ þe pryd of waterford felle; heȓ
all hýs mýght went to noght; heȓ-of come the Englysshe hope
& comfort; & to the Iresshe, dred & wanhope; ffor hýt was neuer 12
theȓ-to-for I-herd, that of so fewe men, so grett a slaght was done.
Bot lyder consaylle thay dýddeɴ þeȓ-after, that turned ham to
mych cruelte; ffor whaɴ the maýstrý was al har, & al har fomeɴ
ouercome, In þe fyght wereɴ ytake well thre score meɴ & teɴ, 16

Seventy
men were
taken
prisoners;
and it is
debated
what to do
with them.

that ham yoldeɴ, & wereɴ the heghest & the rychyst of al the sitè,
such þat þay mýght haue had for ham the sitè delyuered, or els
as myche catel as thay wolden desyȓ.  Heruy of Mountmorthy,
that to haɴ was ýcome, hým thrydsome of knýghtes, & Reymond, 20
vp dyuers domes stroueɴ what meɴ sholdˊ do wyth har prysons[3];
ffor Reymond trauayllet about for to dylyuere haɴ, as a maɴ of
reuthful mode, & þus seyd to hys feres: "lordynges, what ys vs

Reymond
tries to
save them;

to done of ouȓ wreched prisoners? I sey nat that man[4] shal on 24
any maner spaȓ hys fomaɴ; bot thay beth nat now fomen, both[5]
beth meɴ nat rebelle, bot yɴ bat.aylle for to defend[6] har contrey
ouercome.  Me thynketh thay beth now yɴ such state, that me
oght bettyr haw mercy of haɴ & yeve haɴ lyfe, for to yeue otheȓ 28
ensample to be boxoɴ, thaɴ cruely to do haɴ to deth, whaȓ-
throgh þat otheȓ, throgh ferdnesse of trust, þe lasse to yeldˊ haɴ
to vs."  Whaɴ Reymondˊ had such wordes I-seyde, yn al þe folke

but Hervey
opposes
him.

was moste wi[lle][7] to graunt ham lyf, Arose vp Heruy amonge 32

---

[1] MS. lyfe.    [2] MS. sleue.    [3] pryson = prisoner.    [4] MS. maner.
[5] but: Sed hi non hostes jam, sed homines.—Op. v. 250.    [6] MS. defond.
[7] The ink has perisht: 'et murmure populi cum quodam quasi favore sub-
secuto.' Gir. Camb., Exp. Hib. c. xv.—Op. v. 252, Rolls Series.

hoste was dys-comfite *and* toke ham to flyght / The othyr ham ~A.D. 1170.~
folwid' into al the Playñ, and leyde on ham.  So that in lytyl
space of tyme thay kylld' of ham v. C. *and* mo; and the most *ab altis in*
Parte of the othyr fellyn adovñ into the see, of the hey Rokys, *mare rupi-*
*bus prae-*
and dreynt ham-selfe // In this fyght was a knyght that was *cipituti*
*sunt*
callid' William ferrand, that did ful wel *and* abowe al othyr; *infiniti.*
¹he was a man that hade semblant as thegh he were on tho
mych yuel; and therfor he Putte hym-Selfe at tymys ther the
moste Peryl was.  For he roght not thegh dethe come betwen
hym and his Sekenys, or hit were mych grow on hym¹ /
Here the Pryde of Watyrforde felle; here al his myght went to *superhia*
noght; her-of come the Englysh hope and conford'; and to the *cecidit.*
Irysñ, dred and wanhope.  For hit was neuer ther-to-fore herde *horror ..*
that, of So few men, so grete a slaghte was done.  But a lewid *desperatio.*
consaylo thay diddyn, that ther-aftyr turned ham to myche
cruelte.  For whan the Mastry was al hare, *and* al hare enemys
ouercome, Iu the fyght weryn take wel iij° score men *and* teñ that *septua-*
*ginta cives.*
ham yeldyn, *and* weryn the beste and the rycheste of the Cite,
Such that thay myght haue hade for them the Cite delyuerid'; or
els as mych ryches as thay wolde desyre.  Heruey of montmurthy, *pecuniam*
*infinitam.*
that to ham was come, hym thyrdsome of knyghtis, *and* Reymond',
vp-on dyuers consaylis thoghten what thay sholde do wyth har
Prysoneris.  For Reymond laborid' for thar delyverance, as man
of pitefull herte / And thus sayd to his fellowis : "Lordynges, what
is vs to done wyth oure wrechid' presoners ?  I Sey not that man *de captiris*
*nostris.*
shal on any maner spare his enemys; but thay byth nat now
enemys; but byth men not rebell, but in bataill forto defende
har contrey ouercome.  Me-thynkyth thay byth now in such state,
that we owyth bettyr haue mercy of ham *and* yeue ham lyfe, forto *potius ..*
*pietas ad*
yeue othyr ensampill to be boxume, than cruely to do ham to *exemplum,*
doth; wher-for otheris wil truste the lasse to yelde ham to vs." *quam cru-*
*delitas ad*
*Whan Reymond' Hade Suche Wordys y-Seyde, and al the fello- *tormentum.*
[* Fol. 7 a.]
shippe Was most about to graunt ham lyfe, Aros vp heruey ney

---

¹⁻¹ vir carne quidem infirmus, sed corde firmissimus : imminentem, ut videbatur, leprae malitiam morte nimirum praevenire desiderans tam praematura
quam praeclara.—*Op. v.* 249.

A.D. 1170. hame al, & thys ham̄ seyd: "Inogh̄ Reymond openly to vs hath

'Enough of Mercy! spoke of mercy & almes-dedes, vnked landes I-wonne, & nat wyth

Did Alexander and Caesar win by it! slagh̄ & wyth brenny[n]ge. Wheder Alexander & Iulius Cesar, that weren̄ lordes of al þe world, wonnen londes by such wey, 4 I wold Reymond wold me answer. Whan thay comen̄ to vs vel

arrayede to fyghten̄, If þay hadde I-won ouer-hand & vs ouercome, wolden thay, for almesse & for reuth, haw had mercye of vs? nay, I trow nat. þerfor out-chese on̄ of two: Other do manly thynge, 8

Either kill the rebels quietly, wher-fore we bene ycome; & the folke þat ys rebbell ayeyn vs, wyth-outten any noyse, wyth wepne hertely brynge out of dawes; Other, yf we shollen̄ do almes dede on hem̄, & ham̄ sparen̄, as

or go home!' Reymond hath seyd, out we wend to our shyppes, & turne ayeyn̄, 12 & let we the wreched men hold har lond, & brouken wythouten

As no gallows are handy, the rebels are drownd. any chalange." Heruyes dome lyket bettre than Reymondes; & weren the Cyteȝeyns to deth Idemed. Thay ne hadden no wone of warytres; & þerfor þey ladden ham̄ to þe clyf of þe see, & put 16 ham̄ adoun, & drent ham.

### [CHAPTER XIV.]

Earl Richard Struguil [*Fol.7 b.] The men-tyme, the Erl Rychard, wyth the power that he had arayed, was y-come to south wales; & wham̄ he hadde wyth * gret reuerence y-done hys pylrimage at sent dauyes, he put 20 hym to saylle, & hade good wynd, came ẏnto Irland with two

lands at Waterford, Aug. 23, hundret knythtes & other, mor than a thousand. He arryued at weyseford on seynt Bertylmewes euen̄: Than was fulfẏlled a

fulfilling prophecies of Merlin and the Irish Saint Moling. prophecye that Merlyn̄ seyd of hys comynge; 'þe brond shal 24 come to-fore þe borned fyr; And rygh as the spark maked the brond come, Also þe brond shal make the fyr come after.' Anoþer prophecye, seẏnt Molynge seyd of that same: 'A mych man shall erne to-fore; & þe most heeddes of desmond & ek of leynestre 28 he shal defouly; & wyth streynth he shall noblych the wey opne to the wepned.' Amorow, whan the tẏthẏnge of ham̄ was

Reimund joins him. They assault Waterford, Tuesday, Aug. 25. I-spronge, Reymond went hẏm to the Erle with furtẏ knẏghtes with mych gladnes; & amorow, after þe holy-daye, Thay went 32 comynly al to þe syte of Waterford, & assaylled the toun ful fersly; & twyes thay weren̄ rebuked, & ful stalwarhlẏ, of þe Cyteȝeyns. Reymond, that by purueaunce & graunt of ham al was ymade

amonge ham al, *and* thus ham Sayde: "I-nowe Reymond opynly to A.D. 1170.
vs hath Spoke of mercy and almes-deddes, vn-kyd landis to wynñe
*and* nat wyth Slaght *and* wyth brennynge. whedyr Alexandyr *and*
Iulyus Cesar, that weryn lordys of al the worlde, wonnen londis
by such wey, I wold Reymond wolde me answere. whan thay *Cum ad*
commyn to vs wel arrayed' to fyghten, If thay had the bettyr, *and* *nos expug-*
vs had ouercome, woldyn thay, for almesse and for Pite, haue had *instructis*
*aciebus*
mercy of vs? Nay, y trow not. ther-for chese oñe of two: Othyr *adue-*
*nerunt.*
to do manly thynge, wher-for we ben come; and the Pepill that is
rebel ayeynnes vs, wythouten eny noyse, wyth wepyn hertely berewys ham of lyfe / Othyr, yf we shall do almysdede on them,
and ham spare, as Reymond hath Sayd, go we to oure shippis, *and*
turnne ayeyne, *and* lete we the wrechyd' pepil holde har lond', *and*
kepyn wi*th*out any chalange." Herueyes Iugement Plesid bettyr *membris*
*confractis,*
than Reymondes; *and* weryn the Citteseynnes to deth demyd: *in maris*
Thay had no galosis; and therfor thay laddyn ham to the clyfe *praecipi-*
*lium dati*
of the See, and put ham adouñ, *and* drovnde ham al. *sunt.*

[CHAPTER XIV.]

The men-tyme, the Erle Ry*chard*, wyth the Power that he *Capitulum*
had' arraied, was come to Suth Walis; *and* When he had *xiiij^m.*
wi*th* grete reuerence done his Pylgrymage at Seynt Dauyes, he
Put hym to sayle, *and* had good wynd', come into Irland wy[th]
two hundryd' knyghtis *and* othyr, more than a thousand'. he
londid' at Weysford on Seynt Bartolomewes evyn. Then was
fulfillid' a pprophesy that Merlynge Sayde of his comynge: "The *prophetia*
brond shal come to-for the brennynge fyre, And ryght as the *Merlini.*
Sparke makid the brond come, Also the brond shall make the
fyre come aftyr." Anothyr prophesy, Molynge Sayd of that same: *prophetia*
"A mych man shal erne to-for; *and* the moste hedis of desmond *Molyng.*
and also of leynystre he shal defeuly; and wyth streynth he shal *capita con-*
*culcans.*
nobelych the wey opyn to the wepenyd:." A-morrow, whan the
thythyngis spronge, Reymond went to the Erle wi*th* fourty
knyghtis wi*th* mych gladnys; and amorrow, aftyr the holy day
thay went holy to the Cite of Watyrford, and assaylid' the toun *bis viri-*
ful fresly ; *and* twyes they weryn rebukyd'; *and* ful boldely, of the *liter*
*repulsi*
Citteseyn*es.* Reymond, that by Purueyaunce and graunt of ham *fuissent.*

D 2

A.D. 1170. *prince*, & forman of al the host, sawe & awayted a place good for
to assaylle : he cryed & cleped the wepned men to the assaut,

They take & þay egrely assaylleden, & braken yn-to þe sytè, & folke-mele
Waterford. slowe the men yn weyes & yn houses, & wan þe Cỳtò.    In 4
rathnyldes touꝛ weren twey rȳche men ytake, bot þrogh prayeꝛ
of Macmorgh, that thedeꝛ was than I-come, he was y-hold alyue.

Mac-      Macmorgh broght hys doghtyꝛ *with* hȳm, Eue by name, & spoused
murgh's
daughter  hyꝛ to the Erle, & maden fast sekernesse betwen ham.    Wan thys 8
Eve is    was ydo al, þe Erle left men for to kepe the cytè, & turned hym
married to
Earl      *with* the hoste to deuylyn.
Struguil.

## [CHAPTER XV.]

Macmorgh wyst that myche of the poweꝛ of haꝛ lond
was I-come to helpen ham of dyuelyn, & hadden beset 12

They      all þe wodde weyes & þe narow weys thetherward : he left tho
march,    weȳes, & lad the hoste throght the montaȳnes of Glyndelagh, al
thro'
Glenda-   harmeles, rȳght to the sytè.    These cyteȝeyns, oueꝛ al otheꝛ, hated
lough hills,
to Dublin. weren of hym, & that was no wondeꝛ; ffor ẏn some tȳme thay 16
slowen hys fadyꝛ yn the cytè; & *after* the harme, thay dȳdde hym
mych sham, foꝛ thay burryd an hounde *with* hym yn the pute
that he was yn I-leyde.    Thay sent messagers to þe Erle, &
namely the Erchebysshop laurence, & besoghten pees; & as thay 20

Reimund   weren spekyng of pees, on oon half was Reymond, & on the otheꝛ
and Miles halue a ful hardy knȳght, Myles of Cogan, *with* ẏonglȳnges well
of Cogan
assail and coueytouse of battaylle & of gettyng.    Thay assaylled the Cytè,
take
Dublin.   & breken In, & wan þe Cytè, wyth gret slaght of þe sȳtȝeyns. 24

[*Fol.8a.]  *Natheles, the best *parte* of ham, wyth þe rychest & the derwarthest
thyngys þat thay hadden, yn botes escapeden, & wenten yn-to þe

Hasculf   north ylondes, wyth hastoyl, that was maȳstre yn the cyte, &
and the
richest folk har lodesman.    That day byfel two Muracles yn the cyte : that 28
escape.   on of the Croice, yn the modeꝛ chȳrche of þe trȳnȳte, whyche the
Cytȝeyns wolden haue I-ladde *with* ham yn-to the ylandes yn
the see; & for nothynḡ, thay ne myghth yt wecchen out of þe
place.    That otheꝛ, of a sergeant that hadde I-robbet the erche- 32
bysshoppes paleys, & þer-*after* come to-for þe rode, & offred a peny :
fyrst, & efte-sone, & at eueꝛy tym, the peny stert aẏeȳne to hym.
he bethoght hȳm that god was nat wel I-quenyted of the robbery

al was made Prynce and forman of al the hoste, Saw and a-waytyd A.D. 1170.
a place goode forto assayle.   he cried *and* callid the wepenyd men
to the assaute and' thay egyrly assaylid, and brakyn Into the Cite,
and kyllid the men in weyes and in houses, and wan the Cite.   in
rathnyldys toure weryn two ryche men take, *and* thay both were
be-hedyd.   Macsaghlyn of olan was also take, but throgh Prayer Melaghlin
of Macmurgh, that ther was than y-come, he was holde alyue. O'Phelan
Macmurgh broght his doghtyr wyth hym, Eue by name, and but kept
Spousid' hyr to the Erle and madyn fast syckyrnys betwene *Ham // alive.
Whan this was done al / the Erle Lefte men forto Kepe the Cite [* FoL 7 b.]
*and* turnyde hym with the hoste to deuelyn //

[CHAPTER XV.]

Macmurgh vndyrstode that myche of the pepill of the Capitulum
contrey was come to helpe ham of the Cite of deuelyn, xvᵐ.
*and* hadde be-sette al the wodd-weyes and the Narrow-weyes vias nemo-
thedyrward.   He lefte thay weyes, and lad the hoste throw the rosas et
montanys of Glyndelagh, al holde and sound, tyl thay come to the arctas
Cite.   The Citteseynes ouer al othyr hatid Macmurgh; *and* they
wer hatyd of hym: and that was no wondyr.   For in some tyme
thay slowyn his fadyr in the Cite; and aftyr the harme, thay dyd
hym moche shame, for thay buryed an hounde with hym in the cum cane
buryles that he was In-leyde.   Thay send messangeris to the Erle, cires tumu-
*and* namely the archebyschope Laurance, and besoghten Pees; and larerunt.
as thay weryn Spekyn of pees, on oone halue was Reymond and on
the othyr syde a ful hardy knyght, Miles de Cogan, with yonglynges
wel couctos of batail and of getynge: They assaylid the Cite, and
brokyn In, *and* toke the Cite with grete slaghte of the Citesenes.
Natheles, the beste parte of ham, with the rychest and the wourdyest
thynges that thay haddyn, in botis escapedyn, and wentyn into the naves et
north ylondes wyth hastoyl, that was Captayn in the Cite, and har scaphus ..
gouernoure / That day befel two Miraclis in the Cite: that one, of intrantes
the cros in the Cee churche of the trynyte, wych the Citteseynes
wold haue take wyth ham into the Ilandys in the see / And for
no thyng thay myght not take hit out of the place.   That othyr,
of a Sergeant that had yrobyd' the archebysshope-is Place; and i sicut in
ther-aftyr come to-for the rode, *and* offerid a peny: fryst, and Topo-
aftyr, and in euery tyme, the peny styrte ayeyn to hym.   he graphia'
bethoght hym that god was not aplesid of the robery that he had decla-
ratur.
Op. v. 129.

A.D. 1170.
that he had y-do: he turned hým than, & let take al that he had y-nom [1], & bar hyt ayeyn, & went to þe rode & offred; &

Earl Struguil leaves a force in Dublin,

hy[s] offrynge the[r] abode. Whan þe Erl hade a few dayes I-ordyned for the stat of þe Cytè, he left ther Myles de Cogan, 4 keper of þe Cytè & of þe contre, & a partye of þe meyne wýth hým.   And by entycement of Macmorgh, that bethoght hym of þe old enmyte that he hade to the kynge of Mithe, he went hym

and ravages Meath.

to þe contrey, branten, slowen, & robeden, & broghten the contre 8 to noght, for none ne durst hym wythe-stond.   Oconghur of

O'Conor of Connaught

Conaght saw that he was the next—as man that seethe hys neghbors hous berne, he may drede of þe sparkes — he sent Messangers to Macmorgh yn thys wordes: "Ayeyne þe fourme 12

reproaches Mac-murgh,

of our pees, thou hast imad come yn-to thys lond mých out-comen folke.   þe whýlle that thou held the ýn thý leynystre, we hyt tholleth euynly; Now thou, as man that naght ne the thynkest on thyn oth, ne no reuth ne hast of thyn ostage, the 16 merres I-sete of thyn eldren lond, vnryghtfullyo uergoste.   Make thýn out-comen men wýth-draw, & turne aýeýne, or els sothly we shul the send thy sones heede."   Macmorgh thys herd, & yaf hým a prout answar, & sent hym to sey, that he ham wold hold, 20 & send after more & eke more; that he nold neuer reste týl he hadde I-wonne Connaght, wyth the kýnge-dome of al þe lond, as hys eldren sumtým hyt hadden to-for hým.   Oconnoghur had

and cuts off his son's head.

her of grete dyspyte, & sore was atened, & let smyth of sonnes 24 heed, þat he had hym Itake fore ostage.

[CHAPTER XVI.]

A Council of the Irish clerics is held at Armagh.
The country's ill has come from enslaving English children.
[*Fol.8b.]

Aftyr this, worth gret spech ýn-to all þe lond, & mých ferdnesse of the out-comen men.   Than gaddered ham al to-gedderes, al the clerkes & the wysmen of þe lond at 28 ardmagh; & of thys folkes comyng, was mých I-spoke, & longe dalyaunce.   At þe laste, comýnlý thaý accordeden al her-to, that, for the syn of þe folk, thys mesaduentur ham ys býfal; namely, that whan thay fonden englysshe-men chyldren to syllen, that 32 chepmen & robbers woldene brynge to the lond, thay * were wonet to by ham, & do ham yn thraldome ; & that throgh goddýs owne

[1] MS. ymon.

done. ho turned hym than, *and* toke al that he toke wyth hym, A.D. 1170.
and bare hit ayeyñ, *and* went to the rode, and offerid; *and* his
offerynge ther abode. / When the Erle had a few dayes y-ordaynyd
for the state of the Cite, he lefte there myles de Cogan, kepere of
tho Cito and of tho contrey, and a partey of the meynne wyth
hym.   And by entycement[1] of *Macmurgh*, that be-thoght hym of
tho olde enemyte that he had to the kynge of Myth, he went hym
to the contrey, brantyn, Slouedyñ and robedyñ, *and* broghten the
contrey to noght, for non ne durst hym wythstond.   Oconghoure
of connaght Saw that he was the nexte, (as a man that seth his
evyncrystyñ his house brenne, he may dred the sparkys;) he send
messangeres to *Macmurgh* in these wordis: "Ayeyne the forume of
oure pees, thow haste made come into this londe mych strange
pepill.  the whyle that thow helde the in thy leynystre we hit
tollid euynly.   Now thow,—as man that noght rekyth of his
trouth, ne no pite hauest of thyn hostage,—the meris y-sette[2] of-
thyn eldryñ lond, vnryghtfully *ouer-goste*[3].   Make thy strangeres[4]
Wyth-draw, and turne ayeyne; othyr ellys Sothly we shall the
sende thy Sonnys hede."   *Macmurgh* this herde, and to hym yaue
a prowte answere, *and* Sende hym to Say, that 'he ham wold holde,
and send aftyr more, and eke more, / ande that he wold neuer
reste, til he had take *and* conquerid al connaght, wi*th* al the
kyngdome of al the lond, as his predessessouris had to-for hym.'
Oconghoure here-of had grete indignacioñ, and gretly ther-of was
grewid; And he comandid to Smyte of his Sones hede, that he yufe
hym for an hostage.

[1] *instinctu.*
As Mac-
murgh
hated
O'Rourke
of Meath
(p. 2–4),
Meath is
wasted.
*in insulam*
*advocasti..*
*aequa-*
*nimiter*
*sustinui-*
*mus.*
[2] *metas*
*positas ..*
[* Fol.8a.]
[4] *insolenter*
*excessisti*

indignans
Rothericus

### [CHAPTER XVI.]

Aftyr this, Spronge grete Spech in-to al the lond, *and*
mych dreded tho strange comen men.   Than gadderid
ham to-gederes al the clerkys and the wysmen of the land at
Ardmagñ; and of this pepil-is comynge, was mych Speche and
longe delyaunce.   At the last, comynly thay acordid al herto,
that, for the synne of the Pepill, this mys-aduenture ham ys
by-fall, specialy that whan thay foundyn Englysñ-men childryn
to sill, that Marchandis and roberes wold bryng to the lond,
thay were wouod to by ham, and pute ham in thraldome; And

Capitulum
xvj<sup>m</sup>.

*tam a*
*mercatori-*
*bus, quam*
*praedoni-*
*bus atque*
*piratis*

A.D. 1170.

The English, rather than suffer, would sell their children.

wreth hyt was, that as syllers weren̄ to-fore y-broght yn thraldome, also the byggers sholden after: ffor̄ hyt was somtym̄ that the folke of englond—The maner of har kyngdome was al I-hole—whan thay had non̄ other̄ thynge that þay myghten take to, rathar̄ than thay wold any myssayse tholy, Thay wer̄ I-wont to syllen̄ har̄ chyldren & har̄ other̄ kynnesmen̄, both̄ ynto Irlond & ynto other̄ londes. Ther̄-for̄ hyt may well be soth, that as the byggers, also þe syllers, oft serued wel, throgh̄ so loly gyltes to be y-broght yn thraldome.

The Irish resolve to free all English slaves.

Ther̄ hyt was yn þat consaylle be-heght, & by assent of al comynly I-set, that al the englysshe-men̄ yn þe lond that yn thraldome weren̄, shold ben̄ delyuered, & frely let goo whodyr̄so they wold.

[CHAPTER XVII.]

Reports are spread in England of Fitz-Gerald's keeping Irish land.

Henry II forbids ships to go to and from Ireland; and orders all English-men home.

Her-aftyr spronge tythyngges of the Erle & of þe englysshe-men̄ ynto englond; &, as maner ys, myche me made more; & that the Erl hade apropred to hym, nat only leynestre, bot other̄ londes also, that, by no ryght ne by law, to hym̄ ne to hys wyf longen̄. The kynge sent anoon, & forebeed that, 'out no lond that were yn hys power̄, ne shold no shyppen passe yn-to Irland, ne no maner thynge for to brynge; & al men̄ that yn-to Irland war̄ comen, shold ayeyn come yn-to englande, wyth-yn þe next estre, or̄ they sholden be dysheryted & ex[y]led out of lond for euer.' The Erl saw that he & hys weren̄ narow belad, both of hys men that hym wold leue, & eke that nothynge ne most hym come out of other̄ landes, of þynge that hym nede was: by comune rede of hys men, he sent Reymond ouer to the kynge that was fer̄ yn gascoyne, & thus hym sent to say:

Fitz-Gerald sends to Henry II in Gascony, and yields his Irish conquests to him.

"By thy leue, lord, yf y am welle vndyrstond, y went ynto Irland for to help thy trew man, Dermot Macmorgh; þerfor, that al that of hys herytage, other̄ of oþers yn þe lond, almyghty god me hath I-sent, as hyt come of thy graunt & of thy good wylle, also, I wyll that hyt to the turne, to do ther̄-wyth what the lyketh."

[CHAPTER XVIII.]

Thomas a Beket is martyrd.

Reymond went to the kynge with such mandement; & the whyle that he folwed the kynges court, abydynge hys answer̄, Thomas, the erchebysshoppe of Cantrebery [1], was martyred

[1] (*In margin, in a later hand:* The archebushop of canterbury called Tho. Beckett. 1171.)

that, throw godis his owyn wreth hit was, that as the sylleris A.D. 1170.
weryn to-for broght in thraldome, also the byeris sholdyn be
brogh[t] in thraldome aftyr / For hit was somtyme that the
pepil of Englond the maner of har kyngdome was al y-holde:
Whan thay had none othyr thynge that thay myght take to,
Radyr than thay wolde suffyr any dyssese, thay wold syll har *priusquam*
childyr and har othyr kynnes-men, both into Irland *and* into *inopium*
othyr landis.   Therfor hit may wel be trouth that, as the byeris, *ullam aut*
also the Silleris, ofte Scruyd well, throgh So wicked doynge, to be *sustinerent.*
broght in thraldome.   There hit was in that consayll promysyd,
*and* by assent of al comynly y-Set, that al the Englysh-men
in the lond that in thraldome weryn, shold ben delyuerid, and
frely lette goo whedyr So thay wolde.

### [CHAPTER XVII.]

**H**Ere-aftyr spronge tythyngis of the Erle and of the *Capitulum*
Englysh-men into Englond; *and* as the maner is, of mych *xvij^m.*
thay mad more; and that the Erle had approperid to hym, not only *suma de*
leynystere, but othyr londis also, that, by no ryght ne lawe, to hym *magnis*
ne to his wyfe partenyd // The kynge sende anone, and comandid *semper*
that 'no shippe, out of no lond that Partenyth to hym, sholde Passe *majore,*
into Irland, Ne no maner thynge forto brynge; and al men that *vulgante.*
Into Irland war comyn, sholde ayeyñ goo into England wythin the
nexte Estyr, Othyr they sholde be disherytid *and* exilid out of
lond for euer.'   The Erle saw that he and his weryn narrow bylad, *in arcto*
both of his men that hym wold leue, and also that nothynge shold *jam*
come out of othyr landis of thynge that he had ned to / he toke *positos.*
consayle of his men, and Sente Reymond ouer to the kynge, that was
fore in gascoyñ, and thus hym Sende to say: " By youre lycence *si bene*
lord, yf y be wel vndyrstond, y wente into Irland forto helpe yowr *recordor,*
trew man, Dermot Macmurgh.   Therfor, that al that of his [*Fol.8 b.]
heritage, othyr of otheres, that y haue in the Land, that almyghty *sic ad*
god to me * Hath sende, as hit come of youre graunt *and* of youre *eandem*
good wyle, ¹ also y wille that Hit be turne to yow, to do ther-wyth *pro libito*
whate Plese yow." *vestro*
*nutuque*
*radliit.*

### [CHAPTER XVIII.]

**R**Eymond went to the kynge *with* such mandement; *and* *Capitulum*
the whyle that he folwid the kynges courte, abydynge his *xviij^m.*
answere, Thomas, the archebisshope of Cantreberry, was martirid

A.D. 1170. yn englond, nat wyth-out mych blame to al þe lond-folk, both

Arch-
bishop
Beket
sufferd
seven years
in exile,
personally,
lered & lewed. That erchebysshopp, *after* many-fold martyrdome
that he þolled, negh seuen yeꝛ that he was banshed out of englond
for the ryghtes of holy chyurche, In sore & many wepynges, yn 4
double heeꝛ about hys body—þat oñ, yn styd of shyrth; that oþer,
yn stydde of breche—nyght & day yn holy prayeꝛ & redynge

and also
thro' his
persecuted
kinsfolk,
yn holy wrytte; & o thynge that meste sorow broght to hys
hert, that al hys kyñ, men & wommen, yonge & old, wommen 8
lyggyne yn chyld-bed, & old men that fore eld yroked weren yn
heꝛ cradelys, & all otheꝛ, clerkes & lewed, that me myght wytt
that sybrede or otheꝛ frendshypp haddeñ to hym, al thay wereñ
I-dryue out of englond; & al they that wereñ of eld that þay 12
myghty othes swerꝛ, swaren vpon the masse-boke that, as sone
as thay come ouer the see, thay shold go to þe erchebysshoppe,

[*Fol.9 a.]
who
sufferd
for him.
& shew hym the * wrechednesse that þay suffred for hys sake;
ffor he sholď, for reuth of ham, turnen hys hert, & graunt þe 16
kynges wylle of þynge that he desyred. *After* such martyrdomes,
and many otheꝛ þat he tholled yn hys lyue, whyche no manly

Then came
his chief
Martyr-
dom.
hert may bethynke to ful end, the hey martyrdome, that broght
hys soule to þe blysse of heuyn, & hys body to wyrshyppe yn hert, 20
otheꝛ many þynges be-týdden that men Aght well vnderstond;
þat ayeyns hys fomen yede, opyn heed, & opened þe chyrch durꝛ
whyche the monkes hadden I-loke, & seyd þat 'meñ ne shold
no castell make of holy chyrche'; & hys holy croune bade ayeyn 24

He was
slain in
Canter-
bury
Cathedral
by four
knights,
before the
Altar.
the naked swerdes for to smyte, & that yn the modyr chyrche,
heghest of al þe lond, & to-foꝛ the weued, that he of fouꝛ knyghtes,
wodeꝛ than wood houndes, *th*olled fouꝛ woundes yn the holy crou*n*,
& [n]on wit*h*out,—so as þe crou*n* ogñt betokne of *proteccion* to 28
clergy,—that he deth tholled yn the north syde of þe chyrche,
whyche betokneth Ih*es*u cryste*s* passyoñ. & thus goddys owne
knyghte, wythouten any ferdnesse, tholled deth; yn hys lyf of thys

The
Apostle
Thomas
died on
Dec. 21;
Beket on
Dec. 29.
world, chaunged wel selyly for þe lyf that eu*er* shal lest wit*h*out 32
end. And as seynt Tomas-ys day, Apostle, ys þe fyft day afor
yold, so ys thys Thomas day þe fyft day afteꝛ. That Thomas
was candel I-set yn þe este of þe world; Thys Thom*a*s yn þe west.
[That] was lyght to aly chyrche yn hyꝛ yough, as [Thys] yn hyꝛ eld; 36

in England, not wyth-out grete reprefe to al the land-pepill, both A.D. 1170.
lerid and lewid.    That archebisshope, aftyr manyfolde martyrdome
that he Sufferid, / ney vij^e. yere that he was banneschid' out of *septennalis*
England for the ryght of holy church, In sore and many wepyngis, *fere exilii.*
In doubill here about his body,—that on in styd of shyrt, that *tam femo-*
othyr in styd of breche,—Nyght and day, in holy prayeris and *rali quam corporali.*
redynge in holy writte.    And o thyng that meste Sorrow wroght *nec aetati parcente,*
to his hert, that al his kynnes-men, yonge and old, women lyggynge *nec sexui*
in chyldbed, and olde men that for elde yrokyd weryn in her *tam misera-bili san-*
cradelis, and al othyr, clerkys othyr lewid, that thay mygh[t] know, *guinis*
that weryn of his kyn, Othyr frendshipe haddyn to hym, al thay *universi proscrip-*
weryn dryw out of Englond.    And al thay that weryn of elde, *tione.*
that thay myght othys swere, Swaryn on the masboke, that 'as Sone
as thay come ouer the See, thay shold go to the archebyschope, and
Shew hym the mesury that thay Sufferid for his Sake;'  For he
shold, for Pite of ham, turnen his hert, and graunt the Kynge his
wyll of that, that he desyrid.    Aftyr Such martirdomes, *and* many
othyr that he sufferid in his lyfe,—the whych in no mannes hert
may be thoght to ful end;—The hey martirdome, that broght his
Soule to the blysse of hewyn, and his body to vyrchip in Erth,
Othyr many thyngis be-fel that men aght wel vndyrstond; that *quod ipse furibunviis*
ayenes His enemys yede, opyn hede, *and* oppenyd the church-durre, *hostibus*
whych the Monkes haddyn y-loke, and sayd that 'men shold not no *templi fores*
castel make of holy church.'    And his holy crovne bare ayeyn tho *aperuit, et*
makyd Swerdes forto smyte, and that in the modyr chyrch, beghist *aperto vertice*
of al the lond, and to-for the auter / that he of foure knyghtes, *gladiis occurrens.*
wodyr than wode houndis, tholled Foure woundes in the holy croun,
and [n]on wyth-out,—So as the crovn oght to be know tokyn of *et nullum extra.*
protexcion to clergy,—that he deth Sufferid in the north syde of the
church, whych be-tokenyth Ihesu crystes Passion.  and thus godis owyn knyght, wyth-out eny ferd, sufferyd' deth; and his lyfe of
this world, chaunged' for the lyfe that euer shal leste wythout end.
And as seynte thomas-is day the apostyl, is the V. day afor yolde, [1] *ille*
So is this Thomas-is day, the V. day aftyr.  That thomas was candil *nascenti ecclesiue*
y-sette in the Este of the World; This thomas in the weste.  [1][That] *lumen dedit, hic*
was lyght to holy churche in hyr youth, as [This] in hyr elde; and *senescenti.*

A.D.
1170-1.
As the
Apostle
gave his
blood for
the early
Church, so
Beket gave
his for the
aged one.

& as he [the Apostle] commenced holy chyrche with hys blode whan che was arerynge, Also thys, [Beket,] whan she had longe I-stond & wox yn eld, & redy was to falle, wyth hys blode he ryght hyr vp, & sette hyr yn ryght stydde. And as he t[oke hym] selue to 4 quellers ffor to arer þe seknes of holy chyrche, also thys ne douten nat to taken hym-self to kene swerdes, & lydder men hondes, for þe fredome of holy chyrche to sawe vnwemmed. The fourme of hys martyrdome, twey verses a latyn shortly comprehendeth, that 8 thus mych ben to vnderstond : "ffor crystes spouse, vnder crystes

Among all
saints, for

tyme, yn crystes chyrche, crystes owne leman deyed." Amonge al the halwen that almyghty god wroght yn erth, of selcouth myraclys for to showen har holynesse,—as the blynd to see, the 12 lame to gon, þe dombe to speke, the deue to hyr, lasers to clense, paralys to festnen, y-dropesie & al other manere yueles to helen, the dede to areren, yuel gostes to quethen, & al þe four elementes to har commaundement hadden,—he alon was y-wyrshypped with 16

[1 that
tofore]

Beket
alone were
all kinds of
miracles
performd.
He got a
man fresh
eyes and
genitals.

Merlin's
prophecy
of Beket.

[*Fol.9 b.]

al these, & more þer-to, thar-to-for[1] was nat herd ne sey; ffor a man that hade hys eghen I-draw out of hys heed, & hys manly menbres y-kytte of & y-cast awey, come to hys tombe; & progh besechyng of hym, god hym sent newe. Of thys holy martyr, 20 Merlyn seyd thus yn hys prophecye : "A newe martyr shal aryse with newe myracles, that yn the worldes endyng, yn the west of þe world, by specyal vertue, mannys lymmes out I-draw & out I-corue, ayeyn shald make come. Sorow shal turne ynto yoye, 24 whan þe sonnes shal sle þe fadyr yn hys modyr wombe; prynces & hey men * shal come out of þe este yn-to the weste, & lout ham to þe newe martyres fot-stappes." Al þys was openly I-seyd of þe holy martyr seynt Thomas ; he was þe whet corne þat fel yn 28

Beket died
at 48 [that
is, 53-4],
on Dec. 29,
1170.
[T. MSS.
L. T. Ha.
Cl. n. Op.
v. 262 n.
4.]

Macmurgh
dies in
May, 1171.

erth, & mych fruyt forth broght. In þe yer of burth-tyme .xlviij.; of hys sacryfiynge .viij.; of hys exil .vij.; yn the end of Decembre, yn þe yere of our lordes yncarnacion .M.C.lxxj.; & was poppe of Rome, Alexandre the thyrd ; Emperour of Almayne, ffrytheryke ; 32 kynge of ffraunce, lowys. Whan the wentyr was I-passed, Dermot Macmorgh deyed, þe begynenyng of may, & was bured at ffernes. A man grett of body ; hardy yn fyght amonge hys folke ; of lange & lome cryynge yn fyght, hys voys was somdel hors; leuer hym 36

as he commencid holy church wyth his blod whan she was arerynge, A.D.<br>1170-1.
Also this, whan she had long stond, and wox in elde, and redy was
to fall, wyth his blode he put hyr in good state, and therin
confermyd hyr.  And as he toke hym-selfe to them that hym
berewid the lyfe, forto arere the sekenys of holy church, Also this
doutyd not to take hym-Selfe to s[h]arpe Swerdes, & wickyd men [*Fol.9 a.]
hondes, * For the fredome of Holy church to Saue Vn-Wemmede. *ut eiusdem*
The fourme of His Holy martirdome, two Versis of Latey̆n Sortely *formam conservaret*
comprehendyth, that thus mych ben to vndyrstond: "For crystis *illaesam.*
Spouse, vndyr crystis tyme, in crystis churche, crystes owyn leman *verus*
died." / Amonge al the holy Scyntes that almyghty god wroght for *amator obit.*
in erth of voundyrfull miracles, for to Show har holynes,—as the
blynd to se, the lame to gone, the dombe to Speke, the deue to *quod separatis*
hyre, leperes to clense, Paralyse to festnen, ydropesye and al othyr *membris et*
maner sekenes to hele, the dede to arrere, the vickid Spyrytys to *proiectis, inaudito*
ouercome, And al the iiij^e. elementes to har comaundement haddyn *more repossit.*
—he alon was y-wyrchippid *with* al thes.  For a man, that his
eghen was hym berewid, *and* his manly membris y-kute of and
cast away, come to his tombe; and throw besechynge of hym, god
hym sende newe // Of this holy martyr, Merlynge sayd thus in his *Nota de Sancto Thoma.*
prophesy : "A new martyr shall ryse, *with* new Miracles, that in
the worldis endynge, in the weste of the world̃, by Special vertu,
manes lymes out y-draw and out y-corue, a-yeyn shal make come.
Sorrow shal make come Into Ioy, whan the Sonnes shal sle the *cum matris in utero*
Fadyr in his modyr wombe.  Princes and hey men shal come out *patrem*
of the Este into the weste, *and* lout hame to the new martyr-is fote- *filii trucidabunt.*
stappis."  Al this was opynly Sayd of the holy martyr Scynte
thomas.  He was the whet-corne that fel in Erth, *and* mych frute
forth broght.  In the yere of his berth-tyme, xlviij. ; of his Sacry-
fyynge, viij.; of his exil, vij^e.; in the Ende of Decembre, in the yere
of oure lord-is Incarnacion, Ml. Clxxj; and was Pope of Rome,
Alexandre the iij^e.; Emperoure of almane, Fryderik ; Kynge of
Fraunce, Lowys // Whan the wyntyr was ypassyd, Dermot Mac- *Descripcio*
mur*gh* dyed in the begynnynge of May, *and* was buried at Fernys. *Murcardi. (Op. v.*
A man grete of body; hardy in fyght amonge his Pepill; of lange *and* *237-8.)*
ofte cryinge in fyght, his voyce was Somdel hors; Leuer hym was

A.D. 1171.
Mac-
murgh's
character.

was that man hym dredet than loued; þe noble & þe ryche he
wold brynge to noght; the mek [1] & the *pouer* he wold rere; al men
ayeyns hym, & he ayeyns al.

[CHAPTER XIX.]

Hasculf,

Aftyr that, about whyt-sontyde, hastoyl, that was some 4
tyme maystre of deuylyn,—as man that fayn was about for

with
Norsemen
in forty
ships, led
by John
the Mad,
lands

to awreke hys old tene,—come wyt men of northwey & of þe north
ylondes, wit*h* ful grett folk, yn furty grett shyppes, & arryued
yn þe hauen of amlyffy, wit*h* haꝛ lodes-maꝏ, that hete Ioħn the 8
Wood.   Thay wenten out of haꝛ shyppes, men well I-wepned,
sum wit*h* longe swerdes, some wit*h* Iren pletes & round sheldes
well I-bound about wit*h* Iren, swerdes & speres & axys ynowe,

& marches
to attack
Dublin.
Miles of
Cogan and
the English
meet him,

& comeꝏ well ordeynly foꝛ to assaylle the tou*n* on the eest half. 12
Miles de Cogan, kepeꝛ of þe Cyte, kyndly stalwardly, & hardy,
wyth wel choseꝏ folke, went out ayeyns ham, and yaf ham fyght;
bot stronᵹ hyt was, to hold fyght ayayn so many wit*h* so fewe:
thaꝏ had he I-lost some of hys meꝏ; & O knyghtes theyᵹħ was 16
I-cut wit*h* þe kappe of hys haubergeoꝏ wytht a dynt of a dennysħ
ax.   nede he most turne yꝏ ayeyne at þe yate, tyll that Rychardꞇ
de Cogan, Myles brotheꝛ, wythe few men, that whylle stylly went
out at the south yate, & sharply becryed ham behynd, & smote 20
vpon ham.   throgh that, þat he come so fersly vpon ham, thay weꝛ
so afrygh, that thay wyst nat oꝏ whych syde thay shold kepe the

rout the
Norse, and
drive them
to their
ships.
John the
Mad is
slain.

fyght: yn a lytell whyl thay waꝛ dyssconfyte, & toke ham to flyght
toward haꝛ shyppes.   these otheꝛ come ham betwene, & slowe ful 24
many: theꝛ was Ioħn the Wood I-slayn, & ful mych folk wyth
hym, throght Walter de Redlesford, that ful stalwarth was yn the
fyght.   Hascoyl was I-take fro the shyppe theꝛ he was to I-flow,
& I-broght alyues yn-to the Cyte, & hys lyf I-*graunted* for 28
raunceoꝏ; bot as he stode yn court to-foꝛ Myles, he put forth

Hasculf
threatens
his con-
querors,

lyddyrly a *prout* word & seyd, "wyt lytell poweꝛ we comen now,
& thys nas bot assaye of our myght; bo[t] yf I lyue, aꝛ hyt be lange
to, shal come otheꝛ so mych as þese."   Whan thys was I-hardꞇ—for 32
yꝏ the ma*n*nys tonge hys oft lyf & deth, & me seyth eke, 'Tonᵹ
breketh boꝏ, thegh hym-self ne hawe none'—Myles bad that

tha[t] a man hym dreddyd than lowyd ; the nobil and the ryche A.D. 1171.
he wold brynge to noght ; the meke and the Pouer he wold awaunce ;
al men ayeynes hym, and he ayeynes al men //

[CHAPTER XIX.]

Aftyr that, about whitsontyd, Hastoyl, that was Somtyme *Capitulum*
Maystyr of Deuelyn,—as man that fayne was about forto be *xix*.
awengid of his old wreth,—come wyth men of North-Wey and of
the North ylondys, wyth many pepil, in fourty grete shippys, and *sexaginta*
londyd in the hauyn of Amlyffy, with har captayne that was callid *navibus.*
Ihoñ the Woode¹. Thay wentyn out of har shippis, men wel *1 Insano*
wepenyd, Some with longe Swerdys, Some with Iryñ Platys and *rel Vehe-*
roune sheldys, wel bound aboute with Iryñ, Swerdys and Speres *menti.*
*alii*
and axes ynow, and comyn wel ordeynly forto assayle the toun on *laminis*
*ferreis arte*
the Eeste haluo. * Myles de cogan, Kepere of the Citey, Kynly *consutis.*
Boldo and Hardy, Wyth Welle schosyn pepill, went out ayeynnes *[*Fol.9 b.]*
*innatae*
ham and yafe ham fyght ; but stronge hit was to holde fyght ayeyn *animorita-*
so many with so few ; than had he lost Some of his men ; and o *tis au-*
*dacia.*
knyghtes thegh was kut with the lappe of his haubergeoñ, with *cum panno*
*loricae*
a stroke of a dennysh axe.   nedes he moste turne aye at the yate, *praecisa.*
tyl that Richard de cogan, Miles-Is brodyr, with few men, that
whyle went out at the south yate, and sharpely becryed ham *ipsos a*
*tergo*
behynde, and Smote vpon ham.  throgh that, that he come so Fresly *acriter*
vpon ham, thay were so aferde, that thay wyst not on what Syde *exela-*
*mando,*
thay sholde kepe the fyght / In a lytyll whyle thay wer dyscom- *percussit.*
fyte, and toke ham to flyght toward har shippis.  thes oper come
ham be-twen, and kyllid ful many.  ther was Ihoñ de woode *Johanne*
y-slayn, And ful mych pepil with hym, throw Water de Redeles- *quoque*
*vehementi.*
ford, that ful bolde was in that fyght.  Hastoil was take fro the
shipe ther he was to flede, and brogh[t] alyues into the Cite, and
his lyfe gravntid for Rauncecoun ; but as he stode in courte to-for
Miles, he sayd lewidly a prowte worde : "Wyth lytil pepil we come
now, And this was not but assay of oure myght ; but yf y lyue,
ar hit be lange to, shal come othir so mych as thes."  Whan this
was herde,—For in the manes tonge is ofte lyfe and deth ; And as *In manibus*
*linguae,*
hit is Sayd, Tonge brekyth bone, thegh hym-Selfe ne haue non,— *mors et*
*vita.* Prov.
Miles commandid that he shold anone out be-laddo, and to Smyte *xviii. 21.*

A.D. 1171. me*n* shold hym anoo*n* out lede, & smyte of þe heed.   & thus, fo*r*
and is
beheaded. hys hauteyn & prout spech, he lost þe lyf that tha*r*-by-fo*r* mekely
hym was grau*n*ted.

[CHAPTER XX.]

[Fol.10a.]  Sone aftyr thys, many of thay that weren y-come 4
As Henry            yn-to Irland wyth the Erl, & eke to-fore,—for the kynges
II's edict    byddynge that come to ham, as hyt ys to[l]d a-foo*r*,—leften the
leaves
Struguil      Erl, & wente*n* yn-to england.   The peple of yrland saw the erl
bare of
men and       narow beladde, both of hys me*n* That hym left, & of vytalle that 8
food,         trukked, whe*r*-of he hade grete plente the*r*-by-fore out of eng-
the Irish     land.   Thay gaddered ham to-gedders myche folk, al þe prynce
muster a      of the lond, wi*th* al hu*r* poe*r*, & besegeden deuely*n* o*n* eue*r*y
big army,
and besiege   halue; & that was throgh procury*n*g of laurence, Erchebysshoppe 12
Dublin.       of dyuely*n*, as men seyd, for loue of hys folk.   he sent also hys
Gothred,      le*tt*res, wi*th* Oconghours le*tt*res, kynge of Connaght, to Gothred,
King of       kyn*g* of Manne, & to othe*r* prynces of þe nort*h* ylondes, for to
Man, and
others,       be-sete the hauy*n* of dyuely*n*; & large yiftes & *p*resentes ham 16
              yaue, & myche more hem behete, for to helpe ham.   &, for thay
              drede ham of al such mane*r*e of aventu*r*es, Throgh that, that the
              englysshe-men hadden so wel I-conquered vpo*n* þe yrysshe, Thay
with thirty   come*n* the rather ham to help; & yn lytell whyle came .xxx*ti*. 20
ships, beset  shyppys ful of stalwarth men wel arayed to fyght, & besette*n* the
Dublin
Harbour.      haue*n* of amlyffy.   Whan the Erl & hys men were*n* well twey
After two     monthes beley*n* yn the syte of dyuelyn, & to ham come non helpe,
months'
siege, and    nethe*r* of þe lond ne on waty*r*, & vytaylle fast ham slaked; & (as hyt 24
when food     ys oft I-found, selde be-falleth oo*n* harme that more [ne come]) come
is scarce,    Donald, Macmorghes sone, of okenseley, to The Erl, & told hym
news          for that Rob*er*t steuenes-son was beseget yn hys castell that he had
comes that
Robert        rered at þe carryke, of þe Cyteȝeyns of weysford & the men of ken- 28
Stevenson     sely, well þre thousand men; & few men had wyth hy*m*; [&, but
is besieged
in Carrick    hym] come socours by the þryd day, that of hym, ne thay that
Fort.         wi*th* hym were*n*, neu*er* no more to thynke.   Tn the syte of dyuelyn,
Maurice       we*r* that tyme be-left wi*th* the erl, Moryche fytz-Geraud & Reymond, 32
and Rei-
mund Fitz-    that fro*m* the kynge was come*n* newly; sory for ham-self & for
Gerald
are in        hars: & thegh þey weren yn grett angwysshe fo*r* ham-seleue, thay
Dublin.       ware*n* y*n* wel more fo*r* ha*r* good brothe*r* & for hys, that amonge

of his hede.  And this had he for his prowde Spech loste the lyfe A.D. 1171.
that thar-by-for mekely hym was graundid.

[CHAPTER XX.]

Sone aftyr this, many of them that weryn come into Irland
with the Erle, and also tofor,—by the kynges comandement
that come to ham as hit is to-for told,—leften the Erle, and wentyn
into england.  The pepil of Irland Saue the Erle narrow by-lad,
both of his men that hym lefte, and of vytayle that trukked,
wher-of he had gretto plente ther-before out of Englond.  Thay
gaderid ham to-gederis mych pepill, al the princes of the londe
with al har Power, and be-segedyn Deuelyn on euery syd.  and
that was by procvrynge of laurance, Archebishope of Deuclyn, as
men sayd, for loue of his Pepil / Also he sendo his lettres, with
o-conghoure-is lettres, kynge of connaght, to Gothrede, kynge of
Man, and to othyr Princes of the northe ylondes, for to be-Sette
the hauyn of Deuelyn ; and large yeftys and presentis ham yaue,
and mych mor ham promysid, forto helpe ham.  and, for thay dred
ham of al Suche aventures, Throgh that, that the Englysh-men
haddyn So wel conqueryd vpon the Irysh, Thay comyn the radyr
ham to helpe.  and in lytyll whyle came xxxti. shippis, ful of bold
men wel arrayid to fyght, and be-setten the hauyn of amlyffy.
whan the Erle and his men weryn wel two monthys besegid in the
Cite of Deuelyn, and to ham come no Soccovr on lond ne on watyr,
* And Vytayle ham falid, (and as Hit ys oft founde, Selde befallyth
one Harme that more ne comyth aftyr, and euer gaderyth to helpe
more and more,) Come Donald, Macmurghes sone of Okensely, to the
Erle, and toldo hym, for that Robert Steuenes-Sone was besegid in
his castel that he had rerid at the Karrike, of the Citteseynes of
weysford, and the men of Okenseley, wel iije. Mt. men; And few
men had with hym; and, but hym come Socoure by the thyrd day,
that of hym, ne thay that with hym weryn, neuer no more to
thynke.  In the Cite of Deuelyn, wer that tyme lefte with the Erle,
Morice fiz Geraud, and Reymond, that from the kynge was come
newely, Sory for ham-Selfe and for haris.  and thegh they wer in
grete angwysche for ham-Selfe, they weryn in wel more for har
good brodyr, and for his, that amonge his enemys was besegyd, in

E

*Marginal notes:*

Capitulum xxm.

ridentes Hibernici comitem et suos, tam suorum jactura, quam victualium defectu .. jam deficientes.

[* Fol. 10 a.] sed cumulante semper in commoda fortuna sinistra.

quasi tribus virorum milibus

tam suorum quam sui non meliocriter anxietate turbati.

A.D. 1171.

Maurice Fitz-Gerald harangs his men:

hys fomen was beseyget, yn place febly I-garnset, but a dych & a hegge of thornes vpoñ, & lytell ost ston-wal. Moryce arose vp to-fore the erl & the knyghtes, & seyde: "Nat to delytes, ne ydelnes set to drawen, come we nat yn-to thys lande; both[1] for to sechen aduentures, & prouen ouȓ streynth vpon peryl of ouȓ heedes. We haue I-stond awhyle & heghest, & now we bene

"We were the highest: we are now the lowest.

y-turned to the lowest, for so goth þe sykenesse of thys world; euery gladnesse ys endet wyth sorowe, & euery selth hath wnselth at þe end. After þe bryght day, cometh the durke[2] nyght; &

[* Fol. 10 b.]

after, the durknesse of * þe nyght ys awey I-dryuen with þe lyght of þe sone. Ar thys, the ouer-hand was yn all styddes ouȓ, & plente of alle good; nowe beth so belokeñ, that non help vs ne

"No help can come to us.

may come, noþer by lond ne by watyȓ. On oþer halue, Robert steuenes-sone, whos herdy herth. opened vs þe wey yn-to þys land, ys beseged feȓ wyt hys fomeñ yñ folk place. What ybyde we? haue we any hope that ouȓ lond-folk vs come to helpe? thaȓ-to ne tryst we nat; foȓ we beth now yn such law I-sette, þat as þe Iresshe weȓ, aȓ thys, to the englyshe, also þe englysshe beth now

"Let us fight! Tho' few, we've heart, and can beat our naked foes."

to þe Iresshe. thaȓ-foȓ gow owt stalwartly, assayllen ouȓ fomen! thegh we few be, we beñ meñ of herth, & wel I-wepned! ne shal neuer naked rascayll, thegh þey many be, haue myght ne poweȓ vs to wyt-stond." Whan moryce hadde thys I-seyd, Reymond, þat was I-smyte wyth the same sorow of herth, seyd to ham þe same wordes, & mych moȓ, 'that thay wolldeñ allerformest smyth vpon þe kyng of konnaght, & hym that was heed, & formest & heghest

The English sally out, in three small divisions against 30,000 Irish.

of ham alle.' Al that theȓ wereñ, heldeñ herto, & ren astryf to wepne ham, & leppeñ to hors, & deled ham a thre, thegh thay fewe wereñ. In þe formest, was Reymond with twonty knyghtes; In þe otheȓ, myles wyth .xxxti.; In þe þryd, the Erl & morice, with fourty knyghtes & Squyerys; & men an-hors & a-foot, to euery of these I-sete, as hyt wold by-falle: thay went ham out of þe syte stylly, about noon-dayes, & with so few meñ assayllydeñ añ hostes of .xxxti. thousand. Reymond, amonge the fyrst, smote vpon

Reimund Fitz-Gerald fights best.

ham; & feyȓ to-foȓ al otheȓ: he smote tweyne throgh-out wyth a speeȓ. Reymond & Moryce twey sonnes, Geraud & Alexandeȓ,

[1] but.  [2] MS. druke.

place febilly garnesyd, but a dyche and a hegge of thornys vpon, A.D. 1171.
and a lytil stone wal.  Moryce aros vp to-for the Erle and the
knyghtes, and sayd: "Not to delytes, ne ydylnes, come we nat into *Non ad*
this land; but forto sechyn adventures, and proven oure Streynth *delicias,*
*viri, non*
vpon peril of oure hedys.  we haue stond awhyle, and hygh ; and *ad otia*
*rocati.*
now we ben turnyd to the louyst; for So is the schavnge of this
world.  the end of euery gladnes is Sorrow.  And euery Surnesse
hath vnsurnes at the ende.  Aftyr the bryght day, comyth the
nyght; and aftyr, the durkenes of the nyght is a-way dryven with
the lyght of the Sone.  Afor this, the ouerhand was in al places
our, and plente of al goode.   Now ben we So belokken, that none *Auxilium*
*nobis, nec*
helpe vs ne may come, nothyr by lond no by watyr.  On the *mare*
othyr Syde, Robert Steuenes-Sone, whos bolde hert openyd vs the *mittit, nec*
*classis*
way into this lond, is besegid fer with his fomen in febyll place. *inimica*
Whate abyde we ? haue we any hoppe that oure lond-pepil wil vs *permittit.*
come to helpe ? tharto ne trust we not / for we byth now in Such
lawe y-Sette, that [1] as the Iryssh wer, or this, to the Englysh, Also *ut sicut*
*Hibernicis*
the Englysh byth now to the Iryssh.  Wherfor go we out boldely *Angli, sic*
assaylyn oure enemys ! thegh we fewe be, we ben men of herte and *et Anglis*
*Hibernici*
wel wepenyd ! ne shall neuer nakyd raskayl, thegh they many be, *simus.*
haue myght ne powere vs to wythstond."   Whan Morice had this
sayd, Reymonde, that was Smyte wyth the Same Sorrow of herte,
sayde to ham the same wordis, and mych mor, 'that thay woldyn
alther-formyst Smyte vpon the kynge of connaght / and he that was
hede *and* formyst of ham al.'  Al that ther weryn, heldyn herto, and
went to wepyn ham, and leppyn to hors, and delyd ham on thre,
thegh thay few were.  In the formyst, was Reymond, with twonty
knyghtes ; In the othyr, Milis, with xxxti. In the thyrd, the Erle
and Morice wy[th] fowrty knyghtes, *and* Morice with fourty
knyghtis *and* Squyeris ; *and* men an-hors an[d] a-fote, to euery of
thys y-sette, as hit wolde befall.   thay went ham out of the Cite *hora quasi*
*post*
Softely, about noon dayes, and wyth So few men assayledyn an *nonam.*
hoste * of xxxti Mt. Reymonde, amonge the fyght, fryst Smote vpon [* Fol. 10
ham, and ferre to-for al othyr.  he Smote two throgh-out with b.]
a Spere.  Reymond and Morices two Sonnes, Geraud and alex-

---

[1] In the margin, 'as we byth ynglys on to the yryssh, so we byth yryssh on
to the ynglys.'

A.D. 1171.

The little English host rout the 30,000 Irish,

thegh thay wer fyrst y-sete yn þe latest of þe host, throgh kynd stalwardnesse hertly smytteñ out to the formest, & many dydden to deth. Alle þe other fresshely foloweden after; & yn lytell whylle dysconfited al þe hoste, & sloweñ so many, that no tonge ne myght tell. Oconnoghour, þat that tym satte yn bathe, vnnethe escaped: thay folwed the dyscomfytur oñ euery halue

and return to Dublin with great spoil. They march (too late) to aid Fitz-Stephen.

tyll þe nyght ham leth. Than thay turned ayeyne, & name har pelfre, gold & syluyr, clothes & wepne & hors, & wenteñ wyth mychel gladnesse yñ-to þe syte. Amorow þay lefte good kypynge yn tho syte, & turneden toward weysford by Odroon, wyth baners y-lacet, for to socour Robert steuenes-sone.

### [CHAPTER XXI.]

[Fol. 11 a.]

Fitz-Stephen's scanty garrison defend themselves bravely.

The mene time, the folke of Weysford, wythe þe power of Okensely, wel thre þousand men, ayeyn har othes I-swer & har trowth, Robert steuenessoñ al vnwardly, with fyue knyghtes & a few bow-men I-found withyn hys feble castel, thay stynt nat to assaylle. thay defendet ham full stalwarthly, thegh they fewe wer; & namely a knyght that hete Wyllyam Not, aftyr Robert, ouer al other best dydde. Whan thay myght nat wyth streynth spede, thay bethoght ham that wyth falshed & wyth treyson they wold

The Irish deceive them;

come wyth-yn ham. Thay sent to þe dyche twey bysshoppes, that on of Weysford, that other of kyldur, & other mo wyth ham yn habyt of relygyoñ; thay broght with ham massebokes, & Corpus domini, & relykes many, & sworne vp-on ham al, & vpoñ

swear Dublin is taken, and its Chiefs slain.

They offer the garrison a safe transport to Wales. Their false words are believd, and the garrison are slain or imprisond.

har owne soules, that 'dyuelyn was Itak; & þe Erl & morice & Remond, &_ the englisshe-men, euerychon I-slawe; the host of leynestre & of Connaght comyng to ham-ward; & for good of hym, thay wer to hym y-come; that he shold yeld vp his castel, & me shold saue hym lyf & lym, & al his & al har good; for he was ham so fre & so meke lord, me shold trewly brynge hym & his ouer in-to Wales ar the grete hoste of his fomen to hym comen, that nothyng nold spar hym.' Robert leued har speche & har fals othes; he came out & yeldet hym & his, to ham & to har trowth. Thay wer no raþer out I-comen, that me ne name ham euerychone; & some thay sloweñ yn þe place; some þay vndide & betten lidderly & boudẹn; & wyth ham selfe I-bounden, kesten

andyr, thegh they were fryst Sette in the laste of the hoste, throgh *A.D. 1171.*

kynly bolul[1] hertely Smyten out to the formyst, *and* many dyddyn *innatae*
*tamen*
to deth.   Al the othyr freschely folwedyn aftyr; And in lytyll *strenuitatis*
Space of tyme dyscomfyted al the hoste, and slowyn so many, that *indicio ..*
no tonge myght tell.   Oconghoure, that that tyme Satte in bathe, *['¹ for*
*bolnys,'*
vnneth Escapid.   thay folwid the dyscomfiture on euery halue tyll *59/¹4.]*
the nyght ham lette.   Than thay turned ayeyñe, and toke har *victualibus*
*et recturis,*
pilfre, gold and Syluyr, clothis, and wepyn and hors, *and* wentyn *spoliis*
with myche gladnes into the Cite.   A-morrow thay lefte good *quoque*
*et armis*
kepynge in the cite, and turned toward Weysford by Odrooñ, wyth *onerati.*
baneres ylacyd, forto Socoure Robert Steuenes-Sonne.

### [CHAPTER XXI.]

The men-tyme, the pepil of weysford, with the Power of *Capitulam*
okenseley, wel iije. Mⁱ. men, aycȳn har othis Sworne and har *xxjᵐ.*
trouth, Robert Steuenes-Sonne al vn-wittynge, with v. knyghtes *Stephani-*
*dem im-*
and a few bowmeñ, sownde within his febil castel, thay stynte not *provisum.*
to assayle.   thay defendyd ham ful boldely, thegh they fewe were;
and Specialy a knyght that was callid William Not, aftyr Robert,
ouer al othyr best dyd.   Whan thay myght not with streynth
Spede, thay bethoght ham that with falshede and with treysone *ad con-*
*sueta*
thay wolde come within ham.   Thay Sende to the dyche two *fallacius*
bysshopis, that one of weysford, that othyr of kyldare, and othyr *tela fig-*
*mentaque*
mo with ham in habit of religioñ.   thay broght with ham masbokes *dolosa con-*
*currunt.*
añd Corpus domini, *and* relykis many, and Sworñ vp-on ham al,
and vpon har owyn Soulys, that 'Deuelyn was take; and the Erle,
and Morice *and* Reymond, and the Englyssh-men, euerychoñe were
Slayñ; and the hoste of leynystre and of connaght comynge to ham-
ward; and for good of hym, thay were to hym come; that he sholde *Stephani-*
*dae ipsius*
yelde vp his castel, and thay wold Sawe his lyfe, and al his, and al *commodi*
har good; for he was to ham so fre and So meke lorde, they wold *causa.*
trewely brynge hym and his ouer into walis, or the grete oste of
his enemys to hym were come, that nothynge wolde hym Spare.'
Robert belewid har Spech and har fals othys.   He came out, and ² *alii rer-*
*beribus,*
yeldyd hym *and* his, to ham and to har trouth.   Thay were no *alii vero*
radyr out-come, than thay toke ham euerychone; and Some thay *vulneribus*
*graviter*
Slowyn in the Place; Some thay vndide and bettyn vickydly²; *and* *afflicti.*

A.D. 1171.   willych In preson.  Nat long ther-after, come soth tythyngges of
The Irish   the dysconfytur of dyuelyn, & the Erles comyng toward ham.
traitors
burn Wex-   the thraytours, whan thay hyt wysten, thay setten har own toun
ford, and   of weysford afyr, & barnen hyte; & wenten ham-self, with wyf & 4
go to the
Island of   chyld, & al har oþer good & har presons, ynto þe Iland of begger-
Begeri,
with Fitz-  yng, þat hys I-sete yn the entre of the hauen of Weysford.  Þe
Stephen.
In the pass  host of leynester come ayeyns hym yn Odrone, & yaf hym fyght
of Odroon,  yn a paas of o thykke wood, strange yn hym selue, & comerous. 8
Striguil
defeats a   Ther wer many of the Irysshe y-slaw yn that fyght; & þe Erl &
Leinster
force.      al hys camen hole & sound yn-to þe pleyne, sawe o man that he
            þer forlese; & meyler, our al other, as hys wone was, stalwardly
The Wex-    hym thar byladde.  ❡ After that, as thay comyn toward Weys- 12
ford men
threaten to ford, comen men ayeyns ham, & tolden ham the aduentur of
kill Fitz-  Robert, & of the tounes bernyng, & seyden ham sykerly, that 'yf
Stephen
&c.  The    þay to ham wold vend anoon, þay wold sle har presons, & send
English
hear of the ham the heeddes.'  Whan thus was y-hard among the oste, who-so 16
loss of the had I-hard þe wepynge, & the wenynge, & the sorow that thay
Carrick
garrison,   mad, he myght wel sygge that 'neuer-more sych reuth was amonge
and weep
for it.     men I-sey.'  he was man that noon other was hys eunynge In all
            goodnesse [1], & ensampell to all knyghtes that any stalwarthnesse 20
[* Fol. 11  wold begynnyge;  * ffor yn-Wales & eke yn Irland many aduentures
b.]
            both god & yuel had I-fond, that ofter weren hys aduentures hard,
Robert      thegh thay som tyme welcomen wyth hym.  He was man mych
Fitz-
Stephen     of body, [2]fayr vysage, soft & rody, nat ful becumliche; grete 24
described.  meet-yeuer, large & fre throgh al thynge, & of grett solace yn
            Iappynge & pleynge; bot to mych, & vnmesurable, he yaf hymself
Richard,    lecherye [2].  The Erl was man of suche manere; [3]he was samroed,
Earl of
Striguil    with grey eghen, wommanes vysage, & sproty, smal spech, 28
described.  short nek [3]; on al other manere he was of fayr body, & alonge
            fre & meke; ham that he hade nat to yeue to, he quemed ham
            with fayr spech: out of wepne, he was as redy to otheres byddynge

─────────

[1] O virum, virtutis unicum, verique laboris exemplum.—Op. v. 271.

[2-2] vultuque decenti; et statura paulo mediocritatem excedente: vir
dapsilis et largus, liberalis et jocundus, sed vino Venerique trans modestiam
datus.—Op. v. 271-2.

[3-3] Vir subrufus, lentiginosus, oculis glaucis, facie feminea, voce exili, collo
contracto.—Gir. Camb. Op. v. 272.  Rolls Series.

boundy[n]; *and with* hym-Selfe y-bound, kesten vnmercyably in A.D. 1171.
pryson[1]. Not lange ther-aftyr, come trew thythynges of the dyscom-
fyture of Deuelyn, and the Erlis comynge toward ham.   the
traytoures, whan thay hit Vndyrstode, thay Setten har owyn toune
of weysford' afyre, and brentyn hit / And wenten hame-Selfe, *with*
wyfe and chylde, and al hare othyr good and har prisoneres, into the *ad insulam*
Iland of begeryn, that is at the Entrest of the hawyn of weysford'. *Begeri . . .*
the Hoste of Leynystre come aycynys hame in odroon, and yafe *sancta*
ham fyght in a paace of thyke wodde, strange in hym-[\*] Selfe, and [\* Fol. 11
comeros[2]. Ther wer many of the Iryssh Slayn in that fyght; ande *a.]*
the Erle and al his came hole and Sounde into the Playn, Saue
o man that he there forlese.   And Meylere, *ouer* al othyr, as he
was woned, boldely hym there bore / Aftyr that, as thay comen †*ex parte*
toward weysford, came men toward hame, and toldyn ham the *quoque*
*proditorum*
aduenture of Robert and of the tounes brennynge, and †Sayd ham *firmiter*
*asserentes,*
Surly, that 'yf thay wolde to ham wende anoone, thay wolde sle har *quod si*
prisoneres, and Send ham tho hedys.' Whan this was herde amonge *ad illos*
*accedere*
þe hoste, who-so hadd' herd the wepynge, and the lementacion and *forte prae-*
*sumant,*
the Sorrow that thay made, he myght wel say that 'Such Sorrow *praecisa*
was neuer amonge men Sey' // He was man, that none othyr was *sibi suorum*
*capita*
his cunynge in al goodnesse, and Ensampil of al knyghtys that any *statim*
*cuncta*
boldnys wolde begynne. for in Walis, and also in Irland', many *remittent.*
aduentures both good and euyl had fovnde, that ofter weryn his *Descripcio*
*Roberti*
aduentures hard, thegh thay Sometyme wel comyn *with* hym. he *fiz Steuen.*
was man myche of body, fayr vysage, Softe and rody, not ful be- *A big man,*
comlych; good mette-yeuer, large and fre throgh al thynge, and of *liberal, but*
*lecherous.*
grete Solace in Iaypynge; but to mych, and vnmesurably, he yafe
hym-Selfe to Lechery //

   The Erle was man of Such manere: he was wyth-out doute of *Descripcio*
*Ricardi*
grey eighen, womanes visage, *and* Sproty, smale Speche, Short *Comitis.*
neke: on al othyr maner, he was a fayre body, and alonge fre and
meke. thay that he hadd not to yew, he plesyd *with* fayre Spech[3].
Out of wepyn, he was as redy to other*es* byddynge, as thay to hym.

[1] in carceres, et vincula contruduntur.—*Op.* v. 271.
[2] quamquam in sui natura arcto nimis et invìo, concidibus tamen plurimum
arte munito.—*Op.* v. 272.
[3] Quod re non poterat, verborum suavitate componebat.—*Ibid.*

A.D. 1171.

Description of Richard, Earl of Striguil.

as other to hys: alle thynge he dydde by rede of hys men, & nothynge wyth-out. Out of bataylle, he had more of knyght than of host-leder; yn bataylle, more leder than knyght; & yn al aduenturs of bataylle, he was stydfast, ful connynge, & tokne of 4 recet to al hys host; & for non vnhap he ne amayed hymself, ne yn wanhope ne fel; ne for ne good chaunce, he ne made hym the prutter ne þe more hautayn; bot euer-more, yn al aduen[tu]rs, of stydfast herth & trewe.

8

## [CHAPTER XXII.]

The Earl of Striguil

Whan the erl hadde I-hard the trayson þat was I-done to Robert, wytht myche sorow of hert he went hym with the host to Watyrford; & þer he fond heruy of mountmorthy, that than wase newen I-comen out of englond from þe kynge, 12 & broght wryttes, & eke by mych amonested the erl that he

sails to England, and finds Henry II at Newnham, Glostershire, ready to cross to Ireland. The Earl yields Dublin and all haven-towns to Henry,

shold wend to the kynge. he hade shyppe redy, & good wynd; he name heruy with hym, & went ouer; come to the contre of clandechestre, to Newenham, ther he fond the kynge with mychel 16 host, redy to pass yn-to Irland. & after myche speche betwene ham ymade, & myche dalyaunce, throgh heruyes modelyng & comynge about þe erle, & eke hys besechynge, the kynge name of hym manred for to hold leynestre of hym; & the Erl graunted þe kynge, 20 dyuelyn, & all the hauen tounes vpon þe see, with har Candredes & castelles þer-vpon y-set; & that other parte of hys conquestre, he & hys heyres sholden holden of þe kynge & hys heyrs. Whan thys was al on thys manere I-done, the kynge toke the wey yn-to 24

who goes to Pembroke, and waits there for a favourable wind.

south Wales, & cam to pembroke; & ther yn þe contre abode with hys host longe whyle, ar he had wynd for to passe. The whyle that he was thar, he hadde houndes & haukes, as man that mych delyted yn suche game. .O. day he went by the strond of þe see, 28 & bar a mych goshawke of northwey vpon hys hand. Than sat vp-on an hegh clyff ouer the strond, a faucon gentel, negh hys nest,

[* Fol. 12 a.]

ther he was woned to brede. The *goshake sawe the faucon, & a-bated to hym. the kynge that saw; & kest hym of hys hand; & 32 he nam hys flyght toward the facon, hym sore to henten: the

Henry's Norse goshawk

facon sawe hym comynge, & nam hys flyght an hoghe, & escaped of hym; þe goshawke turned ayeyne to þe kynges hand; & ar

Al thynge he did by consaylo of his men, and nothynge with*out* / ᴀ.ᴅ. 1171.
Out of battayl, he had more of knyght than of hoste-leder; in
battaylo / more ledder than knyght / and in al aduentures of *In praelio*
battayle, he was stydfaste, ful conynge, and tokyn of recette to al his *positus,*
*firum suis*
hoste ; and for no vnhape he was not aferde hym-Selfe, ne in van- *recupera-*
*tionis et*
hope ne felle ; ne for no good chaunce, he was not the Pruttyr, ne *refugii*
*signum*
the heyer ; but eu*er*-more, in al aduentures, of stydfaste herte and *manebat.*
trewe.

[CHAPTER XXII.]

WHan the Erle had herde the trayson that was done to Cap*itulum*
Robert, with mycho Sorrow of herte he went with al the ˣˣⁱʲᵐ.
hoste to watyrford; and ther he founde heruey of montmurthy,
that that tyme was come out of England frome tho kynge, and
broght writtes, and Eke mych amonneschyd the Erle that he sholde
wend to tho kynge.   he had ship redy, and good wynd; he toke
heruey with hym, *and* went ou*er*; come to the contrey of clandecestre,
to New-Enham, ther he found the Kynge with gretto hoste, redy to
Passe Into Irland.  and aftyr mych Speche betwen ham made, and
myche delyaunce, throgh herueyes medlynge and comynge about the *circum-*
*ventu*
Erle, and also his besechynge, the kynge toke of hym concayle forto *pariter et*
holde leynystre of hym ; and the Erle graunted the kynge, deuelyn, *interventu*
and al the hawyn tounes vpon the see, with hare candredes and
castelis there-vpon sette ; and that othyr Parte of his conqueste, *He  [* Fol. 11
and Hys heyres sholde Holde of the Kynge and [his] Heyrys.  Whan  b.]
this Was on this manere done, the kynge toke the way into South
walis, and came to Pembroke[1] ; and ther in tho contrey abode with
his hoste longe tyme, ur thay had wynd to Passe.  The whylo that
ho was there, he hadd houndes and haukys, as man that mych
delytyth in Such game.  O day, he went by þᵉ see stronde, and bar
a mych goshauke of Norwey on his hande.  Than Sate vpon an hey
clyfe ou*er* the stronde, a faucon gentyll, ney his neste, ther he was
wonyd to brede.  the goshauke Saw the faucon, and abated to hym *lucra*
*projecit*
hym forto smyte.  the faucon saw hym comynge, and toke his flyght
an hey, and Escapid of hym.  the goshauke turnyd ayeyn to the

_____

[1] Et Penbrochiam veniens, pulcherrimam in brevi Milverdico portu [Milford
Haven] classem conjunxit.—Gir. Camb. *Op.* v. 273.

A.D. 1171.
is kild by
a Welsh
falcon.

he myght fully take to hym, the facon smote to hym from an heyght, & forcleue hym the rygge, & kest hym adoune dede at the kynges foote. Al thay that hyt saw, hadden ther-of myche wondyr. Than bade the kynge, that fro that tyme, the bryddes of that facons 4 neste shold euer-mor be I-kepte to hys owne be-houe; & so thay wer, euery yeyr; & yn al hys kynge-dome wer non so good facons I-found, ne so bold.

[CHAPTER XXIII.]

O'Rourke,
king of
Meath,

assaults
Dublin,
early in
September,
but is
beaten off
by Miles
of Cogan;
and his
son is slain.

The while that thys was, Roueryke, the kynge of Myth,— 8 awayted that the erl was out of lond; & Reymond & lytel folk was beleft ar dyuelyn, the syte & þe contrey for to kepe,— with mych folke come to dyuelyn about myd-heruest, & assaylled the walles of þe syte with gret streynth & loly crye, & wend 12 wel to haue I-take þe syte, & al þat þer-In was. bote ther streynthys & stalwarthnesse, hyt mote nedes shewe hymself: Myles de Cogan & hys men preuely wenten out, & smote grymly vpon ham, so þat yn lytell whyl thay weren al dyscomfyted. Bot 16 roury hymself vnnethe escaped; & hys sone, a welle stalwarth man amonge hys folk, was thar I-slawe, wyth many other.

[CHAPTER XXIV.]

Nota: de [1]
primo
aduentu
Regis An-
gliae in
hiberniam

Henry II
lands at
Waterford
on Oct. 18,
1171,
fulfilling
prophecies
of Merlin
and St.
Moling.

Aftir this, whan the kynge had I-dyght al that nede was to so noble comynge ynto Irlond, he went to seynth 20 dauyes; & besoght the holy man, seynt dauy, with grett deuocion & mych wurshyppe. And tho weder hym come, & wynd at wylle. He put hym to saylle; passed the see, hool & sound; & arryued at Waterford on seynt lukes day, with fywe houndred knyghtes, 24 & men, an hors an a foot, fulle many. Than was fulfylled a pro- phycye that Merlyn seyd: "out of þe Este shal come a fyr bernynge, & shal Irlond al about for-swely." And seynt Molynge seyd þus: "Out of þe eeste shal come a stronge thondred, & shal 28 smyte yn-to þe weste, & al the streynth of Ormond adoun brynge." He arryued, the yer of hys kyngedome, senthe; of hys elde .xl.;

[1] Later note in right margin: 'For in Martilogis the king brought 400 great shippes into Irelande, and in short time subdued the whole lande, beinge governed by 5 kinges, all which submitted to the king, except the king of Connaght, who kept himself in woods and marishes.'

kyngys hand'; and, Ar he myght fully take to hym, the faucon smote *A.D. 1171.*
to hym from an hey, and for-clew hym the bake, and kest hym doune *¹ singulis rex annis,*
ded at the kynges fote. Al thay that hit Saw, ther-of had grete *circa nidi-*
wondyr. ¹Than comandid' the kynge, that fro that tyme, birdis of *ficationis tempora,*
that faucon-is neste shold euer-more be kepe to his owyn behow; *propter falcon s*
and So thay were, euery yere. And in al his kyngdome wer *terrae*
none So good faucones y-found, ne so bolde. *illius, qui marinis*

[CHAPTER XXIII.] *in rupi-*
*bus exclu-*

T He mene-tyme that this was / Roueryke, the kynge of *duntur,*
mythe¹,—be-helde his tyme, and that the Erle out of lond was, *consuevit.*
*and* Reymond' *and* lytil peple was lefte at Deuelyn, the Cite and the *Capitulum xxiijᵐ.*
contrey to kepe,—wyth mych pepyl come to deuelyn about myd
hervyst, and assaylid the wallis of the Cite with gret Streynth and
grymly cry, and wend wel to haue take the Cite, and al that therin
was. But ther streynthis *and* bolnys, hit mote nede Schow hym- *Sed quo-*
Selfe : Miles de Cogan and his men priuely wentyn out, and smote *niam virtus*
grymly vpon ham, so that in lytyll whyle thay weryn al dys- *claudi nescit ; et*
comfytcd'. But Roury hym-Selfe vnneth Escapyd'; and his Sonne, *ignis op-*
a wel bolde man amonge his pepil, was ther Slayn, with many *pressus, in flammam*
oþer. *erumpit.*

[CHAPTER XXIV.]

A ftyr this, whan the kynge had dygh al that nede was to So *Capitulum xxiiijᵐ.*
nobyl comynge into Irland', he went to Seynt Dauyes, and
besoght the holy man, seynt Dauy, with gret deuocion *and* myche
wyrchippe. and then wynde and weddyr hym come at wille. he *Nota de*
putte hym to sayle, and passyd the see, holde and Sounde ; and *primo aduentu*
londyd at Watyrford' on Seynte Luke-is day, with fyue hundred *Regis Anglie in*
knyghtes, and men an hors and a foote, ful many. Than was fulfillid *hiberniam.*
a prophesy that Merlyn Sayd thus / "Out of the Este shal come
a fyre brennynge, and shal Irland al aboute forswely." And seynt
Molyngo sayd thus, "Out of the Este shal come a stronge thondyr, *Veniet ab*
and shal smyte into the weste, and al the streynth of Ormond *aurora turbo*
adoune brynge." he londyt, the yere of the kynge-dome, the Senfte ; *validus.*
of his age, the xl ; of our lordys incarnacion, Mᵗ. Clxxij ; *and* was

¹ rex monoculus Medensis Ororicius . . . cum multitudine magna, circa
kalendas Septembris, Dubliniam venit.—*Op.* v. 274.

A.D. 1171. of ouꝛ lordes Incarnacion .M.C.lxxij ; & was poppe, Alexander the thryd ; Emperouꝛ, ffryderyke ; kynge of ffraunce, lowyse.

[CHAPTER XXV.]

*Henry II has Fitz-Stephen*

The kynge abode at Waterford a fewe dayes. Thedeꝛ come the sytʒeyns of weysford, & broght to hym Robert ₄ steuenesse-sone, as for gret seruyce, & yn hope of good reward ; ffor as myche as he come yn-to Irlond, lond to conqueꝛ, wythout auctoryte of hegheꝛ prynce, & yaue otheꝛ, ensample for to comen ynto the lond. The kynge, at the byggynnyge, told of hym grete ₈

[* Fol. 12 b.] * vnworthynesse ; & edwyte hym, with grete thretynge, of that grete boldnesse ; & lete take hym, y-bound as he was, & gyued hym to

*put in prison.* anotheꝛ, & put hym yn Rathnyldestouꝛ for to kepeꝝ. Soine

*The King of Cork does homage to Henry II ;* þer-afteꝛ come the kynge of Corke, Dermot Maccarthy, & yeld ₁₂ hym to the kynge, & dydde hym homage, & swaꝛ hym hold othes, & delyuered hym ostages for to be to hym hold & trew, & beꝛ hym truage euery yeꝛ of hys land. ffrom thus, the kynge went wythe the hoste to lysmore, & theꝛ was twey dayes ; & fro ₁₆ thus, went to Casshle. Thedeꝛ came donald Obreeꝝ, kynge of

*so do the King of Limerick,* lymeryke, to hym vpoꝝ the watyꝛ of ssur ; & for to hawe pees, yeld hym to þe kynge yn al manere as Maccathy hadde done. The kynge set kepers both at Corke & at lymeryke ; & to hym ₂₀ comen the hoste of both contrees aftyr Maccathy & Obreen, & yeld

*and all the best folk of Munster.* ham to þe kynge, & becomen hys meyn by othes & ostages ; so that theꝛ was none that waꝛ of any name yn al Monestre, that by hys good wylle ne yeld hym to the kynge. Whan thys was al I-done, ₂₄ the kynge, with mych wyrsshyppe & wyth ryche yiftes, lete euery

*Henry II returns to Waterford,* maꝝ wend yn-to hys owne lond, & went hym-self by Tybrach ayeyne to Waterford. þer was ayeyne Robert y-broght to-for hym. The kynge saw hym, & bethoght hym of þe gret goodnesse þat ₂₈ was yn hym, & of hys stalwarthnesse & hys hardy hert ; of many good seruices that he & hys hadden I-done, wyth mych trauaylle & grette perille of lyue : he had grett reuth of hym yn hys hert ;

*pardons Fitz-Stephen, and restores him his lands.* &, throgh besechynge of hegh men, al hys wreth, wyth good hert ₃₂ he hym foryaf, & delyueret hym out of prysoꝝ, & lete delyuer hym hys londes þat hym wereꝝ be-nomeꝝ, of Weysford & of þe

pope, Alexandyr the thyrd; Emperoure, Frederike; kynge of A.D. 1171. Fraunce, Lowys.

## [CHAPTER XXV.]

THe Kyng abod at Watyrforde a few Dayes. Thedyr come [Fol. 12 the Cytteseynys of Weysford, and broght to hym Robert Steuenes-Sonne, as for grete Seruyse, and in hope of good reward, for-as-mych as he came into Irland, lond to conquere, wythout auctorite of heghyr Prince, and yaue othyr ensampil forto come into londe. The kynge, at the begynnynge, tolde of hym gret Vnuorthynys; and reprewid hym, with grete tretynge, of that grete boldnes; and lette take hym, bound as he was, and gywid hym to anothyr, and Put hym in Rathnyldys toure forto kepyn. Sone ther-aftyr come the kynge of Corke, Dermot Maccharthy, and yelde hym to the kynge, and dyd hym homage, and Sware hym olde othis, and delyuerid hym hostagis forto be to hym holde and trew, and ber hym truage euery yere of his land. From thens the kynge went with the hoste to Lysmor, and ther was two dayes; and fro thens went to Cassell. Thedyr came Donal Obreyne, kynge of Lymerik, and to hym on the watyr of Sure; and for-to haue pees, yelde hym to the kynge in al maner as Macchardy hadd done. The kynge Sette keperes both at Corke and at Lymerike; and to hym come the Best of both contreis aftyr maccharthy and Obren, and yelde ham to the kynge, and be-comyn his men by othis and hostagys, so that ther nas none that was holde of any reputacion in al Monester, that by his good wyll ne yelde hym to the kynge. Whan this was al done, the kynge, with mych vyrchip and wyth ryche yeftys, lette euery man wend into his owyn lond, And wente hym-Selfe by Tybraght ayeyne to watyrford. ther was ayeyn Robert broght to-for hym. The kynge Saw hym, and bethoght hym of the grete goodnesse that was in hym, and of his boldnys and his hardy herte, of many good seruyces that he and his haddyn done with mych trauayl and grete Perel of lyfe. He had of hym grete Pite in his herte; and, throw besechynge of good men, al his wreth with good herte he hym for-yaue, and delyuerid hym out of prisone, and delyuerid hym his londys that of hym wer take fro, of Weysford

*[margin notes:]*
a.]
Capitulum
xxv.
quasi sub
praetextu
obsequii,
eo quod
Hiberniam
citra ipsius
assensum
primus
introcerit,
aliisque
maliq-
nandi
occasionem
praebuli-
terit,
vinctum
et cap-
tivum
adducunt.

rex videns
virum
tantis for-
tunae peri-
culis, et
toties, ex-
positum.

A.D. 1171.  contrey about.  Some syggen that the kynge lete to-draw the
Master     traytours that hym betrayed ; Bot Maystre Geroud ne telleth
Gerald
says no-    nothynge þer-of ; & ther-fore I ne tel hyt nat to sothe, bot hyt
thing of    oght well be so.                                              4
traiters
being                              [CHAPTER XXVI.]
drawn and
quarterd.  Whan þe kynge had thus I-do, he left at Waterford, Robert
           beranardesson, wyth mych meyne; &, by Ossery, name the
           wey toward dyuelyn.  In that wyage, the kynge of Ossery came
           to hym, & yeld hym to the kynge; & whan he hade I-bydde 8
           awhylle at dyuelyn, theder come Al þe heghest Iresshe-men of
The Kings  leynestre, & besoghten pees, & yolden ham to the kyng.  Roryke
of Con-
naught     O'conghour, the kynge of Connaght, ayeyns the kynges messagers
and Meath  at the watyr shynnen,—that ys to wytten, hugh þe lacy & wyllyam 12
yield to
Henry II's Al-delines sone,—ther he yeld hym to þe kynge; & the kynge of
messen-
gers.      Myth Also ; So that ther nas none heght man yn Irland, that ne
           come to the kynges owne body, or sent messagers for to be-comen
           hys man, & yeld hym to hym, sawe only thay of vlnestre.  Than 16
Prophecies was fulfylled a prophecye that seynth Molynge seyd : " To-for hym
[*Fol. 13  shall foot-*falle þe prynces, & trogh [1] boxom-fastines [2] the lyme of
a.]        pees shul vnderfonge."  Merlyn seyd an-other : " Tho is lyght, the
of St.     foules of the Iland shollen togedder fle ; & the most of ham, with 20
Moling
and        har wenges I-brant, shollen ouerthrowen yn thraldome ; the fyf deles
Merlin.    shollen be broght yn-to on, & the syxt shal ouercome the strengest
The Irish  places of Irland."  Whan the mydwynter came, many of the heghest
nobles
wonder at  comen to þe kynges court to feste ; & myche wonder ham thoght 24
the fine   of the noble seruice that þey þer saw, & of the myche plente of
meals and
decorations mete & of drynke, of bordes I-sette, & fayr clothes vpon; the hegh
at Henry   seruice of panetrye & buttellerie, & ryche vessels of gold & syluer;
II's feast.
           the many manere metes of kechen, on the manere of Englond, 28
           whych thay had neuer þer-to-fore I-sey.  After that þe fest was
           heghly & fayr I-hold, euery man went wyth gladnesse yn-to hys
           owne.  In that tyme, weren bowemen at ffynglas I-horberowed,
Sacri-     & wenten ynto chyrche haye, & hewen adoun trees, that seyntes 32
legious
bowmen     by old tyme hadden þer I-sete : þer came sodeyn deth vpon ham,
die sud-   euerychon.  [See Giraldus's Topogr. Hibern. Opera, v. 135.]
denly.

---

[1] A later overline h is above the tr. of 'trogh.'          [2] or 'fastmes.'

and of the contrey aboute.  Some sayne that the kynge lette to- A.D. 1171.
draw the traytoures that hym betrayed.  But Maystyr Geraud ne
tellyth nothynge ther-of ; and therfor y ne tell hit not for throuth,
but hit oght wel be so.

[CHAPTER XXVI.]

W han the kynge had thus done, he lefte at watyrford, Robert  Capitulum
  Barnardessonne, with mych pepill ; and, by Ossory, toke his   xxvj<sup>m</sup>.
way to Deuclyn.  In that vyage, the kynge of Ossory came to hym,
*and* yolde hym to the kynge.  and whan he had bydd awhyle at
deuelyn, thedyr came all the heghyst Irysh-men of lcynystre, and
be-soghten pees, and yeldyn ham to the kynge.  Roryke Oconghoure,
the kynge of connaght, ayeynes the kynges messaungeris at the watyr  *nunciis*
of shynnyn,—that is [to] Say, hugh de Lacy *and* William aldelines  *regiis . .*
                                                                      *occurrit.*
Sone,—ther he yelde hym to the kynge ; And the kynge of Myth also ;
So that ther was no man of any reputacioun that he ne come to the
* Kyngys owyn Body, or Sent messangeres forto Becomyn Hys man, [*Fol. 12
Saue only thay of¹ vllyster //  Than was fulfillid a prophesy that  b.]
Seynt Molyng sayd : " To-for hym shal foote-fall the pryncys, and, *procident*
                                                                     *principes,*
throgh buxumfastnys, the lyme of pees shal vndyrfonge " // Merlynge  *et fucato*
sayd anothyr prophesy : "To his lyght, the foulys of the yland  *sub foedere*
                                                                 *pacis*
shullyn to-geddyr fle ; and the mest of ham, with har wynges  *amorem*
                                                               *conse-*
y-brante, shullyn ouer-throwyn in thraldome¹.  the fywe delys  *quentur.*
shal be broght into one, and the Syxte shal ouercome the Strongyst  *sextus*
placis of Irland" / Whan the Mydwyntyr came, many of the heghest  *Hiberniae*
                                                                   *moenia*
men comyn to the kynges courte to feste ; *and* mych wondyr thay  *subrertet.*
had of the nobil seruyce that they ther Sawe, and of the mych plente
of mete and of drynke, of bordys sette, and fayre clothis vpon ; the
hey Seruice of panetrye and buttellerye, and rych wesselis of golde
and Syluyr ; the many maner metys of kechen, on the maner of Englond, whych they had neuer ther-to-for Seyn².  Aftyr that the feste
was ryaly holde, euery man went wyth gladnys into his owyn.  In
that tyme weryn bow-men at Fynglas y-herberowid, and wentyn
Into church-hay, and hewyn adovn trees that Seyntys by olde
tym had ther Sette : there came Sodayn deth vpon ham eueryon.

¹ corruent in capturam.      ² Why wasn't this crane bit english ! 'carne
gruina, quam hactenus abhorruerant, regia voluntate passim per aulam vesci
coeperunt.'—*Op.* v. 280.

A.D. 1172.
Henry II,
wishing to
purify
Irish life,
assembles
the Clergy
at Cashel.

The lond was than yn good pees by-for þe kynge, &
þe pees wel I-hold: the kynge had wel y-hard that þe
folk of the lond was of vnclene lyf, & aycyne god & holy chyrche;
he thoght that he wold brynge the folk ynto better lyf, & myche 4
desyr hadde ther-to; he leth assembly al þe clergye of þe londe
at Casshell, & that me enquered & herd openly the fylthede of
the lond-folk yn whych thay ladde har lyf; & setten hyt yn wrytte,
vnder the bysshoppes sele of lysmore, that was eke legat of þe 8
court of Rome, & heghest of dygnyte ouer al thay that ther wer;
& þe statutes of holy chyrche Whych yit men halte, yn þe manere
þat holy chyrche ham holte yn Englond, he lete thar sette: whych
statutз, yn the wordes that thay weren ther I-swewed, ys non 12
harme thegh me expresse ham here :—

### NARACIO. [CHAPTER XXVIII.]

NARACIO.

The Synod
at Cashel,
under the
Romish
Legate,
the Bishop
of Lismore.

In the yer of our lordes Incarnacion M.C.lxxij, the
forme yer that þe kynge of england, henry, Irland wan;
Crystyen, bysshoppe of lysmore, & legat of þe court of Rome[1]; 16
Dougher, Erchebysshoppe of Casshell; laurenз, Erchebysshoppe
of dyuelyn; Cathel, erchebysshoppe of Connaght; wyth leed
bysshoppes, Abbotes, priours, & many other prelates of holy
chyrche yn Irland, throgh the same kynges commaundement 20
comen to-gedder yn þe See of Casshel; &, for þe state of holy
chyrch to brynge yn-to better fourme, helden ther har conssaylle.

To thys conseyl, comen these from the kynge I-sent: a noble man
Statutes or
Constitu-
tions made
at it:—
1. Irish-
men shall
put away
[† Fol 13.
b.]
their
concubine
kins-
women,
and marry
legally.
2. Children
shall be
baptized in
church
fonts.
Rolf, abbot of byldewdys; Ralf, Erchedekene of landaf; Nychol 24
the prest, & other many, the kynges clerkes & hys messagers.
The statutes or constytucions of that consaylle ben these here
I-wrytten, & by the kynges auctoryte I-stablet.  ℂ The fyrst ys,
that crysten men In Irland shvllen leuen har kynnes-wommen 28
† & her sybbes, whyche þay have ar thys I-hold to har wylle out of
spoushode, & lawfully spouse other wommen, & spousebede lawfully
hold[2]. That other ys, that the chyldren, at þe chyrche dorre
shullen ben I-primseined[3] of the prestes hond, & yn þe holy 32
fantstones yn har moder chyrches to be I-fulled[4]. The thrydde,

[1] Late sidenote in MS.: 'Establishment of orders for the Clergy, and matters of Religion.'

[2] repudiato cognatarum et affinium contubernio, legitima contrahant matrimonia, et observent.—Op. v. 282.    [3] catezizentur.    [4] baptizentur.

The lond was than in good pees by-for the kynge, and the pees wel holde. the kynge herde that the pepil of the londe was of vnclen lyfe, and aycyu godd and holy churche. he thogh[t] that he wolde bryng the pepil Into bettyr lyfe; and mych desyr had therto. he Sende for al the clergy of the lond at Casshel; and that he Enquerid and herde opynly the fylthed of the lond-pepill in whych thay lad har lyfe; and Setten hit in writ, vndyr the Bischopis sele of lysmore, that was also legat of the courte of rome, and heyghest of dygnyte ouer al thay that there were. and the Statutes of holy church, whyche yit men halte[1] in the maner that holy church ham holte in England, he lette thare Sette: Whych Statutes, in the Wordis that thay weryn ther Shewyd, is none harme thegh y expresse ham here :—

*Capitulum xxvij<sup>m</sup>.*

*tam enormitatibus quam spurcitiis.*

*Statuta Cassellensia.*

*[1] quae adhuc extant.*

[CHAPTER XXVIII.]

IN the yere of oure lord-is incarnacyon M<sup>t</sup>. Clxxij, the fryste yere that the kynge of En[g]land, henry, Irland conquerid[2], Crystyn, Byschope of Lysmore, and Legate of the Courte of Rome; Dougher, Archebyschope of Cassel; Laurance, Arcebishope of Deuelyn; Cathel, Arcebyschope of connaght; with othyr Byschopis, abbotis, pryorys, and many othyr prelatys of holy church in Irland, by the same kyngys comaundement comyn to-geddre in the Cee of Casshel; and, for the State of holy church to bryng into bettyr state, heldyn ther har consayle. to this Consayle comyn thes frome the kynge, that is to say: a nobyl-man Rolfe, Abbote of byldewais; Ralfe, Archedekyn of landaf; Nycol the Preste, and othyr many of the kyngys clerkys and his messagers // The Statutes or constytuciones of that consayle ben this her writtyn, And by the kynges auctorite Stabelid // The fryst is, that crystyn men In Irland sholde lewe j<sup>o</sup>. har kynnys-women, whych thay haue ar this holde to har will out of Spoushode, and lawfully spouce othyr women, * and Spoushode Lawfully Holde // The Seconde is, that the chyldryn at the church ij<sup>o</sup>. dore sholde be y-primscined of the prestes honde, and in the holy fantstonys in hare modyr chyrchis to be yfullid. The thyrde, that iij<sup>o</sup>.

*Capitulum xxviij<sup>m</sup>.*

*Catholicus Tuotuenensis (Conactensis, Harl. 177).*

*Nicolaus capellanus.*

*cognatarum et affinium.*

*[*Fol. 13 b.]*

[2] conquesid, MS.

F

A.D.
1171-2.
3. Tithes
to be paid.
4. Church
lands to be
left in
peace.

5. Clergy
not to pay
any of
kinsmens
fines for
Man-
slaughter.
6. Wills to
be made
openly.
Property to
go to family
in thirds,

or halves.

7. As to
funeral
services.
8. All folk
to go oft to
Church.
All Ser-
vices to be
in the
English
way.

In winter,
no ships
can get to
Ireland.

that euery crysten man lawfullych pay hys tethynges to hys paroche chyrche, of corne & of al other thynge that a yer hym aneweth[1]. ℂ The ferthe, that al þe londes of holy chyrche & har possessiouns, of al herthly askynge be quyte; & namely, that no 4 kynges ne other heye men, ne her sonnes, ne her meygnees, mette ne herbrowe yn chyrche londes, ne ask, ne wyth streynth ne be so hardy to take; & that Cursed me[te] that four syth a yer was wonet to be asked yn chyrche tounes, & of the next neghbors, neuer eft 8 be asked. ℂ The fyft, that of manslaghttre that lewed men doth, whan man maketh fyn with hys foman, the clerkes that ben hys kynnes-men, no þynge ne yeue ne yeld ther-to; bot, as thay ben gyltles of the dede, also be thay harmles of þe payement. ℂ The 12 syxth, that whan a man ys seke, he shal make testament openly to-for hys prestes of the parorch, & to-fore hys neghbors; & after hys dettes & seruauntes hyre out take, dele hys catel a thre; yf he hath wyf & chyldren, that on to hys spoused wyf, that other 16 to hys shyldren, The thryde to hys testament. And yf he hath non chyldren by spouse, the good be y-deled bytwene hym & hys wyf, euery Ilyche; & yf the wyf deyeth, the goodes be I-deleth a thre bytwene the housbond, & the chyldren, & the wyf. ℂ The 20 .vij. that whan a man other a woman deyeth, har wathe[2], & the seruyce of holy chyrche, & the buryeng, be man-shyply I-done. ℂ The .viij. that al men & wommen wyrshyppe holy chyrche, & oft go to chyrche; & holy chyrche yn al seruyce be gouerned on the 24 maner that hyt ys yn England. In al these thynges, the kynge ynto the lond come, many defautes wer yn the land I-found, & mych horynesse or oryble synnes that me ne aght nat to speke of, that—throgh grace of god, & by the kynges purueyaunce & hys 28 myght—weren amendet, & yn better wonne I-broȝth. ℂ The prymat of Ardmagh was nat at thys conssaylle, ne theder myght come, for he wase old Man & feble; Bot he come ther-after to dyuelyn, & graunted yn al thyngͤ the kynges purueyaunce. In 32 thys tyme was the weder so stronge, & the wynd so aweyward, that yn al the wyntyr ne myght no shyppe com ouer yn-to Irland.

[1] 16th century side-note: ‘the privileges and frydom gyven to the church, and londs ther of.’    [2] ? mistake for ‘wache,’ or th used for k, as on p. 67, l. 4.

euery crystyn man lawfully pay his thethis to his Parashe church,  A. D.
of corne, and of al othyr thynges that a yere hym aneweth // The  1171-2.
iiije. that al the landis of holy church and har Possessiones of al  *animalium,*
Erthly askynge be quyte; and namely, that no kyngest, ne othyr hey  *frugum,*
men, ne her Sones, ne her menyes, mete ne herbrow in church  *ccterarum-*
londys, ne aske / ne with streynth ne be So hardy to take; and that  *tionum.*
Cursed met that foure tymes a yere was wonyd to be askyd in  nothynge.]
church tounes, and of the nexte neghbores, neuer aftyr to be axed[1].
The Ve, that of manslaghtre that lewid men doth, whan men makyth  ve.
fyne with his enemy, the clerkys that ben his kynnys-men, nothynge  *quolies*
ne yeue therto; but, as thay ben gyltles‡ of the dede, also thay be  *inde cum*
harmeles of the pament.   The vje. that whan a man is seke, he  *inimicis*
shal make testament opynly, to-for his preste of the parash and  *suis com-*
to-for his evyncrystynnes and aftyr his dettis and his seruauntes  *ponunt.*
vagis out-take, dele his catel athre.   yf he haue wyfe and chyldryn,  [‡ MS.
that on to the Spousyd wyf, that othyr to his chyldryn, the thyrd  glytles.]
to his testament.   And yf he haue no childe [by] Spouse, the good be  [2] *inter*
y-delid' betwen hym and his wyfe, euery y-lyke.   and yf the wyfe  *ipsum et*
deyeth, the good be y-delid at thre[2], betwene the hosbonde, and the  *liberos*
chyldryn, and the wyfe / The vije, that whan a man oper woman  *bipartiri*
deyeth, har wache, and the seruyce of holy church[3], and the burienge,  vije.
be wyrchiply done // The viije. that al men and women wyrchip  viije.
holy church, *and* ofte go to church; and holy church in al seruyce be  [3] *et missa-*
gouerned' on al maner that hit is in England.   In al thes thynges,  *rum et vigi-*
the kynge Into the lond come[4], many defautes were in the land found,  *liarum ex-*
and mych felth or orribil synnys that y ne oght not to Speke of,  *multimoda*
that,--by the grace of god and by the kynges purueyaunce and his  *malorum*
myght—weryn amendid, and in bettyr state broght // The Primat  *genera.*
of Ardmagh was not at this consail, ne thedyr myght come, for he  [5] Harl.
was olde man and febill.   But he come ther-aftyr to deuelyn, and  177 ends a
graunted in al thynge the kynges Purueyaunce[5].   In this tyme was  chapter
the weddyr so stronge, and the wynd so aweyward, that in al the  here too,
wyntyr ne myght no shipp come ouer Into Irland.   the kynge  and leaves
out the
Archbp.'s
white cow.]

[1] et quod de villis ecclesiarum cibus ille detestabilis, qui quater in anno
a vicinis comitibus exigitur, de cetero nullatenus exigatur.—*Op.* v. 282.
[4] Tabl. abs.—Nam ante ipsius adventum in Hiberniam.—*Op.* v. 283.

A.D.
1171-2.
The kynge went to Watyrford, & abode ther a whyle, & ful mych
desyre adde for to hyr tythynges from beyont see. & of the

[* Fol. 14
a.]
Henry II
gets the
best Irish-
men on his
side.
knyghtes that he fond *yn Irlaud, he drogh to hym sleghly for
o coste the beste: as Reymond, Myles de Cogan, wyllyam Masturel, 4
& other, for to make hys part þe strenger, & the Erles parte the
fobler[so]. ❡ After the myd-lente, come shyppes yn-to Irland, that

A.D. 1172.
He hears
bad news:
hard tythynges hym broght, & lydder, bothe out of engeland & out
of fraunce, And normande, & other londes; ffor ynto Normandy 8
weren ycome twey cardinalles, from the poppe Alexander y-sent
(that oon heght Albertus, & that other Theodynus), for to serchen
& enqueren of the holy martyres deth, seynt Thomas: ryghtful
men, as me vnderstond, & to that lawfully y-chosen / natheles thay 12
weren Romayns; & such folweth oft coueytyse; &, bot the kynge

the proba-
ble Inter-
dict on his
land, and
come the rather to ham, the kyngedome of england, & al the londes
that he was lord of, sholden be entredyted. & (as me fynd oft [1],
good aduentures comen oft slowly & aloon, bot mesaduentures 16
ne cometh neuer-more aloon;) wyth thay tythynges comen other
mychel wers, & of more perylle; ffor the kynges sone, henry, the

the
treasonous
conspiracy
of his sons.
eldest, whyche he so fayne was obout to crowne kynge of England,
& other tweyn of hys bretheren, (that throgh yought & foolrede 20
hym folwed, & many drogh to ham, both of england & of beyond
þe see,) waren I-swore to-gredder to entre vp-on the kynge, & bynyn
hys londes, The whyle that he was yn Irland: & wel may be
that hyt was I-purueyed bytwen ham, ar he ynto Irland wente.  24

He is
grievd,
❡ Whan the kynge thys herd, he was [2] yn grete anguysshe.
sory he was at the begynnyge, þat he, gyltles, was I-retted of the
holy mannes deth; sore he was afred that hys londes shold bene
I-shent throght that lydder dede of hys sonne; sore hym for- 28

as he
wanted to
fortify Ire-
land,
thoght, that he the lond of Irland so sone most fore-lete, whyche
he hade y-cast for to streynth with castell, & stable yn pees, the
next somer that was to comen. Of al thys, he was yn many
thoghtes; & spake ther-of fyrst to hymself, þer-after to hys men. 32

and keep
it.
Aftyr many redes, he sent some of hys ynto England by-fore hym;
& ther-after he puruyed how he myght sykyrlychest kepe Irland.

---

[1] MS. est.                    [2] MS. way.

wente to watyrford, and abode ther awhile, and grettely desyr hadd A.D.
forto hyr thythyngis from be-yont see.    And of the knyghtes that 1171-2.
he found in Irland, he drew to hym wylely for o Purpos, the beste,
as Reymond, Miles de cogan, William Masturel and othyr, forto A.D. 1172.
make his parte the strongyr, *and* the Erlis parte the febelier / Aftyr
the myd-leynte, come shippis into Irland that[1] screwid thythynge*s* *nares ad-*
hym broght / out of England, and out of Fraunce, And Normandye, *reniunt,* *tam graci-*
and othyr lond*es*.    For into Normandy weryn come two cardynalis, *tatis nun-*
from the pope Alexander Sende,—that one was callid Albert, *and* *ciae, quam* *pravitatis.*
that othyr Theodoin,—forto serche and e[n]quere of the holy martires
deth, Seynt Thomas.    (ryghtful men, as y-vndyrstode, and to that
lawfully chose.) [2]Natheles, they were Romanys ; *and* such * folwyth [* Fol. 13
ofte covetys[2] ;   and, But the Kyng*e* come the Sondyr to Hame[3], the b.]
Kyngdome of England, *and* al the londys that he was lord of[3], *[3] nisi citius* *eis rex*
Sholdyn be Entredytyd, and (as y fynd ofte, good aduentures comyn *occurreril.*
ofte Slowely and aloon, but mysaduentures ne comyth neu*er* more
al-oon,) Wyth thay thythyngys, comyn moche wors, and of moche
more P*e*reyl.    For the kynges sone henry, the eldyst, whych he So
fayn was to crovne kynge of England, *and* othyr two of his
bretheryn (that throw youuth and fooly hym folwid, *and* many drew *fratrum*
to hame both of England *and* of beyonde See,) war*e* Swern to-giddre/ *puerili* *lerilate*
to Entyr vpon the kyng*e* and take his landis, The whyle that he *secuti,*
was in Irland': And hit may wel be, that hit was Purveyed'be-twen *pravissimo* *consilio.*
ham, ar he into Irland went // Whan the kyng*e* this herde, he was in
grete a[n]gwysche :  Sory he was at the begynnynge, that he, gyltles,
was yretted of the holy manys deth[4].    Sore he was aferd, that his
londes sholde ben shente throw that vngoodly dede of his Sonnes.
Sore hym forthoght, that he the londe of Irland' so sone moste leue,
whych he had Purposid to streynth wyth castelis, and stabil in pees, *tam incas-*
the nexte Som*er* that was to come.    Of al this, he was in many *tellure* *quam*
thoghtys, and spake therof fryst to hym-Selfe, theraftyr to his men. *firma stabi-* *lire pace.*
And aftyr many cousalys, he Send Some of his men into England
to-for hym ;  And there-aftyr he Pvrueyed' how he myght Svrly kepe
Irlande /

---

[1] thad, MS.          [2-2] sed tamen Romani.—*Op.* v. 285.
          [4] se tanta tam immerito suspicione notari.—*Ibid.*

A.D. 1172.

Henry II
leaves
Leaders
at Dublin
to keep
Ireland,

and sails
from Wex-
ford on
Easter
Monday.
At St.
Davids, in
Wales,

a Welsh-
woman
complains
to him,

[Fol.14 b.]

he goes on,

and she
appeals
for ven-
geance on
him, to the
stone of
Lechlavar,
the
'speaking
stone'
(prophesied
of by
Merlin

which lies
over a
stream N.
of the
church
yard.

As a corpse
was carried
over it, the
stone
spoke.

He left at dyuelyn, the cyte & the contray to kepe, hught de lassy, wyth .xx.^ti knyghtes ; Robert steuenes-sone, & Moryce fytz Geraud, wytht other .xx.^ti at Waterford ; hunfrey de boun, Robert Bernardesson, & hugh de Gundeuyl wyth .xl.^ti 4 knyghtes ; At weysford, wyllyam Al-delines-sone [1] & phylppe de Breuse wyth .xx.^ti knyghtes. And a morow after Estre day herly, he dydde hym to saylle at Weysford, & arryued at seynth dauyes, sone after none. Whan he come a lond, he went 8 wyth grete deuoccion to the mody̅r̅ chyrche, as a pylgrymage, a-foot, with a burdon̅ yn hys hond. Come the chanons of the chyrche ayeyne hym at the whyte yate, & with fayr processioun, with mych reuerence, & with mych manshype, hym receyued. As 12 þe processyoun yede a rewe to-for hym, come a walche womman, & fel hym to þe feet, & made a myche mone, yn hyre langage, of the bysshope of that place. The [kynge] stode, & herd hyr mone ‖ of an ynterpretour-es mouth that hyt hym told ; & fo̅r̅ he 16 went forth, & dydde hyr no ryght anoon as tho wolde, she smote hy̅r̅ handes to-gyddre, & bytterly began to crye tofore ham Al, a walshe langage, " A-wreke vs to-daye, lahlauar ! A-wreke ou̅r̅ kynred & ou̅r̅ folke of thys man ! " Thay that vnderstode hyr 20 speche, put hyr away, & fore-bade hyre cryynge ; & sho so myche the more cryed yn the same manere, & hoped to an old prophecye that Merlyn seyd : " The kynge of england that shal wyn Irland shal be I-woundet yn Irland of a man with a rede hond ; & as 24 he cometh ayeyne by south wales, he shal deye vpon lehlaua̅r̅ : " Þat was þe name of a stone, that lay ouer a streme by north the chyrche heye of seynt dauyes, yn stydde of a brygge. The stone was of Marbel wel fay̅r̅, & smothe of mannes geynge, & hadde 28 .x. feet yn leynth, & .vi. yn brede, & a foot thykke. And ys ‘lehlaua̅r̅,’ a walshe, as mych to sygge as ‘ a spekynge stone.’ And hyt was ytold, that som tyme as me ba̅r̅ a dede body ouer that stone, he bega̅n̅ to speke ; & wyth the spech he claue throghout ; & yit 32 the clyft ys, I-sene, & yit yn-to thys day me be-bereth no dydde body ouer that stone. The kynge come to that stone, & bethoght

---

[1] Weisefordiae, vero Guillelmo Aldelini filio, Philippo de Hastinges, et Philippo de Breusa.—*Op.* v. 286. [William Fitz-Audeline.]

H E lefte at Deuelyn the Cite and the contray to kepe *Capitulum*
Hugh de Lacy wit*h* xx*ti*. knyghtes, Robert Steuenes-Sone *xxix*.
and Morice fiz-geraud, wyth othyr xx*ti*.; at Waterford Humfrey de A.D. 1172.
bonn, Robert Barnardes-Sone and Hugh de Gondeuyl, wit*h* xl. *Hugone de*
knyghtes / At Weysford, Willam Aldelines sone *and* Philip de *Gunde-
villa.*
Bruse, wit*h* xx*ti*. knyghtes. And amorrow, aftyr estyr-day, Erly
he did hym to Sayle at Weysford *and* londid at Seynt dauyes
sone aftyr noone. Whan he come alond he went wyth grete
deuocion to the modyr church as a Pylgrymage afoote wit*h* a *devoto*
stafe in hande. Come the chanon*es* of the church ayeynes hym *peregri-
nantium*
at the white yate; and wyth fayre processioun[1], wyth mych *more,*
reuerence *and* wyth mych wirchip, hym resceiwid. And as the *pedes,
baculoque*
Procession yede arew to-for hym, come a Walch woman, *and* fel *suffultus.*
to-for his feete, and made mych mone in hyr Speche of the Bischop
of that Place. He stod, and herde hyr complaynte of an inter-
pretoure-es mouth that hit hym tolde; and, for he wente forth, and *quoniam
jus suum*
did hyr no ryght anoone as sho wolde, She smote hyr handis to- *incon-
tinenti non*
giddyr and bittyrly began to cry to-for ham al in walch Speche: *est assecuta.*
"A-wreke vs to-day, lathlauar! wreke our kynred and our pepil
of this man!" Thay that vndyrstode hyr Speche, Put hyr away,
and forbade hyr cryynge. She so mych the more cried in the [2] *ab homine
cum rubra*
Same maner, and hopid to an olde prophesy that Merlynge sayde[2]: *manu in
Hibernia*
"The kynge of England that shal conquere Irland [shal be wounded *vulnera-*
in Ireland of a man[3]] wit*h* a rede hand, and as he comyth ay $\overline{eyn}$ by *tum.
[3] qui trans*
South walis, he shal dye vpon lethlauar": that was the name of *flumen
Aluni ...*
a stone, that lay ou*er* a streme[4] by north the churchey of Seynte *jacens.*
dauyes, instyd of a brige. The stone was of marbill, [*] Wel fayr [*Fol. 14
a.]
and smoth of men goynge, and was of x fote in Leynth, and vj in
Brede, and O foote thykke. And is 'lethlauar' in walch, as mych
to say as 'a spekynge stone': and hit was tolde, that Some tyme *Lapis
loquax*
that whan ther wase a dede body y-bore ou*er* that stone, he began
to speke; *and* wyth the speche he clewe throgh[5]-out; and yit the *ipso conatu
crepuit*
clyfte as Seyn. And sithyn on-to this day, thay berryth no ded *medius.*
body ou*er* that stone. The kynge come to that stone, and bethogh[t]

[1] canonicorum ecclesiae processionem . . . invenit.—*Op.* v. 286.
[2] alludens illi fictitio vulgari, nec vero Merlini proverbio, quo dici solebat.—
*Op.* v. 287. [5] throght, MS.

A.D. 1172.  hym of that prophecye. & he stode at þe stones end & grymly hyt
Henry II  be-hold ; & awhyle ther-after, boldely yedc ouer a good paas. & whan
walks over
the stone,  he was ouer, he turned ayeyne to þe stone, & deynously þus seyd :
and asks
'Who'll  "Who shal heten-forward beleue Merlyn the leyer?" A man stode 4
now be-  þer besyde & herd, & wold, hys thankes, sauc þe prophetes sawe,
lieve the
liar Mer-  Answard the kynge & seyd, "Thou art nat that kynge that shal
lin?'  Irland conquer ; ne Merlyn ne speketh nat of the." Thus the
  kynge went yn-to the chyrch, yn seynt Andrees & seynt dauyes 8
He hears  wyrshyppe I-sette, & herd hys masse of a preste that was I-found
Mass, and
goes to  fastyngc, as god wold. After masse, he eete hys mete ther, & after
Haverford,  mete wente to hauerford, than ouer .xl. myle ; ffrom thens he wente
and
Normandy.  hastyly yn-to englande ; out of enland yn-to Normandy, & come 12
  to-for þe cardynalls with mych buxumnesse at Custance. Ther,
He swears  after myche dalyaunce & many wordes I-spoke, he excused hym
that he
didn't slay  by othes of þe holye Martyres deth, that he was nat by hym I-slaw ;
Beket, but  bot he ne for-sok nat that he nas for hym ; & þerfor he vndretoke 16
he does
penance,  such penaunce as holy chyrche hym wold loke. þe cardynals, he
  sent ayeyne wyth myche wyrshyppe ; & noon he went to þe marche,
  & ther he spake with the kynge of ffraunce. þer, (throgh besechynge
  of hegh men, & namely of phylepe þe erl of flaundres, that from 20
and makes  seynt James was ryght than I-come,) the pees was made betwene
peace with
King Lewis  the twey kynges, of the wreth that was betwene ham for the
of France.  forseyd martyres deth ; ffor-thy that þe kynge of ffraunce, with
  other mychel & myghty men, name an hand to the erchebysshopp 24
  whan he shold turne ayeyne yn-to England, [ayeyn] the pees
  betwen the kynge & hym. ffor þer was pees thus y-made betwene
  the kynges, al the harme þat the sones with har allyees hadden
  throght to do, was I-lost tyl þe next yere theraftyr.  28

[CHAPTER XXX.]

[Fol. 15 a.]  Wnder this, as the lond of Irland was yn good pees
  vnder ham that weren In leftc, the lond for to kepe,
  byfelle that a day of parlement, at a certeyne place, was betaken
Hugh de  by-twene hugh de lacy, whom the kynge had I-yeue dyuelyn to 32
Laci and
O'Rourke,  kepe with trust, And þe kynge of Myth. a nythe, whan the
King of  parlement shold ben a morow, a knygh[t] that was Moryce fytz
Meath,
meet.  Geraudes neuew, & Robert Gryffyn by name, thoght yn hys

hym of that prophesy, and he stod at the stone his ende, and grymly A.D. 1172, hit be-helde; and a whylo ther-aftyr, boldely yede ouer a good pace. *and* whan he was ouer, he turnyd' ayeyne to the stone, *and* deynously thus sayde : "Who shal, fro this forth, beleue Merlynge *rerbum hoc* the lyer ?" A man stode ther bysyd, and herde, *and* wolde, his *indignanter* thankes, Sawe the prophet-is Saynge, Answerid the kynge and *emisit.* Sayde, "Ye ben not that kyng that shal Irland conquere, ne Merlyng Spekyth not of yow" / Thus the kynge went into the church of Seynt Androwis and seynte dauyes, and herde his masse of a preste that was founde fastynge, as god wolde. Aftyr masse he ette his mette and aftyr mette went to hauerford' than *quasi per* othyr xv myle. Frome thens he went forth hastely Into England, *miliaria duodecim* out of England into Normandy and come to-for the cardynals *abinde* with mych buxumnesse at Custaunce. Ther, aftyr mych delyaunce *distaus.* *and* many wordys spoke, he excusid hym by othys of the holy martyris deth that he was not by hym Slayn, but he forsoke not that he was for hym. And ther-for he vndyrtoke such Penaunce as holy church wolde hym enyoyn. the Cardynalls, he sende ayeyn with mych wirchip; and anoone he went to the *ad marchiam cum* marche, *and* there he spake wyth the kynge of Fraunce. There, *Francorum* (throgh besechynge of good' men, *and* namely of Phylippe the Erle *rege Lodovico ...* of Flandris, that frome Seynt Iamys was than come,) the Pees was made betwen the two kynges, of the wreth that was betwen ham for the forsayd martires deth ; [1] For-they that the kynge of Fraunce, [1] *puta* with othyr mychel men *and* myghty / And vndyrtoke to the *quem Anglorum* archebischope, whan he shold turne Into Englan, ayeyn the pees *rex archi-* be-twen the kynge *and* hym. For ther was Pees thus made *praesuli in Angliam* betwen the kynges, al the harme that the Sonnes, with hare *reddituro* allyences, haddyn thoght to do, was left til the nexte yere *.. fide-jussorem* ther-Aftyr. *donaverat.*

[CHAPTER XXX.]

VNdyr this, as the lond of Irland was in good pees *Capitulum* vndyr ham that weryn lefte, the londe for-to kepe, by-fel *xxx^m.* on a day, that a certayn Place, to a parlement was sette, be-twen Hugh de Lacy, to whom the kynge had yewe Deuelyn to kepe wyth truste, and the kynge of myth. On a nyght, whan *et regem* the Parlement sholde ben amorrow, a knyght, that was Morice *monoculum Ororicium* fiz-geraudes eme, *and* Robert Gryffyn by name, thoght in his *Medensem.*

A.D. 1172. slepe that he saw a mych flote of wylde swyne yernynge vp-on

**Griffith Fitz-Gerald's dream: he saves De Laci, & Maurice Fitz-Gerald.** hugh & moryce; & a boore amonge ham, myche & grysly ouer al other, come toward ham, & with hys tuskes wold haue smytten ham & I-slawe, yf he stalwarthly ne had y-come betwene, & I-slawe the bore, & I-holpe ham bothe. A morow, thay went to þe place ther þe parlement was I-sette, at a place that me hath seth y-cleped 'rorykes hylle':

**The interview is at Rorik's Hill.** ffyrst thay helden har parlement from ferr, by messagers goynge betwen; ther-after thay name sekernesse of othes I-sworne, & comen to-geddre by forward; natheles few, & ylych fale on ether halue, and thay vnwepened,—bot the one, her swerdes; & the other, her sparthes,—& ether of har folke somdel

**Griffith keeps seven trusty knights near.** fer from ham.   Gryffyn, that with Moryce was to the parlement I-come, was ful thought-ful of the vysyon that he sawe. he name to hym seuyn knyghtes of hys owne kyn, than that ho moost truste to har stalwardnesse, & drowen ham on the on halfe of the hylle, as neyght as thay myght leppen vpon har stedes, with sheldes about har nekkes, & speres an-hond; & for a coste, pleneden & prykkeden har hors ayeyn other, so that, yn whych halue the parlement turned, throght encheson of such pley thay myght be fonden Redy.   Roryk & hugh helden har parlement of many thynge; bot of nothynge thay myght nat accord, & begyn

**O'Rourke treacherously attacks De Laci.** to departe a wrethe.   The traytour Roryk had yn hys thoght þe trayson þat he hadde I-purueyed. he made semblant, & draw hym by-halues as for to pyssen, & made tokens to hys men that thay hastely shold come to hym.   Whan he thys hadde I-done, he turned ayeyne wyth hys sparth an hegh, hys wysage al blak with

**Maurice Fitz-Gerald warns De Laci,** ful snel goynge. Moryce was Iwarned of hys neueu, of the vysyon that he sawe; stod, & beheld al thys. he hent out þe swerd, & cryed vpon hugh, & mynyed hym, & dyd hym-self ayeyne the traytour, for to defend hym. The traytour ran to hugh, hym for to smyte; har latymer yed betwene hym & the dynt; & he

**who is saved by his inter-preter, and [|| Fol. 15 b.] escapes alive.** smote hym of the oon arme, fast by the sholdre. Moryce stode, & campled wyth hys swerd ayeyne the sparthe, & lowd cryed to har men. & ar hugh myght be yn any state, hym-self for to helpe, throgh grete hastynge, he felle twys || abak; & vnnethe, throgh helpe of Moryce, that hym defendet thus, Hugh escaped wyth hys

Slepe that he Saw a mych flote of wylde Swyn yernynge vpon
Hug*h and* Morice; *and* a bore amonge ham, mych *and* grymly *horribilem*
ouer al other, come to ham, *and* wyth his tuskys wolde haue *prae aliis.*
smytten ham Slayn, yf he boldely ne had come betwene, *and*
Slayne * the Boore, and Holpyd Hame Both. On the morrow, [*Fol. 14
thay Went to the Place ther the Parlement was sette, at a place b.]
that Sedyn is callid "Rorike-is hille." Fryste thay heldyn har
Parlement from fere, by messageres goynge betwen; ther-aftyr thay
toke Surtey, *and* othis Sware, *and* comyn to-giddyr aftyrward.
Nathcles fewe, *and* ylyke many on euery syde, *and* thay vnwepenyd,—
but the on, her Swerdys; the othyr, her Sparthes,—and her felle- *praeter
chip in euery syde fere fro ham. Gryffyn, that wyth Moryce come to *dios tun-*
the Parlement, was ful thoghtful of the vysion that he Saw; he *tum, inde*
name to hym Sewyn knyghtis of his owyn kyn, tham that he *secures.*
most truste to har bolthenys, and drowen ham on the one halfe
of the hille / as neye as thay myght, Leppen vpon har stedes,
wit*h* sheldis about har nekkes, *and* Sperres in honde, and for oo *ex indus-
Purpos pleydyn and prikkedyn in the felde ayeyne othyr, So that *tria torna-
*mentis*
in what syde the Parlement turnedyn, throgh encheyson of Suche *Gallicis
*praeludia*
Pley, thay myght be foundyn redy. Rourik and Hugh kepten har *faciebant*
Parlement of many thyngis; but in nothynge thay myght acorde,
*and* begon to de-Pert, as in wrethe. The traytoure Rourik had
in his thoght / the trayson that he hadd Purueyed : he made
semblaut, and drow hym be-sydis as forto Pissyn, *and* made tokyn *simulans
*ad min-
to his men that thay hastely sholde come to hym. Whan he this *gendum.*
had done, ho turned ayeyne wit*h* his sparth an hey, his face al *rutta
*pallido.*
blake wit*h* ful snel goynge. Morice was warnyd of his eme by the
vysyon that he sawe; stode, and be-helde al this. he toke out
his Swerde, and cried vpon Hugh, *and* mynyd hym, *and* did hym- *prae-
*muniens et
Selfe agayn the traytoure, forto defende hym. The traytoure rane *suscitans.
agayn hugh, hym forto smyte. har latymer yed betwen hym and *riri inter-
*pretis . . .
the stroke; and he smote of hym the oone harme of, fast by the *letali
shuldyr. Morice stode, and camplid wit*h* his Swerde ayene the *culnere
*brachium
Sparthe[1], *and* loude cried to har men. And ar hugh myght be *amputarit.
[1] *contra
in any state[2], hym-Selfe forto helpe, throgh grete hastynge, he fel *securim
twies a-bac; *and* vnneth, throgh helpe of Morice, that hym defendid *gladio
*confligebat.*

[2] staste, MS.

A.D. 1172. lyf.  The whyll that thys was, Rorykes men ful many come to hys
clepynge, out of dales & wodes about, yernynge to ham wyth
speres & with sparthes, for to brynge hugh & Moryce out of
dawes.  Than Gryffyn & hys felewes comen yernynge vp on har 4

O'Rourke  hors styffly to ham.  þe traytour saw ham comynge, & lep to hors
that to hym was broght, & wold do hym to flyght ; & as he lepe,

is slain by  vp come Gryffyn, & wyth hys spere smote hym & hys hors throgh-
Maurice  out, & slowe hem bothe.  Wyth hym wer I-slayne þay that, yn so 8
Fitz-
Gerald.  mych perylle, the hors hym broght ; & hy[s] heed I-smytten of, &
yn-to england þer-after to the kynge I-sent ; & al hys men yn-to al
the feldes dyscomfyte, & I-slawe ful many.  Rolf, Robertes sone fytz
Stephen, was the other stalwardthest that daye yn the felde [1].    12

[CHAPTER XXXI.]

[Fol.16 a.]  **M**orice was a mane ful wyrshypful & chamfaste ; vysage
Maurice  wel colowred ; becomlyche ; lytel of body, sumdele more
Fitz-  þan lytel, & lasse than metlych.  of hert, & body, wel I-thewed ;
Gerald
described.  nothynge hauteyne.  of k[i]ndly goodnes, he was good ; & leuer 16
hym was be good, than be sey good ; hys maner was euer-more to
He spoke  hold hym methelyche.  man of short spech & lytel, bot of fayr
little,  wordes, as he that more hadde yn hert than yn mouth, more of
wytte & reyson þan of spech.  [2]Nat forthy[2], whan tyme was, & nede 20
to sp[e]ken, to good reyson forth brynge,—as lettred as he was, as
was very  wytty he was[2].  In thynge that byfell to bataylle, swyth hardy,
bold, but
not fool-  & vnnethes of stalwarthnesse any was hys bettre ; natheles, of
hardy,  perille to take, he was nat to hastyf ne to fool-hardy.  bot as he was 24
thus, & of purueaunce thynge to begynne, Also he was stronge &
was strong  stydfast yn thynge Whan he hyt hadde begune.  he was sobre, wel
and sted-
fast.  I-thewed & chaste, lawful, & stydfast, without blame.

A.D. 1173.    [CHAPTER XXXII.]

In April,  **I**n the next auril ther-after, þe yonger kynge henry, þe 28
Henry II's
three sons,  kynges sone, the lyddernysse that he hadde I-thoght to hys

---

[1] The twelve lines on the back of fol. 15, 'a bak (p. 74, at foot) ... felde,'
were first written by mistake on fol. 16, but afterwards struck out.

[2]–[2] Et tamen, cum sermonem res exigebat, ad sententiam dicendam sicut
serus, sic scientissimus.—*Op.* v. 297.    [3] ? MS. Rat fortly.

thus, Escapid wyth his lyfe.   the whyle that this was, Rourik his A.D. 1172.
men, ful many, come to his callynge, out of dalis and woddis about,
rynnynge to ham with Speres and Sparthes, forto berew hugh and *cum jaculis*
Morice the lyfe.   Than gryffyn and his fellouys come rynnynge *binis et securtbns*
vpon har hors styfly to ham.   the traytoure˙ Saw ham comynge, *amplis.*
and lep to hors that to hym was broght, and wolde do hym to
flyght / And as he lep, vp come gryffyn, and wyth his spere
smote hym and his hors throght-out, and slayne them both.   wyth *cum ipso,*
hym were Slayn thay that, in so myche Peril, the hors hym broght / *tribus ejusdem fumi-*
and his hed Smytten of / and into England theraftyr to the *liaribus.*
kynge hit seude; and al his men into al the feldis discomfite, and
Slayn ful many / Rolfe, Robert-is Sone, fiz-Steuyn, was the othyr
boldyste that day in the felde.

### [CHAPTER XXXI.]

MOrice was a man ful wyrchipphul and shamefaste; [1] vysage *Capitulum xxxjᵐ.*
wel colorid; becomlych; lytil of body, sume-whate more *Descripcio*
than lytel and lasse than metlych.   of herte and body, wel thewed ; *Maurici fiz-geraud.*
nothynge couetynge.   of * Kyndely goodnes, He was good [1] ; ande *[*Fol. 15*
Leuer hit Was to Hym to Be good, than to Be sayde good.   his *a.]*
maner was euer-more to holde hym methelyche.   man of Shorte
Speche and lytyll, but of Fayre˙wordis, as he that more had in *plus pec-toris ha-*
herte than in mouthe, more of witte and Reyson than of speche. *bens quam*
Nat forthy, whan tyme was, and nede to Spekyn, to good reyson *oris, plus rationis*
forth brynge,—as letterid as he was, as witty he was. In thynge that *quam ora-*
befel to battayl, Swyth hardy.   But as he was thus, and of *tionis, plus sapientiae*
Purueyance, thynge to begyn, Also he was stronge and stydfast *quam elo-*
in thynge whan he hit hadd begonne.   [2] he was sobyr, wel *quentiae.*
condicionyd and chaste, lawful and stidfaste, wyth-out blame [2] /

### [CHAPTER XXXII.]

                                                                    A.D. 1173.

IN the nexte Aurel ther-aftyr, the yongyr kynge henry, the *Capitulum xxxijᵐ.*
kynges Sonne, the Wickidnys that he had thoght to his
fadyr done / nolde no longyr helle, wyth his two bretheryn that

[1]-[1] vultu colorato, decentique; mediocri quadam modicitate, tam medio-
cribus minor, quam modicis major; vir tam animo quam corpore modificato,
nec illo elato, nec hoc dilutato ; innata vir bonitate bonus.—*Op.* v. 297.

[2]-[2] Vir sobrius, modestus et castus ; stabilis, firmus atque fidelis.—*Ibid.*

A.D. 1173.   fadyr nold no lenger hellen; with hys twey bretheren—that ys to

Henry,      wytte, the Erl of peytou & the erl of brytayn [1]—wenten to the
Richard
and Geof-   kynge of ffraunce, whose doghter he hadde I-spoused, & purchased
frey, get    helpe of hym for to werr vpon hys fadyr. The enchesoñ wher-for 4
French
help, and   hyt was, Mayster Géraud ne telleth nat, ne I ne cañ nat sey; bot
rebel.
         many hegh & Ryche men he hadde to consaylle & to helpe, both

         of England & of beyend the see; many openly & wel; most, illy &

Henry II   dernely. The old kynge, the yonger kynges fadyr, for the fortune 8

         that hym come to oñ euery halue so vnwarly, was ful sorowful.

draws most  ¶ Nathales, throgh gret sleght & hegh herth, he made fayr semblant,
of his men
from Ire-   & heped to god; & oñ euery syde that he myght, yn al maner he
land. They besoght help. He sent messagers ynto Irland, & mad come ouer 12
come to
him at    to hym the meste parte of the knyghtes & of the good meygne þat
Rouen.
[† Fol. 16  he ther hadde I-lefte. Thay come to hym at the cyte of Ruem,
b.]
         & he bethogh hym that † hyt was perylle to leue har lond vnkepet;
He com-   ther he betoke þe Erl Rychard al þe lond to kepe, & setto to hym 16
mits Ire-
land to    Reymond as hys other hand; ffor the erl for-soke al out & out, þat
Earl
Striguil and he that kepynge wold nat receyue, bot yf he hadde Reymond with
Reimund
Fitz-     hym for to helpe.
Gerald.

[CHAPTER XXXIII.]

Most Irish,  The Erle [&] Reymond, with har power, wentten yn-to 20
hearing
of the        Irland; &, for the folk of yrland hade y-hard of the mych
Princes' re- stryff that was betwene the kynge & hys sonnys be-yent the see,—
bellion,
turn       as folk þat styddefast ys yn vnstedfastnesse, & lawfully ham holt
against
Henry II.   to vnlawfulnesse,—the most parte of the prynces of þe lond, ayeyn 24

         har trouth I-found, þay turned ayeyn-to the kynge. The erl hadde

         sone I-spend the traysour that he broght ouer wyth hym; & whan

         the meygñe lacked spendynge, & nat spedden yn prayes takynge

         vnder heruy, that was conestable ouer the meygne, & euer hadde 28

The Eng-   enuy to Reymond, Thay wenteñ ham to the erl comynly by one
lish de-
mand to   accorde, & sey hym wel, that ' bot yf he wold sete Reymond ouer
be put
under Rei- ham, thay wold leue hym cuerychone, & wend yn-to england; oþer,
mund Fitz- that wel wors was, thay wold turnet to har enemyes ayeyns har 32
Gerald.
         heed.' As the meygne wold, Reymond was I-sette ouer ham; thay
They in-
vade      name than hert to ham, & wenten vpon the Ofolanes yn the dees,
Offaly, in
Leinster,

---

[1] Pictaviae scilicet et Britanniae comitibus.—Op. v. 297–8.

is to Say, the Erle of Peytou *and* the Erle of Brytayn, wentyn   A.D. 1173.
to the kynge of Fraunce, whose doghtyr he had Spousid, *and*   *ad Lodo-*
Purchasid helpe of hym forto were vpon his fadyr.  The encheyson   *ricum,*
*Francorum*
wherfore hit was, Maystyr Geraud ne tellyth not / ne I ne can   *regem.*
not say; but many hey men he hade to consayl and to helpe,
both of England *and* of beyonte see; many opynly *and* wel; *multo*
*plures*
[more] falthyr pryuely.  The olde kynge, the yongyr kynges fadyr, *occulte*
for the fortvne that to hym was fal on euery syde so vnwyttyngly, *habens, et*
*fautores.*
was ful Sorroful.  Neuer-the-las, by grete Sotylte *and* hey herte,
he made fayre semblante, *and* trystid to god; *and* on euery syde
that he myght, in al maner he besoght helpe.  he sende messageres
into Irland, *and* made come ouer to hym the meste Parte of the
knyghtes and of the good mennye that he ther lefte.  Thay come
to hym at the Cite of Ruem.  *and* he be-thoght hym that hit was *ad urbem*
*Rothoma-*
Peril to leue har londe vnkepte : ther he be-toke the Erle Richard, *gensem.*
al the londe to kepe, and sette to hym Reymonde as his othyr *custodiam*
*illam sus-*
hande; For the Erle forsoke out and out, that he that kepynge *cipere*
wolde not rescewe, but yf he hadde Reymond wyth hym, hym *omnino*
*renuerat.*
forto helpe.

[CHAPTER XXXIII.]

The Erle and Reymond, wi*th* har men, wentyn Into  *Capitulum*
Irland; and, for þe Pepil of Irland had herde of the grette *xxxiij*.
stryfe that was betwene the kyng and his Sonnes be-yount the
See,—as Pepyl that stydfast is in vnstydfastnes, *and* lawfully ham *gens sola*
*constans*
holde to vnlawfulnes,—the most Part of the Pryncis of the londe, *incon-*
agayñ har trouth y-founde, thay turned agayn the kynge.  The *stantia.*
Erle had spende the tresoure that he broght ouer wyth hym; *and* *deficien-*
*tibus*
whan the fellochipe lackid spendynge, *and* not Speddyn in Prayes- *quoque*
takynge, Vndyr heruey, that was constabil ouer the menny, and *stipendiis.*
euer had envy to Reymond; Thay wenten ham to the Erle
comynly by oone acorde, *and* sayde to hym wel, ' but that he
wolde sette Reymonde ouer ham, thay wolde lewe hym euerichone,
*and* wende Into Englande; othyr, that wel wors was, thay wolde
turne to har enemys agaynes hame ' / And as the menny desyrid,
Reymonde was sette ouer hame.  thay take then herte to ham, *in Offelanos*
*insur-*
*and* wenten vp-on the Ofelanys in the descses, and toke grette *gentes.*

A.D. 1173. & name grett *prayes*, arrayed ham nobly wyth hors & wepne.

Lismore, &c., and take much prey. From thens thay wentten to lysmore, & the cyte, & al þe contre about, robbeden & *prayeden*, & by the see wey senten many grete *prayes* to Watyrford ; & of pylfre & thynge that thay namen, thay 4 fylled .xiij. far costes that weren I-come fro Waterford yn-to the hauen of dongaruame.  As thay wer wynd abydynge, ther come

The English fleet fight a Cork fleet, þe men of Cork from by west, by the see, yn xxxij shyppys, & many men ther-In, for to take thay other.  Ther was the fyght styffely 8 I-yeuen, of these twey fletes yn the see: That oon assaylled that other grymlych *with* stones & *with* sparthes ; the other weren welle I-wepned, & *with*-stode styffly *with* arblastes & *with* bowes.

rout it, and kill its men, and take their prizes to Water-ford. At þe end, thay of Corke weren descomfyted & ouer-come ; her 12 shyppys I-take ; her men I-slawe, & I-caste yn the see.  Adam de herford & phylep de Wellsse, that weren I-sette ouer thay yong-lynges, *with* mo shyppes & grete beyetes of wepne & of pylfre, to

Reimund marches, Watyrford wenten *with* grete yoye.  Reymond herd speke of thys 16 fyght, & tythynges to hym come ; he toke *with* hym xxti knyghtes & an hundreth bowmen, & went by the see wey thederward. Than come to hym tythynges þat dermot, þe prynce of desmond, was, *with* myche hostes, comen to lysmore, to helpe ham of Cork. 20

Dermot daren't face him.

Reimund has 4,000 cattle. Reymond went hym thederward.  Þe prynce that herd, & turned ayeyne, & durst hym nat abyde.  And Reymond went forther yn-to the contrey, robbed & *prayed*, so that he hadde *with* hym at hys turny[n]ge aye toward Watyrford, four thousand kyne ; & as thay 24

[|| Fol. 17 a.] The Irish take some. wer comynge || by narow weyes wyth har *praye*, come the Ireshe-men of þe contray, & henten a party of har kyne, & wenten al quytten *with* ham to wodde.  þe crye arose, & Reymond [1] (as man that euer was formost redy) went aftyr, *with* on *priuisant* man an 28

He pur-sues them into a wood. hors wyth hym ; come to the woddes ense [2], ther the theues weren an hydynge.  Whan he hadde I-faylled of þe preye, & wolde turne ayeyne, hys felewes folyly entyced hym for to wende yn-to þe wodde, & he so dydde.  Whan thay weren wel *with*-yn, 32

---

[1] The Latin text gives this exploit to Meiler : Gir. Cambr. *Op.* v. 309–10,
' et in primis Meilerius, ut erat praeceps semper et probus, satellite quodam comitatus equestri, praedones usque ad silvae condensa est persecutus.'
[2] Ends.

Prayes arrayed ham nobely with hors and wepyñ.  From thens A.D. 1173.
thay wentyn to lysmore ;  *and the Cite and the contrey about, [*Fol. 15
robbodyn and preedyn, and, By the See-wey, Sendyne many gret ᵇ·]
prayis to waterford ;  and of pilfre and of thynge that thay toke,
thay fillid xiijᵉ. farcostes that weryn come from watyrford into *navicnlas*
the havyn of doūn-garvan.  As thay were wynde abydynge ther, *tredecim.*
come the men of Corke from be weste, by the See, in xxxijᵘ. Shippis,
and many men therin, forto take the othyr.   ther was tho fyght *bellicosis*
fressely yewyn of this two flittes in the See.   That oone assaylid *refertae*
                                                                    *viris.*
the othyr grymly with stones and with Sparthis ; the othyr wer ·
wel wepenyd, and wythstod styfly with arblastes and with bowes¹.
At the Ende, thay of Corke weryn dyscomfyted and ouer-come ;
Her shippis take, her men slayne, and caste Into the See.   Adam
do herforde and Philippe² the wellsshe, that weryn sette ouer
thay yonglynges, with  mo shippes and gret begetes of wepyn *cum armis*
and of Pylfre, to Watyrford wentyn with gret Ioy.   Reymond *et oneribus.*
herde speke of this fight, and tythynges to hym come : he toke
with hym xxᵗⁱ. knyghtes and an hundrid bowmen, and went by *per mari-*
                                                             *timam*
the see-way thedyrwarde.   Than com to hym tythyngis that *viam.*
Dermot, the prince of desmonde, was with myche hostys comyn
to lysmore, to helpe ham of Corke.   Reymonde wentyn hym
thedyrward: the prince that herde, and turned agayn, and durst
hym not abyde.   And Reymonde wente Ferdyr Into the³ contrey,
robbid and Prayed, So that he hadd with hym at his turnyngo
agayn toward watyrford, iiijᵉ. Mᵗ. kyne.  and as thay were comynge
by naroweis wyth har Pray, come the Iryssh-men of the contray, *ad silras*
and tokyn a party of har kyne, and wentyn al quyte with ham to *de plano.*
wodde.   the cry aros, and Reymond, as man that euer was formyst
redye, wont aftyr, with one pryuisant man an hors with hym, come
to the woddys syd ther the thewis were an-hydynge.   Whan he had
falid of the pray, and wolde hauo turne agayne, his fellowis folely *jurene in-*
                                                                     *sligante*
Enticed hym forto wende into the wodd ; and he so dide.   Whan *temerario*

---

¹ dum isti lapidibus et securis acriter impetunt, illi vero, tam sagittis quam
laminis ferreis quibus abundabant, promptissime resistunt.—*Op.* v. 309.

² Philippe, MS.

³ the the, MS.

A.D.
1173-4.
Reimund is
attackt,
but cuts
his way
thro' his
foes.

the Irysshe-men rysse to ham on euery halue, & leyd ham on,
& anoon-ryght the yonge man was al to-hakked to-for hym ; he
yarne to snellych for to socur hym, & was assaylled on euery
halue ; & he, as man, hent out the swerd & leyd on about hym, 4
& smot of that man the hond, þat other the arme, þe þryd the
heede by þe sholdres ; thus he opened hym the wey, & come out
to hys men, & broght twey sparthes fast on hys sheld, & thre on
hys hors [1] ; bot all hool & sound, & harmeles of body, he escaped.  8

A.D. 1174.

[CHAPTER XXXIV.]

Whan thys was y-done, & the meygne was noblych
arrayed both byl ond & eke by watyr, come tythynges
to Reymond, that hys fadyr Wyllyam fytz Geraud was dede.

Reimund
goes to
Wales.
Hervey is
made Con-
stable.

Reymond went ouere yn-to Walys, to take seysyne yn hys fadyr 12
landys ; & heruy was the whyle eft [2] y-made conestable of þe
meygne: he wold fayne entremette hym to do some thynge the
whyle that Reymond was out of londe, & made the Erl & the
meyne wend to Cassell for to weren yn Monestre ; he sent eke 16
after the meyne of dyuelyn to come to ham.  And as thay come
throgh Ossery, & laye a nyght yn a place that thay supposed to
be al syker, Obreen, the kynge of thomone, was syker, & awayted

Donnell
O'Brien
slaughters
the Dublin
men.

har comynge by good spies.  he aroos with mych folk vpon hem 20
erly a day yn the morowenynge, & smot vpon ham vnwyttyngly,
& slogh four knyghtes that weren ouer ham, & four hundret
ostmen.  Whan the tythynges her-of come to the Erl, he turned
ayeyne to Waterford with mych shame, & held hym thar as man 24
that was beseget, that he cam nat fro thennes.  And for thys

The Irish
massacre
the Eng-
lish.

aduentur, the folk of Irland wyth oo hert al to-gyddre aresen vpon
the englysshe, & slow ham yn-to al ther thay myght ham fynd.
The kynge of Connaght come eke ouer the shynen yn-to Myd, 28
& fond al þe castels wast & voyde ; he brant & keste ham adoun
to ground, tyl he come ryght to dyuelyn.  The Erl saw þat he
was narow by-ladde : by consaylle of hys men, as the last remedy
of lyue, he sent hys lettres to Reymond ouer yn-to Walys, yn these 32

[1] tres secures Hibernicas in equo confixas, duasque in clipeo portans.—Gir.
Camb. Op. v. 310.          [2] MS. est.

thay wer with-In the Irysh-men rysse to ham on euery halue *and*
leyde on ham, *and* anoone the yonge man was al to-hackid to-for
hym.   He rane forto socoure hym, *and* was assaylid on euery syde.
And he, as man, toke out his Swerde, *and* leyde on aboute hym, *and*
Smote of, that man the honde, that othyr the harme, the thyrde the
hede by the sholdris; thus he oppenyd the wey, *and* come out to
his men, and broght two Spares fasto on his shelde, and thre on his
hors; but al holde and Sounde *and* harmeles of body he Escapid.

A.D.
1173-4.

exserto
gladio,
eiam sibi
vir ani-
mosus riri-
bus ape-
ruit.

[CHAPTER XXXIV.]

A.D. 1174.

Whan this was done, *and* the meyne was nobely arrayed
both by londe *and* also by watyr / come thythyngis to
Reymonde, that his Fadyr willam fiz-geraude was dede.   Reymond
wente ouer into Walis, to take seysyne in his Fadyr landis; And
heruey that tyme was made constabil of the meny.   he wolde fayn
entremitte hym to done sumthynge, the whyle that Reymonde
was out of londe; *and* made the Erle *and* meny wende to cassell
forto werryn in monestre.   He sende also aftyr the meny of
deuelyn to come to ham.   And As thay come throgh Ossory,
*and* lay a-nyght in a place thar thay demyd to be al Sure,
Obreen, the kynge of Thomonde, was Sure, *and* awayted hare
*comynge By good Spies.   He aroose, with mych Pepil, vppon
Hame, erly a day in the mornynge, *and* Smote vppon ham vn-
wittyngly, *and* killid iiije. knyghtis *and* weryn ouer hame, *and*
CCCC men.   Whan tho thythynges herof come to the Erle, he
turned agayne to Watyrford with mych shame, *and* helde hym
ther as man that was besegid, that he came not fro thennes.
And for this aduenture, the Pepil of Irland with oo herte al-
to-giddyr arysen vpon the Englysh, *and* Slowen ham in al places
that thay ham myght fynde // The kynge of Connaght come also
ouer the shynnyß into Myth, *and* found al the Castelis waste *and*
woyde.   he braunt and keste ham doune to grounde, til he come
ryght to Deuelyn.   The Erle Saw that he was narrow bylad: by
consail of his men, as the laste remedy of lyue, he sende his
lettres to Reymond, ouer into Walis, in thes wordis: "As rath as

Capitulum
xxxiiije.

aliquid
agere
videretur.

[*Fol. 16
a.]

qui aliis
praeerant.

unanimiter
insurgunt.

in arcto
jam posi-
tum.

G 2

A.D. 1174. wordes: "As rathe as thou hast I-sey these *lettres*, ne leue nat to

Striguil
asks Rei-
mund's
help, and
promises
him his
sister
Basile.

come to socou*r* vs wyth good myght: & thy desyr of basyle, my
sustre, lawfully for to spouse, anone at þy comynge, wythout faylle
thou shalt haue." Whan Reymond hadde thys I-herd, both for the 4
maydnes loue þat he so longe hadde desyred, & for to proue hys
stalwardnesse, & socou*r* hys lord yn hys mychele nede, wyth Mcyle*r*,
hys emes sone, he dyght hym al þat he myght yn such hast, so

[‖Fol. 17
b.]
Reimund
sails, lands
at Wex-
ford,

that he hadde thretty ‖ knyghtes of hys owne kyn, & thre hundert 8
bowmen, the choyse of al Wales: he put hym to saylle, & arryued at
Weysford yn fyftene shyppes. That same tyme, the men of Weysford
hadden I-*pur*ueyed ham to vndo al þe englysshe, whe*r*-so me myght
ham fynde. Whan thay sawe the shyppes comynge yn þe hauyn, & 12
baneres that thay wel knowe; þroght þat comynge so fersly, that

and brings
Striguil
safe from
Waterford.

trayson was y-lefte; & anoon Reymond went wyth hys men to
Water*ford*, & broght thens the Erl stalwarthly to Weysford.
ffresel, that was kepe*r* of Wate*r*ford, went afte*r* the Erl by þe 16
water of Sur, yn botys wi*th* hys men; &, as þay we*r* yn the waty*r*,
the lydder gyddes that hym shold lode [1], slowe hy[m] & al hys men,
& turned ayeyne to the Cyte, & gadered ham to-gedder al þe

The Irish
in Water-
ford slay
the English
there.

Irysshe-men, & smyt vpon þe englesshe, & slowe al that thay 20
myght fynd yn hous & yn wey, men & wommen, yonge & old,
wi*th*out any sparynge, sauc thay that escaped yn-to Rathe-
vyldestou*r*; & throgh ham was the toun I-saued, tyl the traytou*rs*
þer-after come to pees, & eue*r* ther-after the lasse beleued & loued. 24
Reymond, whan he hadde thys I-se[u]yd the Erl, he miniyed the

Striguil's
sister
Basilia
weds
Reimund.

Erl of hys beheste. The Erl sent anoon to dyuelyn aftyr hys
suste*r*, and went neue*r* from Weysford, fort sho was wi*th* mych
wyrshyp*pe* I-spoused to Reymond. Whan he was I-spoused, & 28
al þe day was Ihold yn yoy, gladnesse, & mych plente of mete
& drynke, & the nyght aftyr, yn delytes of chambre as ham beste

King
O'Conor
destroys
all Meath.

lyked, came tythynges that Oconghou*r*, kynge of Connaght,
hadde I-destrued al myght, & was I-come wyth myche powe*r* 32
yn-to the contrey of dyuelyn. Reymond was nat slowe, nethe*r*

Reimund
marches
after him.

fo*r* loue of hys fay*r* wyf ne for the moche feste, bot anoon
a morowe he toke hys men wyth hym, & went toward dyuelyn.

[1] *for* lede.

ye haue sey thes *lettres*, ne lette not to come to socoure vs with   A.D. 1174.

good myght: *and* youre desyre of Basyle my Sustre, lawefully forto   *et desiderium tuum,*

Spouse, anone at youre comynge, with-out fayl ye shall haue'' //   *in Basilia*

Whan Reymond hadd this herde, both for the maydes lowe that he *sorore mea tibi*

so longe had desiryd, *and* forto prow his myght, *and* socoure his *legitime copulanda.*

lorde in his mychel nede, with Meyler, his emys sone, he dight hym

al that he myght in such haste, so that he myght haue / *and*

hadde xxx<sup>ti</sup>. knyghtes of his owyn kyne,*and* CCC bowmen, the coyse *de electa*

of al Walis. he putte hym to sayle, *and* arryued at Weysforde in *Kambriae juventute.*

xv. shippis. that same tyme, þe men of Weysforde hadd Purveyed

ham to vndo al the Englysh, wherso thay myght ham fynde.

Whan thay Saue the chippis comynge Into hawyn, and bancres

that thay wel knew; throw that comynge So Fresly, that trayson *adventu*

was lefte; and anoone Reymonde went wyth his men to watyrforde, *tum subito.*

*and* broght thens the erle boldely to Weysforde. Fresell, that was *Fretellus,*

keper of watyrforde, wente by the watyr of Sure in botis with his *custos.*

men; and, as they were in the watyr, the liddyr gides that hym *ab iniquis*

Sholdo lede, slayne hym *and* al his men, *and* turned agayn to the *Oolmannis.*

Cite, *and* gaddrid' ham to-geddyr al the Irysh-men, *and* smyte

vpon the Englysh-men, *and* slayne al thay that thay myght fynde

in hous, in wey, men *and* women, yonge *and* olde, with-out any *in plateis*

sparynge, Saue thay that Escapid' into Rathevyldestoure; 'and *et domibus.*

throgh ham was the toune Sawid, tyl the traytorys ther-aftyr

come to Pees, *and* euer ther-aftyr the<sup>.</sup>lasse belewid *and* lowid. /

Reymond, when he hadd thus I-Sawid the Erle, he mvnyed the

Erle of his promes. the erle sende anoone to deuelyn aftyr his *revocatam*

suster; *and* Wente neuer frome Weysforde till that she was, with *a Dublinia Basiliam,*

mycho wyrchipp, Spousid to Reymonde. Whan he was spousid,

and al tho day was holde in Ioy *and* gladnys, *and* mych Plente

of mette and drynke, and the nyght aftyr in delytes of chambyr, *in thalami*

as ham beste plesyde / Came tythyngis that o-conghoure, kynge of *deliciis nocte con-*

Connaght, hadd destrued al Myth, *and* was come with grete hoste *sumpta.*

into the contrey of Deuelyn. Reymond was not Slow, nethyr for *nec vino,*

lowe of his fayre wyffe, ne * for the moche feste; But amorrow He *nec venere, retardatur.*

toke His men With Hym, *and* Went towarde Deuelyn. O-con- [*Fol. 10 b.]

A.D. 1174.
O'Conor
retires.
Reimund
rebuilds his
Castles and
restores
peace.

Oconghour hadde þer-to-forne assayed hys mayne, y-douted hym
the more; he ne abode nat wyth hym, bot was gladde to take
homward. Reymond let restore & arere that was destrued throgh
þe werr, & fale castels ryght vp, & broght yn-to rather state; 4
& for dred of hym, the lond wax yn good pees a good whyle, that
none Iresshe-maiñ ne durst hym styrre, wer to begynne.

A.D.
1173-4.

Henry II
livd in
strife.

[CHAPTER XXXV.]

This while the kynge was yn mych stryf, wel two yer,
ayeyñ hys thre sonnes & har allyes, both yn englande 8
& yn normandy & garioigne; & so was I-peyned with trauaylle
yn wepne & wakynge nyght & day, that no man ne myght more.

The worst
was, that
his trusted
Body-
guard
deserted to
his rebel
sons.

Bot, for ne wors fomanne may be, þañ thay that mañ moste
trusteth to, o thynge was, that meste tene hym dydde : that þe 12
knyghtes that he hadde I-chose, hys body to kepe, yn whose
hondes hys lyf & hys deth he be-taght, for the moste dele euery
nyght wenten to hys sones pryuely; so that, whan the kynge
oft-tymes asked aftyr ham, thay war nat I-founde. Natheles, the 16
bataylle that was of so dotous begynnyge, hadde so good endynge
that, for the vnryght that hys sonnes hym dedde so vnk[i]ndely,

But he won
all fights,

hyt semete bettre tha[t] he soght by power of god, than by erthly
power; ffor yn al places, the ouerhand was hys. And as hyt semete 20
fyrste that hyt was for wreth of seynth Thomas-es deth that þat

[||Fol. 18
a.]

vnhape hym || betydde, Also hyt semed þer-aftyr, Whan he
hadde I-done asseth to holy chyrche, & pees made wyth the
holy martyr, wyth teres & repentaunce of herte, al hys tene, 24

by God's
help.

throght goodys helpe, hym turned to gladuesse : ffor aftyr the
mych tene & traysoñ þat he hadde Itholled al two yer, at þe
laste was þe bataylle I-smytteñ, at the whych, betwen the twey

His sons
were
routed, and

ostes, Ther war the kynges sonnes dyscomfyt, þrogh Rauf de 28
Glanuyl, that was mayster of þe kynges hoste. Ther was I-take
þe kynge of scotland, & þe erl of shestre, & þe erl of leycestre,
& so fele gret men, bothe of england & of beyent see, that vnnethe
me fond prisons to ham. Ther, aftyr al þe trauayl þat þe kynge 32

obliged to
make
peace (a
false one).

hadde, & þe enuy, & þe costes al two yer, come þe sonnes to þe
fadyres pees, & maden asseth, falsly, as hyt was þer-aftyr wel
Ishewed yn deede. Of þus vntrowth, spake Merlyn yn hys

ghoure had thertofor assayed his meny, *and* douted hym the more. A.D. 1174.
he wolde not abyde hym, but was glade to take homwarde. *et castris Mediae . . . dirulis . . .*
Reymonde lette restore and arere that was destrued by the werre; And fale casteles ryght vpe, and broght into radyr state. *and for* *jam reparatis et in* dred of hym, the londe wax in good pees a goode whyle, that none *statum redactis.* Irysh-man ne durst hym not styre, werre to begynne.

[CHAPTER XXXV.]
A.D. 1173-4.

This whyle the kynge was in myche stryfe, wel two yere, agayn his Sonnes *and* har allience, both in Englande and in *Capitulum xxxvᵃ.* Normandy, *and* gascoygne ; *and* So was peyned with trawail in wepyn, nyght and day, that no man ne myght more.  But, for no wors enemy may none be, than thay that a man trusteth moste to, O thynge was, that most angyr hym didd : that the knyghtes that he *illi quoque* hadd chose his body to kepe, in Whos handis his lyfe and his deth *quos cubicularios* he betoke, for the mor Party, euery nyght wentyn to his Sones *sibi milites elegerat.* priuely ; So that, whan the kynge ofte-tymys askyd aftyr hame, thay were not founde.  Natheles, the battayll that was of So doutos begynnynge, hadd So good Endynge that, for the vnryght that his Sones hym didde so vnkyndely, hit Semyd bettyr that he foght by Powere of god, than by Erthely Powere.  For in al Placys, the ouer-hande was his.  And as hit Semyd fryst, that hit was for wrethe of Scynte Thomas-es deth that that vnhape hym befell, Also hit semyd ther-aftyr, whan he hadd done asseth to holy churche, *and* pees made with the hooly martyr, with terys and repentaunce of *propitiante nobili* herte, al his tene (by godys helpe) hym turned to gladnys.  For *martyre* aftyr the mych tene and trayson that he hadd sufferid al two yere, *Thoma, lacrimis et* At the laste, was the battayl Smytten, at the whyche, be-twen the *devotione* two hostys, Ther were the kynges Sonnes dyscomfyte, by Ralfe de *jam placato.* Glanvil, that was Maystyr of the kynges hoste.  Ther was take the kynge of Scotlande, and the Erle of Chestre, and the Erle of leycestre, and So many grete men, both of England *and* of beyonte See, that vnneth thay found prisonys to ham.  Ther, aftyr al the trauail that the kynge hadde, and the Envy, and the costys al two *umbratiliyque magis* yere, come the Sonnes to the faderis Pees, *and* madyn asseth, falsly, *quam vera* as hit was ther-aftyr wel Shewid in dede.  Of this vntrouth, Spake *concordia.*

Merlin of Celidon's prophecy of the Rebellion of Henry II's sons.

prophecyes, & seyde : "The sonnes shullen agylte ayeyn þe fadyr for hys gyltes, & the rather gylte shal be encheson of þe gyltes þat after shullen comen. The sonnes shullen aryse vpon þe fadyr ; & for to awreke hys felonye ayeyne þe wombe, the tharmes shal 4 swer ham togydder. In the man of blode, the blode shall aryse, & wanhoply shal hys pynsynge be, tyl that scotland þe penaunce of hys pylgrymage bewepe."

[CHAPTER XXXVI.]

Henry II had grey eyes, a red face,

The kynge henry the other, was[1] a man saunrede, rounc 8 heed, & round grey eghen ; roghly lokynge, & rede yn wreth ; vysage rede bernynge, grete speche, neke somdel logh of þe sholdres, brest thyk, armes staluarthe, of flesshy body ; &, more

and a big belly, tho, to lessen it, he'd hardly rest his body. All day he was out hunting, and rode a high trotter ;

of kynde than of glotony, grete of wombe ; for he was, as to prynce 12 belongeth, [of] mete, & of drynke ful meen & for-berynge[2] ; &, for to a-quenche that gretnesse, he put hymself to ful mych trauaylle, that wnneth he lete hys body haue eny reste, ether by day other by nyght ; ffor, wynter, & somer, he arose euer more yn the dawn- 16 ynge, & herd fyrst hys seruyce of holy chyrch ; ther-aftyr, most what al þe day he wold ben out, other wyth houndes other wyth hawkes, for yn thay two thynges he delyted hym swyth mych wythal ; & vnnethe he wold ryde any amblynge hors, bot myche 20 trottynge hors, for to trauaylle hys body the more. Aftyr al hys trauaylle a-day, vnnethe he lete hys body haue a lytell reste for to syte to hys mete the whyle that he eete ; & anoon aftyr mete,

at night he stood.

& namely aftyr sopper, anoon he wold aryse & stonde, & so dryue 24 forth al þe meste parte of the nyght, so that al þe court was

When once he'd seen a man, he knew him again.

oft ennyede ther-of. þe man that he ones yn lych beheld, euer eft he hadde knowleche of hym ; & dynge þat he hadde ones herd, euer eft he hyt wold vnderstond ; þe man that he ones hated, 28 vnnethe he wold euer eft[3] loue ; & man that he ones loued, vnneth

---

[1] vir subrufus, caesius (= lentiginosus), amplo capite et rotundo, óculis glaucis, ad iram torvis, et rubore suffusis, facie ignea, voce quassa, collo ab humeris aliquantulum demisso ... corpore carnoso, et naturae magis quam gulae vitio, citra tumorem enormem et torporem omnem, moderata quadam immoderantia ventre pracamplo. Gir. Cambr. Op. v. 302.

[2] Erat enim cibo potuque modestus ac sobrius ; et parcimoniae, quoad principi licuit, per omnia datus. Gir. Cambr. Op. v. 302.    [3] MS. est.

merlynge in his prophesies, and Sayde : " The Sonnes shullyn agylte
agayn the Fadyr for his gyltes ; and the radyr gylte shall be encheyson of the gyltes that aftyr shullyn come.    The Sones shall aryse
vpon the fadyr; and forto aw[r]eke his felony agayne the wombe, the *et ob scele-*
tharmes shal Swere ham to-giddyr.   In the man of blode, the blode *ris vindic-*
*tum in*
shal aryse; *and* wanhoply shal his Pynsynge be [1], til that Scotland *ventrem*
*viscera con-*
the Penaunce of his Pylgrimage bewepe. '                                    *jurabunt.*

[CHAPTER XXXVI.]

The kynge henry the othyr, was a man same rede, rounc *Capitulum*
hede, *and* rounde grey eyyn ; row lokynge, *and* rede in wreth ; *xxxvj^m.*
*Descripcio*
Visage rede, brennynge ; * grete Speche ; neke somdel shorte of the *Henrici*
Soldrys, breste thyke, of fleschy Body ; aude, more of kynde, than of *regis tercij.*
*[\*Fol. 17*
glotony, gret of wombe ; for he was, as to prynce belongyth, of *a.]*
mete *and* of drynke ful meen *and* for-berynge ; and forto aquenche
that gretnes, he put hym-Selfe to ful mych trauayl, [2] that vnneth he *immo-*
*derata*
lette his body haue enny reste, othyr by day othyr by nyght. ˙ For *corpus*
Wyntyr and Somer, he aros euer-more in the dawnynge, and herde *vexatione*
*torquebat.*
fryst his seruyce of holy church ; theraftyr, most part al the day he
wolde be out, othyr with houndys or with haukes ; for in thay two
thyngys he delyted gretly with-al / *and* vnneth he wolde ryde any
hamlynge hors, but mych trottynge hors, for to trauail his body the
more.   Aftyr al his trauayl a-daye, vnneth he lette his body haue
a lytil reste forto sitte to his mette.   the whyle that he ette, *and*
anoone aftyr mette, *and* namely aftyr soper, anoone he wolde arysse
*and* stonde [3], and So dryue forth al the moste Parte of the nyght, So *totam*
*statione*
that al the courte was ofte wery of his wakynge.   the man that he *continua*
onys in lyche be-helde, euer he hadd knowlege of hym ; and thynge *curiam*
*lassare*
that he hadd onys herde, euer aftyr he wolde hit vndyrstonde. *consue-*
the man that he onys hattyd, vnneth he wolde euer aftyr loue ; *and* *rerat.*
man that he onys lowyd, vnneth he wolde euer aftyr hate.   Whan

---

[1] et desperabilis fiet afflictio.—*Op.* v. 301.

[2]-[3] sibi nec pacem ullam nec requiem indulgebat.   Venationi namque
trans modestiam deditus, summo diluculo equo cursore transvectus, nunc
saltus lustrans, nunc silvas penetrans, nunc montium juga transcendens, dies
ducebat inquietos : vespero vero domi receptum, vel ante coenam vel post,
rarissime sedentem conspexeris.—*Op.* v. 302.

Henry II
described.

He lovd
meekness,
and hated
pride.

he wold *euer* eft hate. Whan any vnhappes hym befelle, noman
meker ; efte whan he was yn sekernesse, no man sterneꝭ. Suert
ayeyn the bold, meke wyth ham that were�)̃ vndeꝭ y-broght, hard
amonge hys owne, & *priuely* large amonge vnkouth ; & openly 4
mekenesse & debonerte he louede ; pryde & hauteynesse he hated,
& wold brynge vnder fote.

A.D.
1174–5.

[CHAPTER XXXVII.]

Henry II
does not
forget his
Ireland.

[*Fol. 18
b.]

He gets a
grant from
the Pope,
of the Lord-
ship of Ire-
land, and a
charge to
reform the
folk to the
laws of the
Church,

No[ta]
teno[rem]
bullee
[A]drian.

to with-
stand sin,
and better
bad doings.

Thegĥ þe kynge wer wel longe yn grete nuy & grete
       anguyshe throght hys sonnes, as hyt ys to-fore I-told, 8
natheles, amonge otheꝭ nedes, he ne foryet nat hys Irland. He
lete take the *lett*res that waꝭ Imade yn the consaylle of Casshele,
of the vnclene lyf & the horyble synnes that the folk of Irland
lyueden In, ‖ other-wyse than crysten men oght lyuen; & the 12
*lett*res, al ensealed as thay wer, he sent by hys messagers to the
Court of Rome, to the pope Alyxsandeꝭ that than was; & thaꝭ
he dydde the *pur*chace, that by auctoryte of the pope, & by hys
concent, was to hym I-*gr*aunted the lordshype of the lond ; & þe 16
lond-folke, that crysten shold be, & al clene was out of ryght
reule of crystendome & ryght byleue, to bryngeꝭ yñ-to ryght
lawe of holy chyrch, yn the man*ere* of England. That pryuelege
forth, wyth anotheꝭ, that ratheꝭ was *pur*chaced of þe pope Adriañ, 20
that was to-fore Alexander, was I-sent ou*er* yn-to Irlande by
Nychole, pryouꝭ of Walyngeford, & Wyllyam Aldelines sone;
& was a consaylle of al the clergye of Irland I-gaddered to-gyddre
at Wat*er*ford: theꝭ weꝭ the pryueleges I-shewed & I-radde 24
solempnelych to-fore ham, & I-*gr*aunted heghlygh by consente-
ment of al the comynes. The forme of thay *pr*euyleges, as thay
wer endyted yn the Court of Rome a latyne, ne myght I nat
comly setten yn Englyshe, & þerfor I hyt leue; bot the meste 28
streynth ys thys :—Whan the pope Adryan hadde herd opynly
the euyle lyf, & þe synfule, that þe folk of Irland ladden, wors than
wyld bestes, & out of constytucions of holy chyrch & ryght byleue,
he g*r*aunted the kynge that he shold ynto Irland wend, for to 32
adresse & sprede þe t*er*mes of holy chyrch, for to wythstond & lete
the ruyne of syn, for to Amend the lyther thewes, & sette þe good,

any vnhappis hym be-felle no mano mekyr. Whan he was in sickyrnys, no man sternyr. Smyrte agayn the bolde, meke wyth ham *clemens in subactos.* that weryn vndyr-broght; harde amonge his owyn, ande Pryuely largo amonge strange men; *and* opynly meknys *and* debonerte he *diffusus in* lowyd; Pryde *and* hauteynesse he hatyd, *and* wolde brynge vndyr-*extraneos.* fete.

[CHAPTER XXXVII.]

A.D.
1174-5.

Thegh the kynge *were* wel longe in gret angwysche throgh his sonnes, as hit is to-fore tolde, natheles, amonge othyr nedys, he foryate note his Irlande. he take the letteres that ware made in the Consayl of Cassell, of the vnclene lyfe and the horribil Synnys that the Pepil of Irland lyuedyn In / In othyr wyse than crystyn men oght lyue; and the *lettres*, al Ensealid as thay were, He sende his messagers to the Courte of Rome, to the Pope Alysandyr that than was, *and* thar he did Purchase that, by auctorite of the Pope and by his concent, was to hym grauntyd the lorchippe of the londe, *and* the londe-Pepill that crystyn shold be, and al clene was out of Ryght rule of crystyndome and ryght belewe, to brynge into ryght lawe of holy church, in the man*er* of England. That pryvylege forth, wit*h* an othyr [1] that radyr was Purchasid of the Pope Adriane, that was to-fore Alexandyr, was sende ou*er* Into Irlonde by Nycole, pryoure of Walyngeforde, *and* Willam Aldelines-sone; and was a consayle of al the clergy of Irland y-gadderid to-giddyr at Watyrford. ther wer the pryuy-legis y-shewyd, *and* y-radd Sollempnelych to-fore ham, *and* grauntyd hyghlych of al the comynys. The fourme of thay Pryuylegis, as thay wer endyted At Rome a-latyne, y may not comly sette in Englysh, and therfor y * Hit Leue; But the mest streynth is this: Whan the Pope Adryan Hadd Herde opynly the evyl lyfe, and the synfull, that the Pepell of Irland laddyn, wors than wilde bestis, *and* out of constituciones of holy churche *and* ryght be-lewe, he graunted the kynge, that he sholde into Irland wende, forto adresse and sprede the termys of holy church, forto wythstonde *and* [2] lete the ruene of synne[2], forto a-mende the wickid dedis, *and* sette the good; forto En[e]che religion of crystyndome, So that hit were

*Capitulum xxxvij^m.*

*suae tamen inter agendum Hiberniae non im-memor.*

*ab Alexan-dro tertio, tunc prae-sidente, privi-legium im-petrarit.*

*[1] quod idem rex ab Adriano... perquisi-erat.*

*in publica audientia ejusdem privilegii, cum uni-versitatis assensu solemnis recitatio facta fuit.*

*[*Fol. 17 b.]*

*Nota teno-rem bullae Adriane.*

*[2] et filio-rum plan-taria inde exstir-panda.*

for to eneche relygyoun of crystendome, so that hyt war wyrshype
to god, & helte to the soules; & the folke of þe londe, manshyply
hym shold vptake, & worthly as lorde; saue ryghtes of holy chyrche

But every
house in
Ireland is
to pay the
Pope 1d. a
year.

vnwemmed; & to seynt petyr & þe holy modyr chyrche of Rome, of 4
euery hous a pany to rent, a yer, yn Irlnd, as yn England.  Thys
pryuelege was I-purchased of þe pope Adryan; & a clerk hyt
purchased, that hette [1] Ihoū of Salusbury; & the pope, by the
same clerk, sent to the kynge a gulden rynge, yn name of Seysyne 8
of the lond.  the pope Alexandre next aftyr hym confermed that

All oppo-
nents are to
go to the
Devil.

same yift; & euery eþer of ham amonested & parted from god
almyghty, & betheght þe deuyl al ham that yn any tyme þer-
ayeyne wold come.                                                        12

### [CHAPTER XXXVIII.]

Now again
for our
Knights'
deeds in
Ireland.
Hervey of
Mont-
maurice,
jealous of
Reimund,

Off þe kynge And of hys sonnes, & of the purchace that
þe kynge dede, ys Inowe Itold shortlyche : now we
wyllen turne ayeyne to our knyghten gestes yn Irlande.  The
lond of Irland was yn good pees vnder Reymond-ys kepynge; bot 16
heruy of Mountynorthy,—that euer hadde enuy to Reymond, & saw
that hys selth & hys wyrshype wex euer more & more,—fore he ne
durst nat openly showe the felony that was yn hys hert, he
bethoght that he wold dernely; he made hym semblant of myche 20
loue; besoght ful yorne þat he most allyaunce haue to har kynrede,
& namely, that he moste haue to wyue a gentyl-wommañ, Moryces

doghter, fytz Gereud, that hegĥ Neste.  Thys mayd was hym
Igraunted, & he hyr spoused; & þat þe kynrede sholden the 24
faster be Ibound togydyr, by procurynge of Reymond & of hym
eke, þe Erl yaf helyn, hys sustre, to Wyllyam, Moryces eldest sone :
þe erl sent eke aftyr Moryce, that was than Iwent ynto Walys ;
& at hys comynge, he yaue hym þe haluendele of Ofclañ, & þe 28
castel of wykynlo ; & þat oþer haluendele he yaue Meyler.  In the

tyme þat þe pees was, & þe lond yn good state, byfel that Obren,
the kynge of Thomon, ayeyne hys trouth & ayeyn the kynges pees,
began to withdrawen hym from the kynge, & noght nold be 32
bowynge to hym, ne to ham that wer vnder hym yn þe lond.

---

[1] MS. 'sette' for ' hight, hette, or hete,' p. 94, l. 22 below : ' per Johannem
Salesberiensem,' v. 316.

vyrchipp to god, *and* helth to the Sowlys ; *and* the Pepil of the
londe, manshiply hym sholde vp-take, *and* worthy as lorde ; Saue the
ryght of holy church vnwemyd ; and to seynt Petyr *and* the holy
modyr churche of Rome, of euery hous a peny to rent, a yere, in
Irland as in England. This pryuylege was Purchasyd of the Pope
Adrian. / And a clerke hit Purchasid that was callid Ihon of
Salysbury ; *and* the Pope, by the Same clerke, Sende to the kynge
a golde rynge, in tokyn of Seysyn of the londe. And the Pope
Alexandyr nexte aftyr hym confermyt that Same yfte ; And euery
othyr of ham amoncessed *and* Partid from god almyghty, *and* betoke
the deuyl al ham that in any tyme ther-ayeynnes wolde come.

A.D.
1174-5.

*salva beato
Petro, et
sacro-
sanctae
Romanae
ecclesiae,
sicut in
Anglia sic
et in Hiber-
nia, de
singulis
domibus
annua
unius
denarii
pensione.*

[CHAPTER XXXVIII.]

A.D. 1174.

*Capitulum
xxxviij^m.*

OFf the kynge and of his sonnes, and of the Purchas that
the kynge did, is y-now tolde Sortelych. Now we will
turne agayñe to oure knyghten gestis in Irland // The londe in
Irland was in good pees vndyr Reymonde-is kepynge ; but heruey of
montmorthy,—that euer hadd envy to Reymonde, and Saw that his
goodnes and his wyrchippe [wex] euer more and more,—for he no
drust not opynly show the felony that was in his herte, he be-thoght
that he wolde Pryuely / he made to hym semblant of mych loue ;
be-sogh[t] gretly that he sholde alyaunce haue to har kynryde, and
namely, that he haue to wyue a gentyl woman, Morices doghtyr,
fitz-geraude, that was callid Neste. This mayde was to hym
graunted, and he hyr Spoused: and that the kynred sholde be fastyr
bounde to-giddyr, by procurynge of Reymonde *and* of hym also, the
Erle yaue Ellyn his sustyr, to Willam, Morices Eldyst Sone. the
Erle sende also aftyr Moryce, that was than went into walis ; and at
his comynge, he yaue halfe to hym of Ofelan, and the castel of
wickylow ; *and* the othyr halfe he yaue to Meyler. In the tyme
that the Pees was, and the londe in good state, befel that Obreen,
the kynge of Thomonde, agayn his trouth *and* the kynges Pees,
began to wyth-drawe hym frome the kynge, *and* wolde not be
bowynge to hym, nethyr to ham that wer vndyr hym in the londe.

*Videns ..
ejusque
successus
de die in
diem am-
plius pros-
perari.*

*Nota
matrimo-
nium inter
Heruelum
contrahi et
Nestam
filiam
Maurici
fitz-geraud.*

*medium
Ophelaniae
cantare-
dum ....
cum Wy-
kingelo-
nensi
castro.*

[Fol. 19
a.]
A.D. 1175.

Reymond marches to Limerick; but is stopt by the Shannon.

Reymond told þer-of myche vnworthynes, & yn lytyl whyle gadered to-dedderes [so] hys hoste, so that he hadde an hundert knyghtes & .xx.ti, thro huudret other an hois, & .cccc. bowmen afote, & about al-halwen-tyde went toward lymeryke. Whan thay wer theder 4 I-come, thay hadden grete lette of the grete watyr of þe shynen, that was betwen ham & þe sytè, so that thay myght nat ouer wende: the yonglynges—that wel coueytouse wer ham self to auaunce, her stalwarthnesse to showe, & also wynnynge to gete & to 8 hawe,—weren wel sore a-tened þat thay myght nat ouer to þe syte that was ham so neght, for þe watyr þat was so depe & so streit rennynge betwene, & eke so stony by the ground. As the formest of ham waren houynge vpon þe waterys brynk, was a yonge 12

His nephew, Davy the Welshman

knyght amonge ham, newly I-dobbet, fayr & stalwa[r]th, Reymondes Neuowe, that hete Dauy the Welsse[1]: throgh grete couetyse that he hadde, ouer al other to wyn the formest pryce, ne dredet nat to do hym-self to so horyble perylle of deth; he smote hys hors with 16 the spores, & ouer-threwe adoun ynto þe watyr, þat was so depe & so stony. the horse was myche & stronge, & come sone vp

swims the river aslant;

aboue the watyr wyth hym. he wyssed the hors sydlynge ayeyns the watyr asquynt, & come ouer on the other syde, & cryed to hys 20 men, & seyd that he hadde a ford I-found. bot, for he fond no man

but as only one knight follows him, he swims back.

þat hym wold felowe, bot o knyght that hete Geffrey Iudas[2], he turned ayeyne by that same wey, & þe knyght with hym. he come ouer hole & sound; bot þe knyght, þrogh þe streyntnesse of þe 24 watyr, was I-throw adoun, he & hys hors, & y-drent to-for ham al.

Meiler then

Whan Meyler, that theder was wyth Reymond I-comen, þys saw, he hadde grete enuy that such hardynesse shold be I-teld of any other, & nat to hym: vpon the hors þat hym bar, he put hymself 28

crosses the Shannon.

yn the watyr, & hardylyche, wyth-outten any ferdnesse, passed ouer þe other syde. The cytzeyns sawe hym comynge so al-oon; thay comen ayeyn hym, some for to kepe hym vpward at hys comynge out of þe watyr, for to mak hym turne ayeyne; other, to vndo hym 32 ryght yn the watyr. The knyght was stalwarth, & boldly putte hym vp bytwene twe perylle:—on on halue, þe wode-yernynge

[1] David agnomine Walensis. *Op.* v. 321.

[2] Galfridus Judas. *Ibid.*

Reymonde tolde therof gret vnworthynys, *and* in lytyll whyle A.D. 1175.
gaddrid to-gidderis his hoste, So that he hadd an hundred knyghtes *circa*
and xx<sup>ti</sup>, thre hundrid o𝄆er an hors, and CCCC bowmen afoote ; and *kalendas Octobris.*
aboute al-halwyn-tyde wentyn toward lymerike. whan thay wer
thedyr come, thay hadd gret lette of \* the watyr of the Shynnyń, [\*Fol. 18
that Was Betwen Ham and the Cite, So that thay myght not ouer- a.]
wende. the yonglynges—that wel couetos were ham-selfe to *juventus,*
auaunce, har myght to show, and also wynnynge to gette *and* to *tam lucri quam*
haue,—wer sore greuyd that thay myght not ouer to the cite that *laudis cupida,*
was ham so nyghe, for the watyr that was to depe, and so Streyte *tanquam*
rynnynge betwen, *and* also so stony by the grounde. As the *ad aquas Tantali*
fryste of ham was abydynge vpon the watyres brynke, was *posita.*
a knyght amonge ham newely dobbid, fayre *and* stalwarth, Reymondes Eme, that was callid Dauy the Welsse : throgh gret *horren-*
couetyse that he hadd, ouer al othyr to wyn the formyste price, he *dumque mortis*
dreddit not to do hym-Selfe to so horribill Perel of deth. he *periculum laudis*
smote his hors with tho Sporis, *and* ouer-threw adoûne Into the *amore con-*
watyr, that was depe *and* ful of stonys. the hors was mych *and* *temnens.*
stronge, *and* come Sone vp abow the watyr with hym. he wissed *Cursum*
the hors sydlynge ayeynes the watyr asquynt, *and* come ouer on the *itaque fluminis*
othyr syde, and cried to his men, *and* seyde that he had a forde *lateraliter obliquans.*
founde. but, for he found no man that hym wolde follow, but
O knyght that [was] callid Geffrey Iudas, he turned agayn by that
Same wey (*and* the knyght come with hym) holde and Sounde ; but *militem*
the knyght, throgh the Strey[t]nys of the watyr, was caste doun, he *illum, in redeundo,*
and his hors, *and* drounde to-for ham all / whan Meyler, that *amnis im- petuosi*
thedyr was with Reymonde come, this Sawe, he hadd gret envy *violentia*
that Such boldnys sholde be tolde of any othyr, and noght of hym : *raptum, ad ima sub-*
vpon the hors that hym bare, he Put hym-Selfe in the watyr, *and* *mersumque non re-*
boldely, wyth-out any ferde, Passid ouer the othyr syde. The *duxit.*
Cittescynys Saw hym comynge out of the watyr so al-oone : thay
came agayn hym, some forto kepe hym vpward at his comynge out
of the watyr, forto make hym turne agayn ; othyr, to vndo hym
ryght in tho watyr. The knyght was stronge, and boldely Putte
hym vp be-twen two Perelis :—on oone halue, the wode rynnynge

A.D. 1175.
Meiler is
stoned and
shot at by
the Lim-
erick men.

Reimund

calls on his
troops to

save
Meiler.

He and all
his host
swim the
Shannon,
and take
Limerick.

[||Fol. 10
b.]

Which was
the boldest
of the
three?
Davy,
Meiler, or
Reimund?

watyr so grysly; on other halue, hys fomen, that with stonys & with fawes hym leyden on, both at þe watyr, & vpon the wallys of the toun, þat ryght vpon the watyr stode. He pute hys sheld & hys heed wyth the helme ayeyns the dyntes, & hertely held hym amydde 4 al þat harme, alone, wythout any helpe, ful unseker on al syde: þe crye was ful horyble on euery halue. And Reymond, that was at þe last of þe hoste, as hede & lodesman & prynce of al þe hoste, herde the crye, & wyst nat yit what hyt was. He come anoon hastyly 8 thrughe al þe hoste, tyl he come to þe watyr; & when he sawe hys neueu on that other syde, so narowe byladde, & on al syde besete so narowe, he hadde grete angwysshe yn hys hert; & sharpe & byttyrly bygan to cry to hys felowes: "Men that so stalwaith 12 ben of ryght kynd, & yn so fele Anguysshes with vs hath your streynth assayed, cometh forth, men! the way ys open to-for vs, & the ford that noon of vs ne couth, throgh hardynesse of our y-found. folow we now the herty knyght, that so stronge ys 16 byladde, & let me hym neuer so neygh to-for our eghen be I-shent!"

With that word, Reymond was þe fyrst that put hym yn þe watyr; & al þe hoste aftyr dyde ham yn aduentur, & yn goddys grace, & wenten our al quyte, bot o knyght that hete Guy, & twey fote- 20 men. her fomen flowen ² to-fore hem ynto the Cytè, & thay braken yn aftyr, & wan the cytè, & slowen ful many of þe cytzeyns, & dreyntten. Thay fonden ther so myche gold & syluer & other rychesshe, that for that, & eke for the maystre || that god ham sent, 24 thay told lytel of the perylle & the lostes that thay hadde ther-to- fore. Nowe arede ye, whyche was the hardyest of these thre knyghtes? whether he, that wythout any man to-fore hym, put hym yn-to the watyr for to techen al the other the weye; Ather 28 he, that, aftyr ensample of hym, & the horyble death of ham that weren I-dreynt to-fore har eyghen, passed the watyr, & al-one sette so hardyly hys body to mark amonge so many fomen; Other he, that aftyr ham both, so hardyly & so boldly, with al the hoste, put 32 hym yn so gret perylle? Thus was, as the ³ tyme, lymeryk I-wonne

¹ MS. fawes. Lat. creberrimis lapidum jaculorumque jactibus. Op. v. 322.
² MS. slowen. Lat. fugatis in urbem hostibus, v. 322.
³ ? for 'at this.'

watyr so grymly; on the othyr syde, his enemys, that wyth stones *A. D. 1175.*
and with sawis hym leydyn on, both at the watyr, *and* vpon the *creberri-*
wallis of the toun, that ryght vpon the watyr stode.   he Put his *dum jacu-*
shelde and his hede with the sallet [1], agayn the strokys, *and* hertely *lorumque jaclibus.*
helde hym amyd al the Perclis al-one, with-out any helpe, ful [1] *galeam ictibus*
vnsure on al sydis / the cry was ful horribill on euery syde.   And *clipeumque*
Reymond, that was at the laste of the hoste, as hede and ledder and *praeten-dens.*
prynce of al the hoste, herde the cry, *and* wyst not what hit was.
he come anoone hastely throw al the hoste, til he come to the watyr;
and whan he Saw his eme on that othyr syde, so narrow besette, *acriter ex-*
he hadd grete angwysche in his herte; and sharpe and bittyr began *clamavit: Viri, qui-*
to cry to his fellouys, " Men, that So bolde ben, of ryght kynde, and *bus virtutis*
in so many angwyschis with vs hath youre streynth proued, come *insitum*
forth, men! they way is oppenyd' to-for vs; and the forde that noone *novimus a natura,*
of vs knew, throgh boldnys of oure is founde.   followe now the herty *quorumque in tot an-*
knyght that so stronge is by-ladde; *and* lette we neuer so ney to-for *gustiis ani-*
oure eyyne be shente!" wyth that worde, Reymonde was the fryste *mositatis vires ex-*
that * Put Hym in the Watyr; and al the Hoste aftyr did Ham in *perti*
aduenture, and in goddys grace, *and* wenten ouer al quyte, (but *sumus.*
o knyght, that was callid Guy, *and* two footmen,) [2]her enemys *Nota p̄*
kylledyn to-for hem, into the Cite [3], *and* Slowyn ful many of the *captionem ciuitatis limeric.*
Cittescynes, and dreyntyn [2].   Thay foundyn ther so mych golde and [*Fol. 18
Siluyr, and othyr riches, that for that, and also for the Maystry that b.]
god ham sende, thay tolde lytel of the Perel and the lostis that thay
hadd ther-to-fore.   Now ared þe, whyche was the boldyst of this
thre knyghtes: Whedyr he that, with-out any man to-for hym, put *Elige,*
hym in the watyr forto techyn al the othyr the wey; Othyr he that, *lector, trium ri-*
aftyr Ensampill of hym, and the horribil deth of ham that weryn *rorum au-dentissi-*
drovnde to-for har eyyn, Passid the watyr, *and* al-ono sette so *mum.*
hardy his body, to marke, amonge so many ennemys; Othyr he that,
aftyr ham both, so hardy and so boldely, with al the hoste, Put hym
in so gretto Peril.   Thus was as this tyme lymerike take on

---

[2]—[2] fugatis in urbem hostibus, non sine grandi civium strage, muros statim
irruperunt; et urbe potiti cum victoria, spoliis plurimum ditati et' auro,
periculi damna lucri simul et laudis honore compensarunt.   v. 322-3.

[3] The English copier of this MS. has jumpt from the first ' Cite ' to the
second—see lines 21, 22 opposite,—and put ' killedyn ' = ' slowen ' l. 22 opp.
for ' flowen,' l. 21 opp.

A.D. 1175.
one a tywesday[1]; Watyrford I-wonne one a tywesdaye, & dyuelyn

Three Vic-
tories on a
Tuesday,
the day
dedicated
by hea-
thens to
Mars.
also : noght for o coste was that day awayted þer-to, bot as hyt
byfelle by cas & by adwentuƷ; & nat wythout skyle, ffor the
tywesday, by hethen men day yn the old world, was I-sette to a god 4
that day cleped Mars, & was I-hold god of bataylle; & on that day
thay fonden, þat whoso bataylle besoght, he shold spede betteƷ than
yn oþer dayes.

[CHAPTER XXXIX.]

Reimund
Fitz-
Gerald
Now I wille yowe telle these twey stalwarth knyghtes, 8
Reymond & Meyler, whych thay weren. Reymond was
a man brod of body,[2] somdel more than metlyche, yolowe heƷ &

was a far-
seeing, self-
restraind
man,
sam-crysp, grey eyghen & depe, somdel heyghe nose, neb rody,
wel I-hewed, glad semblant & cleeƷ[2]; man of moche methe & of 12
grete puɼueyaunce; nothynge delycion, nother of mete ne of cloth ;
heet & cool, al I-lyche, wel he myght suffre; man of mych
trauaylle; tholmode yn wreth; as redy he was to serue, to queme
ham that he was ouer, as to be I-serued of ham. Whan he hoste 16
ladde, he was so besy about to kepe the host, that oft he left

watchful at
night,
slepe al the nyght, & wandredde about, spyenge & crynge for to
look þat noon harme ne shold betyde, & for he wold euer fyrst be
redy, yf hyt nede wer. & shortlych to sygge hys thewes & hys 20

liberal,
maneres, he was man free & meke, queynt & puɼueynge; & thegh
he wer swyth hardy & wel taght yn wepne, of quenyntyse & of

and most
skilful in
War.
sleyght yn syght, & of selth yn bataylle, he passed al otheƷ[3]; &
thegh he yn both weƷ myche to preyse, he was betteƷ leder of 24
hoste þan knyght.

[CHAPTER XL.]

Meiler
lookt dark
and stern.
Meyler was a man of durk semblant; blak eghen, &
rogh lokynge; sterne semblant; of body, somdel more than
methlych; ful stalwarth, wel I-brested, smal mydel[4], armes & other 28

---

[1] Later note in margin : 'TheƷ-aftyre hyt was I-socoured one a tywsday.

[2-2] staturaeque paulo plus quam mediocris ; capillis flavis et subcrispis, oculis
grossis, glaucis et rotundis, naso mediocriter elato, vultu colorato, hilari, ac
sereno. *Op.* v. 323.

[3] et quanquam animosus plurimum, et armis instructus, prudentia tamen
rebus in martiis et providentia praecellebat. v. 324.

[4] staturae paulo mediocri plus pusillae ; corpore tamen pro quantitatis captu
pervalido ; pectore quadrato, ventreque substricto. v. 324.

a tyvysday, theraftyr hit was socourid' on a tywysday, waterford A.D. 1175.
was take on a tyvysday, and deuelyn also.   noght for oo Purpos *nec per in-*
was that day wayted therto, but as hit befell by case and by *dustriam*
*haec, sed*
aduenture, and not with-out skylle.   For the tyvysday, by hethyn *casu solo*
*contigisse.*
men tyme in the olde worlde, was sette to a god that is callid Mars,
*and* Was holde god of battayle; And on þat day thay fovndyn, that
who-so battayl be-soght, he sholde spede bettyr that day than in
othyr dayes.

### [CHAPTER XXXIX.]

NOwe y wille you telle thes two bolde knyghtes, Reymond *Capitulum*
*xxxix^m.*
*and* Meyler, whych they weryn // Reymond' was a man *Descripcio*
brode of body, somdel more than metlych, yolowe here, and sam- *Reymundi*
crysp; grey cyyn and depe, Somdel hegh nose, face rody we[l] hewid, *Le gras.*
glad, semblante, *and* clere; man of mych mette *and* of grete Puruey- *Vir mo-*
*destus et*
aunce / nothynge delycious, nothyr of mete ne of cloth; [1] hette *and* *providus,*
colde, al y-lyke, wel he myght suffyr; man of mych trauail; *nec cibo*
*nec veste*
tholmode in wreth; as redy he was to Serve, to queme ham that he *delicatus.*
was ouer, as to be seruyd of ham [1].   Whan he hadd host, he was so
byssy about to kepe the hoste, that ofte he lefte Slepe al the nyght,
*and* Walkid about, Spyenge and crienge forto loke that noone harme
ne sholde befall, and for he wolde euer fryst be redy, yf hit nede
were.   And Sortely to Say his condicionys and his maneres, he was
man fre and meke, queynt and Purueyynge; *and* thegh he wer *providus*
*et prudens.*
Swyth hardy, *and* wel taght in wepyn, of queyntyse and of Sleght [2] *multum*
in fygh[t], *and* of Selth in battayl, he Passid al othyr; and thegh he *quidem*
*militis*
in both were mych to Preyse [2], he was bettyr ledder of hoste than *habens,*
*sed plus*
knyght. *ducis.*

### [CHAPTER XL.]

MEyler was a man of durke semblant; [3] blake cyyne and rogh *Capitulum*
*xl^m.*
lokynge; sterne Semblante; of body, somdel more than [3] *oculis*
metlych, ful bolde, wel brestyde, smale myddyl, armys and othyr *nigris et*
*torvis.*

---

[1]—[1] caloris et algoris ei patientia par: vir patiens irae, patiensque laboris.
Quibus praesidebat prodesse magis quam praeesse, potiusque minister quam
magister videri volens.—*Op.* v. 324. (No Latin here for 'Whan . . . nede were.')

lymmes ful bony, more synowy than fleysly.  he was knyht ful

Meiler was
never
afraid of
any enter-
prise.
He'd
win or die.
But he, and
all the
knights,
robd the
Church.
hardy & enuyouse ; he was neuer aferde ne agryse to begynne
thynge yn fyght that any man oght done hym on, Ather wyth
otheꝛ y-meued [1].  In euery fyght, he was þe fyrst to begynne, & the 4
laste that hyt wold leue.  Al þe stalwarthnese that any man myght
do, he wold passe, or suffre deth ; the maystrye & prys to wynne,
otheꝛ deye,—nothynge he ne sette betwene.  Of al thynge, bothe
these knyghtes weꝛ to preyse myche wyth-al, neꝛ hyt that thay, 8
throgh couetyse, oft byname holy chyrch heꝛ ryghtes ; bot more
harme ys, & mychel to mourne, that defaute haddeñ meste al ouꝛ

Praises of
the Fitz-
Stephens,
Fitz-
Geralds,
St. Davids,
Fitz-
Henrys,
Fitzhughs,
&c.
knyghtes from the forme begynnynge.  What was Robert
steuenessoñ & hys sonnes yn haꝛ tyme ? what, Moryce fytz 12
Geraud & hys sones ? what, Robert debarry, of whom ys to-fore
I-told ? what, myles de seynt dauy ? both Robertes & Moryce
neueuen, that with þe formest boldly come ynto Irland ? what,
Robert fyz henry, Meyleres brotheꝛ ? what, Reymond de Cante- 16
tone ? what, Robert de barry the yonge ? what, Reymond hues-

The
memory of
their pluck
and grand
deeds shall
never die
out.
sone ? what, otheꝛ of the selue gentrye, many & I-nowe, whych
hyt waꝛ stronge to namen al by nam ? for no mane ne myght hyt
bethynk, bot haꝛ stalwarthnesse ne heꝛ good deddes sbold neuer 20
wend out of mynd.  Thay weꝛ a folke & a kynrede, on two halue,
kyndly, stalwarth, & hardy ; on other halue, of þe kynde of ffraunce,

[*Fol. 20
a.]
& theꝛ of wel I-taght yn wepne of myche * nenbre (?) of kynred
& kynd stalwarthnesse euer more to heꝛ ende.  Whan Reymonde 24

A. D. 1175.
hadde I-wonne the sytè of lymeryke, he ordeyned & purueyed
how the cytè myght be best I-kept ; he lete brynge thedeꝛ

Reimund
victuals
Limerick,
and leaves
his cousin,
Miles of
St. David's,
in charge of
it.
vyttaylle on euery halue grete plente, & lefte þer Myles of seynt
dauy, with fyfty knyghtes & squyers an-hors, & ccc bowmen, 28
& with þe other parte of the hoste wyth yoy & gladnesse al
harmles turned ayeyne ynto leynestre.

[CHAPTER XLI.]

Hervey of
Mont-
maurice
euvies
The lond was þan yn good pees vnder Reymondes kepynge, so that non Iresshe-man ne durst hym stur to 32
mysdom.  Heruy of Mommorthy, that euer hadde enuy to hym,

---

[1] Miles animosus et aemulus ; nihil umquam abhorrens, quod aggredi quis
vel solus debeat vel comitatus, v. 324.

lyme*s* full bony, more synowy than fleshy.  he was knyght ful Descripcio

hardy *and* Enuyouse ; he was newyre aferde ne agryse to begynne Melerij.

thynge in fyght that any man ogh don hym on͞, * Althyr wyth [*Fol. 19

othyr ymewyd.  In euery fyght, he was the fryst to Begynne, and þ*e* a.]

laste hit to leue ; al the boldnes that any man myght do, he wolde

Passe, or suffyre dethe.  The maystry and Prysce to wyn othyr dye, *inter mor-*

nothynge he no sette betwen.  Of al thynge, both this knyghtes *tis et*

were to Preyse mych wyth-all, nere hit that thay, throgh covetyse, *triumphos,*

ofte toke holy church ryghtes ; but more harme is, *and* gretly to *dium*

morne, that defaute haddyn meste al our knyghtes frome the fryst *ponens.*

begynnynge. / What was Robert Steuenes-sone *and* his Sonnys ;

What, Robert de barry, of whom is to-for tolde ; What, Morice fiz-

geraud *and* his sonnes ; What, Miles de seynte dauy ; both Robert

*and* Morices emys, that wyth the fryst boldely come into Irland ;

what, Robert fiz-henry, Meyler-is brodyr ; What, Reymonde de

Canteton ; What, Robert de barry the yonge ; What, Reymond Hues- *Quid alii*

Sone ; What, othyr of the same gentil, many *and* y-now, whych hit *tatis ejus-*

were stronge to telle by name ?  for no man ne myght hit be-thynke, *dem quam*

but har boldenys ne her good dedys shold neuer go out of mynde. *qnibus*

¹ They wer a pepill and a kynred, on both sydys, be kynde, bolde and *singulorum*

hardy ; on othyr halue of the kynde of Fraunce, *and* ther-of wel *gesta*

taght in wepyn, of mych nembre, of kynred and kynde bolde, euer- *poterant*

more to her eude¹ // Whan Reymonde hadd take the Cite of lymerike², *laudis*

he ordeynyd *and* Purueyed how the Cite myght be best kepte : he *promereri !*

lette brynge thedyr vytayll, on euery halue, grete Plente ; and lefte *A. D. 1175.*

ther Miles of Seynt dauy, wi*th* fifty knyghtes *and* Squyerys an hors,

and CCC bowmen ; *and* wyth the othyr Parte of the hoste, wi*th* Ioy

*and* gladnys, al harmeles, turned agayn Into leynystre.


[CHAPTER XLI.]

T͟He londe was than in good Pees vndyr Reymondys kepynge, Cap*i*tulum

So that non Irysh-man durst not styr hym to mysdone. *Herreius*

Heruey of Mounmorthy, that euer had Enuy to hym, ne lefte not, *de Monte*
*Mauricii.*

---

¹⁻¹ O genus! O gens! gemina natura, a Trojanis animositatem, a Gallis
armorum usum originaliter trahens.—*Op.* v. 326.

A.D. 1175. he left nat, for the allyauce that was ham betwene, þat he ne
Reimund dydde hym al þe harme that he myght, & opynly shewed than
Fitz-
Gerald, and þe felony that he longe hadde I-borne yn hys hert.   He sent ouer
sends lies to þe kynge by Messagers, [1] & made hym to vnderstond that 4
about him
to Henry Reymond was yn yndygnacion of the kynge; & ayeyne hys owne
II, trouth, so hauteyn I-worth, that he wold al Irland take to hym
& to hys [1]; &, for hys lesynges shold þe bettyr be y-leued, feel
þynges he made hym to vndrestond, & so fayr hyt slyked wyth 8
which the fulsnesse, that hyt somet sothe, al that he seyde.   The kynge—as
King
believes, ofte manere ys that lydder tales ben bettyr I-leued, & lenger
and des- I-thoght, that good—he beleued þe fals mannys talys & wryyngc,
patches
Messengers & sent yn-to Irland four Messagers, that ys to wytten, Robert 12
to bring the power, Osbern of herford, Wyllyam Berynger, & Adam of
Reimund
back. yarnemouth, of whych the twey shold abyde with the Erle yn
Nota de Irland, & þe other tweyn shold wende ayeyne ynto England wyth
aduentu
poweren- Reymond, as þe kynge hym hadde COMMAWNDET.                    16
ter in hi-
berniam.
                          [CHAPTER XLII.]

Hervey de Heruy was a man fayr & lygne, eyghen grey & depe,
Mont-
maurice       ouelyche lokynge, fayr semblaunt, of fayr spech & wordes
wel besete; of body more than methlych, of al lymmes ful
was as fair becomly; bot as fayr & as becomly as he was wytout, as lydder 20
without, as
he was foul & as fals of many maner lastes he was wyt-In; ffor, fro the tyme
within. that he was chyld, he yaf hymself to lecherye; & nat only to many
He was
lecherous, sengle wommen; bot he ne synned neþer spousbrych ne syblynges;
incestuous, he was onful & bakbyter, [2] wreyer, false & traytur, duble of 24
envious,
trea- tonge & nothyng stydfaste, butt yn [2] falsnesse hys speche thoght
cherous, as thogh hyt wer hony & mylk out of hys mouthe, bot euer hyt
was I-meygnet with attyr at þe ende.   Som tym he was stalwarth,
as to knyght longeth; bot aftyr, he yaue hym selue more to 28
a coward, cowerdyse than to knyghthode; & more he couth hym maken,
a braggart,
and a liar. than he was worth [3]; hegh of berynge yn hous, & noght of plente;
of mych speche, & lytel sothnesse.

        [1—1] illi sinistre rerum eventum indicarit: asseverans quoque Reimundum,
        contra regis honorem, et fidem debitam, non tantum Limericum, verum etiam
        Hiberniam totam, sibi suisque jam occupare proculdubio proposuisse.—Op. v. 327.
        [2—2] These words are in a different hand.                    [3] MS. wroth.

for the alyaunce that was ham betwen, that he ne did hym al the A. D. 1175.
harme that he myght, and opynly shewed than the felony that he
longe thoght in herte. he sende ouer to the kynge by messangerys,
*and* did hym to vndyrstonde, that Reymonde was in indignacion of
the kynge ; *and* agayn his owyn throuth, so Hauteyn I-worth, that *Et ut hoc*
he wolde al Irland take to hym *and* to his. And, for his lesyngys *figmentum delator*
sholde the bettyr be belewid, ¹ many lesyngys he made hym to *regiis auribus*
vndyrstonde ; and So fayre hit glosyd wit*h* lesyngis, that hit Semyd *tutius et*
trouth, al that he sayde ¹. The kynge,—as ofte man*er* is, that fals *probabilius praesen-*
talys ben bettyr belewid, *and* lengyr thoght², than good,—he belewid *taret.*
the fals man*es* talys and accusynge, And Sende Into Irland⸗ foure *² memoria diuturnior.*
Messagers, that is to wittyn, Robert de Power, Osbern of Herforde, *Nota de*
Willam Berynger, And adam of Iarnemouth³ ; of the whych, two *aduentu Power-*
sholde abyde wit*h* the Erle in Irland, *and* the othyr two sholde *encium in Hiber-*
wende agayn in-to England, wit*h* reymond, as the kynge hym hadd *niam.*
comandyd.

[CHAPTER XLII.]

HEruey was a man fayr*e* and lygne, eyghyn grey and *Capitulum*
depe⁴, lolych lokynge, fayre semblant, of fayre Speche *xlij^m.*
*and* wordys wel besctte * of body more than metlych, of al *Descripcio Heruei.*
Lymmys wel becomly ; But as fayre and as Becomly as he was *[*Fol. 19*
wyth-out, As wickyd and as fals of many maner lastes he was *b.]*
wyth-In. // Fro the tyme that he was chylde, he yaue hym-Selfe *i promi-nentibus*
to lechery, *and* not only to many Syngyl Women⁵, but he ne *aspectu amabili.*
synnyd neuer spousebrich ne siblynge*s* ; he was onfull *and* bac- *⁵ nec incestus*
byter, wreyer, fals *and* trechoure, doubill of tonge, and nothynge *ullos, nec adul-*
stydfast but in falsnesse ; his spech, as hit were honny *and* *teriam vitans. Vir*
mylke out of the mouth, but eu*er* hit was medlid wit*h* wenym at *invidus,*
the Ende. Sometym he was bolde, as longyth to a knyght ; but *delator, et*
aftyr, he yafe hym [more] to cowardyse than to knyght-hode ; *and* *duplex ; vir sub-*
more he made of hym-Selfe than he was worth ; hey of bery⸗ge *dolus,*
in house, *and* not of plente ; of myche speche, an*d* lytyl trouth. *facetus, et fallax.*

---

¹⁻¹ ad votum effectui mancipandum, in Bragmannorum morem conjuratas ad
hoc catervas Reimundum asserit composuisse. v. 327.
³ Robertum Poerium, et Osbertum de Herlotera, Gulielmum de Bendinges,
et Adam de Gernemies. v. 328.

[CHAPTER XLIII.]

A. D. 1176.

Reimund hears that Donnell O'Brien, King of Limerick, is besieging the English there.

Reymond hym dyght for to wende ynto England, as the kynge hym commandet; & nothynge abode, bot wynd & wedyr at the see: come Messagers, hastyly I-sent from the meygne of lymeryke, & tolden that Obreen, the kynge of thomond, was 4 belyggynge lymeryke with ful grete hostes; &, for þey hadden all the wytaylle þat Reymond ham lefte & eke that thay hadden ther-aftyr I-puchassed yn the wenter-tyme, al I-spendet, me shold ham hastyly send socoure. The Erle was ful anguysshous ham 8 for to socour, & spake þer-of to the meygne, & besoght ham wel yonre (yorne?) theder to go; bot thay war so wroth & so sory for Reymondes wendynge awey, that euerychon, with oo mouth, for-soken alout, that, without Reymond, for nothynge theder thay 12 nold wend. The Erle toke consaylle her, of the kynges messagers;

Reimund marches for Limerick, [*Fol. 20 b.]

&, for the thynge was yn grett perryll, at þe end, throgh bysy besechynge of the erle & eke of ham, Reymond turned ayeyne the baneres toward * lymeryke. And as thay come toward 16 Casshel wyth the hoste,—as myght be, syxty knyghtes, & two hundret squyers & thre hundret bowmen, wythout Iresshe-men

with McMurrough of Okensely and King Donnell of Ossory.

that comen eke wyth ham, as Macmorgh of okensely & dofnild of osserye,—me come to ham, & told ham, fore that þay of 20 thomon hadde I-lefte þe sege of lymeryke, & wer I-comen ayeyns ham, to kepe ham yn the paas of Casshel; & thegh the paas

The men of Thomond barricade the Pass of Cashel against the English.

was stronge yn hymselfe, thay kesten adoun tren, & made dyches thar towr, & hegges vpon, for noon horsman ne shold ouer wend. 24 Whan thay weren negh to the pas I-comen, Reymond deled the hoste a thre. & downyld, þe kynge of Ossery, that ful mychell hated, & foman was to, ham of thomon, saw þe Englyshe hoste— thegh thay fewe wer—of ful good herte, & wel & semly I-wepned, 28

K. Donnell of Ossory appeals to the Anglo-Irish force to fight bravely.

for thay shold be þe trustyer, & the bettre herte haue to hem, & seyd, "Men, that þys lond wyth stalwarthnesse haue I-wonne, assayleth today styfly your fomen! ffor yf, ye, as your won ys, ouercometh, & the maystry haue; our sparthes, furth wyth yowr 32 swerdys, our fomen smertly shulle folowen aftyr; & yf ye—that god forbede!—ben ouercome, syker be ye that we forth with our fomen wyllen turne vpon yowe. Take hede, knygthtes, & vnder-stondeth, your townes .& your castels ben welle ferr hennes, & 36

[CHAPTER XLIII.]

REymond made hym redy to go into England as the kynge hym commaundid *and* nothynge abode but wynde *and* wedyr at the See. Come messagers hastely sende frome the meny of lymerike, *and* toldyn that Obreen, the kynge of Thomonde, was besegyn lymerike wit*h* ful grete hostis; and, for thay haddyn al the vytaill that Reymonde wit*h* ham had lefte, *and* also that thay purchasid sithenys, thay had al spende, And that thay sholde hastely sende ham Socoure. The Erle was ful angwyschous ham for-to socoure *and* Spake therof to the meny *and* besoght ham wel ofte thedyr to go, but thay were so wroth and So sory for Reymondes goynge away, thay euerchone wyth o woyse forsokyn al, that wyth-out Reymonde for no-thynge thedyr thay wolde goo. / The Erle toke consayl her-of of the kynge*s* messangers, and for the thynge was in gret Perel. at the Ende throw besechynge of the Erle *and* also of ham Reymond turned agayn the baners toward lymerike. And as thay come to-ward cassel wit*h* the hoste—as myglit be, Sixti knyghtys *and* two hundrid Squyere*s and* iij*c* bowmen, wit*h*out Iryssh-men that comyn also wit*h* ham, as Macmurgh of O-kensley and dofnyld of Ossery—thay come to ham, *and* tolde ham, [1] fore that thay of Thomon hadd lefte the sege of lymerike, *and* were comyn agayne*s* ham, to kepe ham in the Paas of Casshel; and thegh the Paas was stronge in hym-Selfe, thay castyn adoun trees, *and* made dichis thartowre, *and* heggys vpon, for noone hors-man ne sholde ouer-wende. When thay wer ney to the Paas y-come, Reymond delid the host a thre. And downyld, the kynge of Ossory, that gretly hatid, *and* enemy was to ham of Tomonde, Saw the Englyssh host (thegh thay few were) of ful good herte, *and* wel semely wepenyd; and for thay sholde be the trustier, and the bettyr herte haue to them; *and* sayde, "Men, that wyth boldne*s* this londe haue conquerid, assaylyth this day styfly youre enemys! For an ye, as youre wone is, ouercomyth, and the maystry haue, our Sparrys, forth wit*h* youre Swerdys, oure enemys smyrtly shull follow aftyr. And yf ye (that god forbede!) ben ouer-come, syckyr be ye [2]that we forth wit*h* oure enemys wil turne vpon yow. Take hede, knyghtys, and vndyrstondyth, youre [*] tounys and you*r* castelys Ben wel ferre Hennes, and the flyght ful

*Marginal notes:*

Capitulum xliij*o*.

A.D. 1176.

*quoniam omnia alimenta, tam ibi inventa quam attracta, brumali tempore consumpserant. se illuc ituros absque Reimundo omnes unanimiter contradicerent.*

[1]*audivit Tuhetmonienses, obsidione relicta, ei in passu Cassiliensi obciam venisse; et locum, natura difficilem, confragis arborum et fossatis plurimum exasperasse; sepem quoque fortissimam ex transverso locasse, [2]in vos cum hostibus procul-dubio con- certentur.*

[*Fol. 20 a.]

A.D. 1176. the flyght ful longe, & our maner ys, to helpe ham that ben omost,
& folowe the fleyngc. trysteth wel to vs; bot no lenger than the
ouer hand ys your." ⁋ Whane thys was yseyd, Meyler, þat was
yn the formeste of the host, smertly spronge out, as sparke out 4
of fyr; & al the host aftyr stalwartly com to the pas; & nat
wyt-out gret slaght of ham that wythstoden, opened the way,
& wentten ouer an estre euen, & a thrydde ester day, that ys to
wentten, on a tywesday, as at the other tyme. Also nowe, the 8
host come ynto lymeryk, Reymond lete ryght & arer that, throgh
the sege of har fomen, was I-wasted & destrued. & nat lange
ther-aftyr, he held parlement wyth the kynge of Connaght & the
kynge of Thomon, bot yn oo day bot nat yn o place; ffor the kynge 12
of Connaght held hym yn the watyr of the shynen, yn a myche
logh, yn botys, & the kynge of Thomon was thar negh yn a
wodde. Reymond was betwene two, at kyldalo, as myght by,
syxten myle frome lymeryk. Ther was the parlement so fer forth 16
I-dryuen, that euery of ham delyuered to Reymond good hostages,
& othes many-fold sworne hold & trewe, yn good pees for to hold
euer efte to the kynge & to hys. Whan thys was I-done, &
Reymond turned ayeyne wyth hys hostages to lymeryke, þe 20
prynce of desmond, Dermot Maccarthy, sent by messagers to
Reymond, & besoght hym that he ayeyne hy[s] eldeste sore that
hete Cormoc Olethan—tha[t] wel negh hym out of hys kynge-
dome I-putte—hym, as the kynges trew man, shold helpe; & 24
large yiftes he byhete, both to Reymond & the meygne, wyth that
that thay wold hym helpe. Reymond, as man that had nat loth
wynnynges, ne hymself to auaunce, spake her-of to hys falawes,
& thay alle graunted to don as he wold, & turned the baners 28
toward the Contreys of Cork. by weyes as thay wentten, thay
name many prayes, wher-of the meynge was ful wel apayed, &
mych ther-of was oft I-sent to lymeryk, so longe, that throgh help
of Reymonde, Dermot recouered al hys kyngedome vpon hys sone 32
—of whyche he was negh I-pute owt:—the sone was I-take &
delyuered to the fadyr, & he hym pute yn pryssoun, & nat longe
ther-aftyre hym be-lete take out of pryssoun, & smyth of hys
hede. 36

Meiler Fitz-Henry leads the attack, and forces the Pass on Easter Eve April 3.

They enter Limerick, and repair it.

Reimund, at Killaloe, induces the Irish rebels to swear allegiance to Henry II.

He then agrees to help Dermot Mac-Carthy against his son Cor-mack.

Reimund marches to Cork, and beats Cormack,

who is put in prison, and then beheaded.

Longe. [1] And oure maner is, to helpe ham that ben omyste, and A.D. 1176.
follow the fleynge. trystyth wel to vs; but no longyr than ye haue
the ouer hande" / Whan this was sayde, Meyler, that was in the *Nota quod*
fornyst of the hoste, smyrtly styrte out, as sparke of fyre; and *hibernici*
*non sunt*
al the host aftyr, boldely come to the Paas; *and* not wyth-out gret *amici nisi*
slaght of ham that wythstodyn, openyd the way, *and* wentyn ouer *quandiu*
*forma*
an Estre-evyn, and the thyrd Estyr-day, that is to say, on a *faciet.*
tyvysday, as at the othyr tyme. also now þe hoste come to [1] *Et nos*
*rictoribus*
lymerik, Reymond lette rere that throw the sege of har enemys *semper*
*adhue-*
was wastid' *and* destrued. *and* not lange ther-aftyr, he helde *rentes,*
Parlement wyth the kynge of Connaght *and* the kynge of *solum per-*
*sequimur*
Thomonde, both in oo day, but not in oo Place; For the kynge *fugientes.*
*De nobis*
of Connaght helde hym in the watyr of shynnyn, in a myche *itaque*
logh, in botis, and the kynge of Thomonde was thar negh in a *confidite,*
*sed ric-*
wodd'. Reymonde was betwen two at kyldalo, as myght by, *tores.*
syxtene mile from lymerik. Ther was the Parlement So fer
forth drywen, that euery of ham delyuerid to Reymond good *fidelitatem*
*Anglorum*
hostagis, *and* othis manyfolde Sworn, holde and trew, in good *regi et suis*
Pees forto holde euer aftyr to the kynge and to his. Whan *de cetero*
*inviolabi-*
this was don, *and* Reymond turned agayn with his hostagis to *liter exhi-*
lymerike, the Prince of Desmonde, Dermot Maccarthy, sende by *bendam*
*sacra-*
messagers to Reymonde, and besoght hym that he-agayn his *mentis*
*corpora-*
eldyst Sone that hete Cormok Olethan, that wel ney hym out *liter prae-*
of his kyngdome Putte,—hym, as the kynges trew man, sholde *stitis renu-*
*vaverit.*
helpe; *and* large yftys he Promysyd, both to Reymond *and* the
meny, yf thay wolde hym helpe. Reymond, as man that had no
[1] *Multis*
loth wynnynges, ne hym-Selfe to auctorice, Spake herof to his *itaque tum*
fellowis; and thay al graunted to do as he wolde, and turned the *praedis in*
*brevi quam*
baners toward the contreis of Corke. [1] by weyes as thay wentyn, *stipendiis,*
thay rerid many Prayes, Wherof the meny was ful wel appayed *familia in*
*partibus*
*and* wel arrayed, *and* mych therof was ofte sende to lymerik. *illis abunde*
*refecta, et*
So longe, that by the helpe of Reymond, Dermot recoverid al his *alimen-*
*torum*
kyngdome vpon his sone, of whom he was ney Putt out / the *copia Li-*
Sone was take, and delyuerid to the Fadyr; and he Putt hym *mericum*
*abinde*
in prysone. and not longe ther-aftyr, hym he lette take out of *persaepe*
*transmisra.*
pryson, *and* smyte of his hede.

A.D. 1176.                    [CHAPTER XLIV.]

[Fol. 21a.] **T**he whyle that Reymond was in this maner yn
Reimund
Fitz-                desmon, come a Messager to hym ffrom dyuelyn,
Gerald
hears from    hastyly I-sent, & broght hym a *lettre* from basile, hys wyf; bot
his wife      he that hyt broght, wyst nat what hyt was. Reymond hadde 4
Basile,
              wyth hym a clerk that he wel tryst to; he lete hym rede the
              *lettre* priuelych, that thus myche hym seyde: "To hyre leue
              lord & hyr spouse Reymond, hys basyle sendeth gretynge. as to

that her      hyꝛ selue, wyt thou, lef man, that the grete chek-toth that so sore 8
bad tooth
is out,       me oke, ys I-falle. Wherfore, yf thou any thynge recheste of thy
              self, otheꝛ of me, ne leue nat to come hastyly to me." Whan

i.e. that     Reymond thys herd, he vnderstode that the mych toth that hyr
Earl Stri-
guil is       was I-falle, betokned þe Erles deth; for he lefte hym ful seke at 12
dead, tho'
his death     dyuelyne, whan he parted from hym. And thegh he lange theꝛ-to-
is kept
secret.       fore was ded, foꝛ drede of Iresshe-men he was for-hold tyl
              Reymondes comes, & the meygnees, ynto leynestre. Reymond
              turned sone to lymeryke. & þe sorow that was yn hys hert 16
              with-yn, he, for al hyt, as myche as he myght, with fayr semblant
              makynge with-out; & ful fewe men, he shewed the aduentuꝛ that
Reimund's     so sodeynly was byfalle; & of ham that mooste good kouth, he
Council
advise him    besoght consaylle & rede, what was ham to done. Than was 20
to quit       comenly haꝛ rede such: "what fore the erles deth, what for
Limerick,
and take      Reymondes wendynge out of the lond, that the sytè of lymeryke,
his men to
Leinster.     that was so ferꝛ, & amonge so many enemyes, me shold leue voyde;
              & al the meygne holy led ynto leynestre, þe townes vpon þe see 24
              & the castels for to kepe." Reymond, thegh hym loth weꝛ,
              graunted thys, & stod to haꝛ rede; &, for he ne fond none that
So he com-    aftyr hym wold theꝛ abyde, he betoke Obreen, the kynge of
mits Lim-
erick to      thomon, the Cytè to kepe as the kynges baroun, & toke of hym 28
O'Brien,      efte newe hostages, & many new othes I-swore, the toun harmles
who swears
to keep it    for to kepe, & the pees trewly for to hold. Vpon thys forward,
in peace;
but at once   thay wentten al out of the Cytè, & lefte Obreen & hys men with-yn;
breaks his    & vnnethes thay waꝛ I-passed the brygge, that þe tother end nas 32
oath, and
destroys      I-broken anoon ryght behynd ham, & þe toun, that wel & fast was
the Bridge.   I-walled, & wel I-byld with good housses I-herlerged o wyttaylle
              that on euery half þether was I-broght woll I-stoffe¹, nat without

[CHAPTER XLIV.]

The whyle that Reymond was in this maner in desmonde, come a Messager to hym frome deuelyn, Hastly sende, and broght hym a lettyr frome basyle, his wyfe; but he that hit broght, wyst not what hit was. Reymond hadd with hym a clerke that he trust wel to. / He mad him rede the lettyr priuely, þat thus mych hym sayde: "To hir welbelowid lorde and Spouse, Reymond, his basylle sendyth gretynge. as to hyre-Selfe, wit thou, lefe man, that the grete chektoth that so sore me grewid, is falle; Werfor, yf ye rekyth any-thynge of youre-Selfe, othyr of me, ne leue not to come hastely to me." When Reymond this herde, he vndyrstod by the mych toth, that * Hyr was fall, Betokenyd the Erlys deth; for He Lefte Hym ful seke at deuelyn when he lefte hym. And thegh he lang therto-for was ded, for fere of Irysh-men, he was for-holde tyl Reymondes comys and the menyes, in-to leynystere. Reymond turned sone to lymerike. and the Sorrow that was in his herte wythin, ¹he, for al hit, as mych as he cowthe, made fayre semblant without¹; and to ful few men he shewid the aduenture that so sodeynly was byfall; and of ham that moste good couth, he besoght consayl and rede, what was ham to done. Than was comynly har consail Such, "what for the Erlys deth, what for Reymondys² wendynge out of the londe, that the Cite of lymerik, that was so ferre, and amonge so many enemys, that they sholde leue woyde; and al the meny, holy lede Into leynystere, the tovnes and the castelys vpon the See forto kepe." Reymond, thegh loth hit was to hym, gravntyd this, and stode to har rede; and, for he ne found none that aftyr hym wolde byde there, He yaue Obreyn, the kynge of Thomonde, the Cite to kepe as the kynges barovne, and toke of hym, fryst, new hostagis, and many new othys Sware, the tovñe harmles forto kepe, and the Pees trewely forto hold / Vpon thys, thay wentyn al out of the Cite, and lefte obreen and his men within / and vnnethys thay were Passyd the brige, that the othyr ende nas brokyn anoone ryght behynde ham; and the toun, that wel and faste was wallid, ²and wel bylid with good houses, I-herbergid of wytalis, that on euery halfe thedyr was broght wel Stuffid, not wythout gret Sorynys of herte,

*Capitulum xliiij^m.*
*nota De morte comitis Richardi.*

*quod dens ille molaris et magnus, qui tantum mihi dolu-erat, jam cecidit.*
*[*Fol. 20 b.]*

*usque ad Reimundi famili-aeque redi-tum.*
*⌐ exte-riore vultus hilaritate valde dissi-mulans.*

*totamque familiam integre.*

*Duvenaldo Tuhetmo-niae prin-cipi.*

*²aedificiis decenter ornatam, alimentis undique congestis plane refertam.*

² de[part·ing?] at first written here.

A. D. 1176. grette sorynesse of hert, thay sawe on fouꝛ partyes I-sette afyꝛ;

O'Brien & thys the traytouꝛ Obren shewed openlych how me shal tryst
burns
Limerick. to Iryshemen trouth. ❡ Reymond, with all the meygne, wentt hym
Richard tho to dyuelyn; & the Erles body, that by hys byddynge was I-kept 4
Fitz-
Gilbert, vnburyed, [was buryed] yn the modyr-church of þe Trynyte, to-for
Earl of the swete rode, by procurynge of sent laurence, that was yn that
Striguil, is
buried. tyme erchebysshoppe of dyuelyn.

[CHAPTER XLV.]

Henry II's **A**ftyꝛ that þe Erle was dede, the kynges mes- 8
Commis-
sioners go sagers, that weren aftyr Reymond I-come, vpon newe
back to
him. aduenturs toke new consaylle. Thay lefte Reymond keper of
Irland, & wentten ham ynto Engeland hastyly to the kynge, &
*Nota* the told hym of the erles deth, & the state of the lond. The kynge 12
goodnesse sent than ynto Irlande, Wyllyam aldelinessesone, procuratouꝛ of the
of Geraud.
Henry II lond, with x knyghtes of hys own priue meygne; & with hym, Ihon
sends Wm. de Courcy with other x; Robert steuenessone & Myles de Cogan,
Fitz-Aude-
line and þat al two yeꝛ yn engeland & yn gascoyne nobly hadden with the 16
others to kynge I-be, come þan ynto Irland with xxti knyghtes. Tythynges
Ireland.
come to Reymond that thay waꝛ arryued; & he anoon-ryght went
[*Fol. 21 ayeyns ham with mych gladnesse * & fayr felawshyppe of knyghtes
b.],
Reimund to Weysford. Ther he yeld vp to Wyllyam, as to Seneschal from 20
yields all the kynge I-sent, al the kynges townes, & hys castels, & al the
his towns
and host- ostages of Irland. Wylliam sawe Reymond wyth so many & so
ages.
His fine fayr yonglynges bylad, & beheld Meylleꝛ & other knyghtes of hys
retinue kyn, fayr & rychely y-wepned of o maner vepne, wel thrytty, vpon 24
excites
Fitz-Aude- ful fayꝛ hors, sheldes about haꝛ nekkes, & spers yn hand, pleynge
line's envy, to-geddre ynto al the feldes: he turned hym to hys men, & seyd al
soft, "Thys pryd shal be pute In, ar hyt be lange, & þese
sheldes to-dreued." Ffro that tyme euer aftyr, these & meste al 28
otheꝛ proc[ur]atours yn Irland, as thoght hyt weꝛ by on oth
togeddre I-swore, throgh ond & enuy ne stynt neuer to besech
and he Reymond & Meilleꝛ, Robertes sones, & Moryce, & al that kynrede,
always
works al þe enuy that þay myght & durst; for þys ys euermore haꝛ 32
against wayte & haꝛ aduentur: euer whan grete nede byfelle yn tyme of
Reimund
and the weꝛ, thay war lef & derward, & the formeste to I-clepped, & to
Geraldines. bataylle, throgh hardynes, formest & fyrst redy; whan non ned was,

thay Saw on foure Parties sette afyre.  And thus the tray-toure A. D. 1176.
Obreyn shewid opynly how we sholde trust to Iryssh-men trouth // *corpus*
Reymond, with al the meny, went to deuelyñ; and the Erlis body *comitis*
that by his byddynge was kepte vnburied [was buried] in þe modyr *fuerat re-*
church of the trynyte, to-for the Swete Rode, by procurynge of *servatum*
Seynt laurance, that was in that tyme Archebyschope of Deuelyn. *. . . in ec-*
*clesia . . .*
[CHAPTER XLV.]  *est tumu-*
*latum.*

A ftyr that the Erle was dede, the kynges mes- *Capitulum*
sangers, that weryn aftyr Reymond come, vpon new *xlvm.*
*Nota the*
aduentures toke new consail.  Thay lefte Reymond keper of *goodnys*
Irland, *and* thay went into Inglande hastely to the kynge, and tolde *of Geral-*
*dynes.*
hym of the Erle-is deth, *and* the state of the londe // The kynge *Nota de*
sende than into Irlnd, Willam Aldelinys Sone, Procuratoure of the *adventu*
*Willelmi*
londe, x. knyghtis of his owyn Pryue meny; And with hym Ihon de *Addellini*
Cursi, with othyr x; Robert Steuen-es [sone] *and* Miles de cogan, *Iohannis*
that al two yere in England' and in gascoyn nobely haddyn with *de Cursi,*
*in Hiber-*
the kynge be,come than Into Irland with xxti. knyghtis. Thythynges *niam.*
come to Reymond that thay ware londid'; *and* he anone-ryght went *¹ Super-*
agaynes ham with mych gladnys, *and* fayre felochipp of knyghtes, *biam*
*hanc, in*
to weysforde.  Ther he yaue to Willam, as to Senescal from the *brevi com-*
kynge sende, al the kynges townes, and his castelis, and al the *primam, et*
*clipeos*
hostages of Irland.  Willam Saw Reymond with so many and so *istos*
fayre yonglynges * Bylad, And Be-Helde Meyler and Othyr *dispergam.*
Knyghtes of His Kyn, fayre and riche wepenyd of o maner [*Fol. 21
a.]
wepyn, wel xxxti, vpon ful fayre hors, sheldys aboute har neckys,
*and* sperris in honde, Pleyynge to-gadderes in-to al the feldys.
He turned hym to his men, *and* sayde al softe, "This Pryde shal *Nota de*
be Put In ¹ ar hit be lange, and this sheldys to-dreued." Fro that *geraldinis.*
*Nota*
tyme euer aftyr, *and* thes *and* most al othyr procuratoures in *causam*
*invidie*
Irlnd, as thegh hit were by one othe to-giddyr Sworne, throgh *inter*
hate and envy ne stynte thay neuer to malyngne agaynys Reymond *aldelini*
*filium et*
*and* meyler, Robert-es Sonnes *and* Morices, and al the kynred of *geraldinos.*
geraldines, al the envy that thay myght *and* durste; for this is
euer-more har abydynge *and* har aduenture: Euer whan grete *Semper in*
nede bifel in tyme of werre, thay wer lefe *and* derwarde, *and* the *armata*
*militia*
fryst to be callid for bolnys, *and* to battail fryst redy; whan no *cari.*

A.D. 1176. anoon̄ thay wer̄ loth, & I-pute abake; her̄ felowshyp I-left yn̄ yurne
to harme.  Na the wodde of har̄ gentryce, throgh non enuy ne
myght neuer be I-rotet; for euer ham spryngyth new spourges, of
*Yet the* whych the myght yn the lond nys nat lytelle.  Who beth that 4
*Geraldines* kepeth the contreys? the Geraudynes: Who throgh þurleth the
*won and* hostes? the Geraudynes: Who ben that fomen adredeth? þe
*kept* Geraudines: Who ben that enuy bacbyteth? þe *Geraudines.*
*Ireland.*

*Had justice* Hade thay I-found prynce yn any tyme, that har̄ stalwarthnesse 8
*been done* ham had y-yold, as thay worthy wer̄, yn good pees & stydfast
*them,* hadden I-broght the state of Irland.  Bot thegh thay nededen
*they'd* neuer so well, thay ne hade bot lytele thanke, other̄ noon; har̄
*have held* trauaylle yuel I-yold, & ouerthrow yn har̄ goodnesse, & mysbeleue 12
*the land in* & bacbyttynge of har̄ stalwarthnesse; & to other̄, the prynces
*peace.* trysten, wyt whych no staluarthnese was I-founde, ne no power
hadde well to done without helpe & socour̄ of ham.  And also
*Fitz-* Aldelinese-sone, at hys comynge ynto Irland, he wente from toun to 16
*Audeline* toun vpon̄ þe see, & þrogh soght the Cyttes ther̄ plente was of
*sought his* mete & drynke; bot the monteynes, & þe londes with-In, nold he
*ease, and* neuer come negh̄. gold & syluyre, whar̄-of mych plente was yn þe
*opprest* lond, wel hungrylych he gaderede, to helpe-with pledynge & 20
*the poor,* pullynge of pees men, & nogh of theues ne of reuers.  In that
*not the* tyme, about myd-heruest, Moryce fyzt-Geraud deyed, nat without
*thieves.* gret Sorynesse of al hys, & mych harme & lost to al Irland; ffor
*Maurice* he was a man methefull, suttell, & stalwarth: trewer̄ man ne 24
*Fitz-* stydfaster man̄, ne left he non yn Irland.  ☾ Wyllyam adelinese-
*Gerald dies* sone ran Moryce sones to harme anon, & ne stynt neuer tyl he
*about Sept.* hadde I-take of hym þe Castel of Wykelowe wyth falsnesse.  of
*1.  No* Reymond & Robert steuenesse-sone, he name the londes that thay 28
*truer man* hadden yn the vale of dyuelyn & yn Ophelayn; & other̄ that
*was left in* hadden londes yn̄ pes, he name thay londes to the kynges behoud,
*Ireland.* & delyuered ham londes furthyre yn̄ marche, & yn perryll nexth
*Fitz-Aude-* har̄ fomen: al with vnryght, & by hys owne wyll; ffor ther̄ ys 32
*line robs* nothynge so bold ne so kene as ys that man̄ that ys of noght
*Maurice's* I-come, Whan he ys an-hegh̄ I-broght, & vnkyndely I-sette yn
*sons.* maystry.  ☾ Wyllyam was a man mych of body, & of makynge;

*No one is* 
*so keen as* 
*an upstart* 
*set to rule.* 

*good met-yeuer; fre & corteys by semblant; bot al that he dyde any 36

nede was anoon they were hatyd *and* Putte abake, her fellochip A.D. 1176.
left *and* turne to harme. // Na the wodd of har gentryce, throgh *Nota de*
non envy ne myght, neu*er* be y-roted, for eu*er* ham spryngyth *gerau-*
*dynes.*
new Spourgis, of whych the myght in the londe is not lytell.
What ben thay that kepyth the contrayes ? the Geraudynes.    Who *Qui sunt*
throw thurlyth the hostis ? the geraudines.    Who ben that Enemys *qui pene-*
*trant hostis*
dreddyth ? the geraudynes.    What ben thay that envy bacbityth ? *penetralia?*
the geraudines.    Hade thay found prynce in any tyme that har *Note the*
*harde ad-*
streynth ham wolde yeue, as thay worthy wer to haue / in good *venture of*
pees *and* stydfast thay haddyn broght the state of Irland.    But *Geraldines.*
thogh thay eu*er* so wel had done, thay hadd but lytyll change,
or noone, for her laboure.    But eu*er* thay profited in har goodnys ;
and mysbeleue and bacbitynge, of hare boldnys.    And to othyr
the Pryncis trystyn, wyth whych no boldnys was founde, ne
Power had wel to do / wi*th*-out helpe and Socoure of ham //
And also Aldelines Son*n*e, at his comynge into Irland, he went
from toun to tou*n* vpon the See-syde, *and* throw soght the Citteis *Nota quo*
ther Plente was of mette and drynke; but the montaynys *and* the *tempore*
*mortuus*
londe wi*th*-In, he wolde neu*er* come ney. / golde *and* sylu*er*, wherof *erat ille*
*Mauricius*
mych Plentey was in the lond, wel hungryly he gadderid to-giddyr, *geraldi*
wi*th* pledynge and Pullynge of peese men, *and* not of theuys ne of *filius.*
Robers.    In þat tyme about Mid-heruest, Morice fiz-geraud deyed, *Descripcio*
*Maurici fiz*
not wi*th*-out grette Sorrow of al his, *and* mych harme and loste*s* to *geraud.*
al Irlande // For he was a man meteful, Suttyl *and* bolde : trewer *(See p. 76.*
man, ne stydfastyr man, ne lefte he none in Irlande // Willam *7.)*
Aldelinys sone ran Morices sone to harme, *and* styntid neuer til he
hadd take of hym the castel of Wickelow wyth falsnes.    Of *fraudu-*
*lenter*
Reymond *and* of Robert Steuenes-sone, he toke the londys that *eripuit.*
thay hadd in the vale of Deuelyn, *and* in Ophelan; *and* othyr that
hadd londis in Pees, he toke thay londys to the kynges be-howe, ____
[1] *Asperius*
and delyuerid ham landys furthyr in Marche, *and* in Peril nexte *nihil est*
har enemys, al wi*th* vnryght *and* by his owyn will.    For ther is *humili,*
*cum surgit*
nothynge so bolde ne so kene, as is that man that is of noght come, *in altum.*
*Claud.*
whan he is an-hey broght, *and* vnkyndely sette in Maystry [1] // *Eutrop. i.*
Willam was a man mych of body *and* of makynge, good mete- *181.*
[*Fol. 21
* yeu*er*, fre and corteyse By Semblant.    But ale that He did any b.]

1

Bad char-
acter of
William
de Fitz-
Audeline.

to wyshype al hyt was yn spyinge, felonye, & trecherye; euer he
shedde attyr vndyr hony.  To-day he wold do the wyrshyp⁊,
to-morow he wold the reue & do shendshype; the meke & þe
lotles he vndedde, þe sterne & the hawtcyn he plessed; softe with 4
wyld men, & hard with pees men; of fayr spech, soft, fals,
trecheur; argh & enuyous, dronklewe & lecheour.

A. D. 1177.

[CHAPTER XLVI.]

John de
Courci sees
Fitz-
Audeline's
rascality.

Iohan de Courcy saw that al thynge that Willyam
dydde was couetise And  trecherye, & that he nas 8
nothynge trewe to ham that vndyr hym wer, ne dredlyche to
the mysdoynge.  he chase hym of the meygne of dyuelyn a few,
bot thay wer good & stalwarth & hardy throgh al thynge, so

He gets
troops from
Dublin;
invades
Ulster,

that he hadde xx^tiij knyghtes, fyfty squyers, & fotmen as myght 12
be by ccc, & went hym ynto Vlnester, whare non engeleshe-man
I-wepned to-for hym was I-seye.  Than was fulfylled a prophecye
of Merlyn, that thys seyd: "A whyt knyght, syttynge on a
whyt hors, berynge fowles yn hys sheld, shal formest assayll 16
Vlnestre."  Thys I hon was a man ful whyt, & rood þan vpon
a whyt hors, & bar yn hys sheld, ernes I-peynted.  he went hym
throgh Myth & throgh Vryel thre dayes goynge; & the forth

and takes
Down.
King Mac
Donlevy
flees.

day erlych, come to doune without any lete of any foman. 20
Vnwyttynge he come; In he wente. dyuelyn, the kynge, was
shorthlych a-fryght of so derne comynge, left the toun & flow; the
meygne, that was myssayse & hungry, fond ther mete & drynke
Inowe, & pylfre of gold & syluer & clothes, & eke whar-wyth thay 24
war wel arrayed, & har hert wel comforted.  Into the toun was

The Pope's
Legate,
Vivian,
tries to
get rid of
De Courci,

than I-come a legat of Rome, that hete Vyuyen, & was y-come out
of scotland.  Thys legat was youre aboute, pees to make betwene
the kynge & Iohn: myche he spake & mych he hym profred, & 28
more he behete, & trewage to beren euery yer to Englyssh-men, by
so that he wold the lond leue, & turne ayeyne.  Myche he spake
ther-of, & mych hym bysoght; bot noght he wold hym hyr, ffor hys

who means
to win or
die.

thoght was al I-turned, the lond for to wyn, or the lyf to forlese. 32
Donleue saw that he, wyth fayr spech ne fayr beheste, noght ne
myght spede; he sent anoon aftyr hys folke, & within the viij day
he gadered to-gyddyr an hoste of ten thousand men, stalwarth

to wyrchyppe, al Hit was in Spyinge, felony, and trechery; euer *Descripcio*
he shed Venym vndyr hony. Tho day he wolde do the wyrchipp; *Willelmi*
to-morrow he wolde the rew, *and* do shenshipp. the meke and the *Aldelmi.*
buxum he vndid; the sterne and hawteyn he Plesyd; Softe with
wylde men, harde with Pees men; of fayre spech, Softe, fals
trechoure; feynte *and* Envyous, dronklewe *and* lecherere.

[CHAPTER XLVI.]                          A. D. 1177.

IOhan de Cursy Saw that al thynge that willam did *Capitulum*
was couetyse and trecherye, and that he was nothynge *xlvj^m.*
trew to ham that vndyr hym were, ne dredfull to his enemys.
He chose hym of the meny of Deuclyn a few, but thay were good
*and* bolde, and hardy throgh al thynge, So that he hadd xxij^ti
knyghtis, fyfty Squyeres, *and* footmen as myght be by thre hundrid,
and wente hym to vllyster, whar noone Englysh-man wepenyd to-
for hym was seyn. Than was fulfillid a prophesy of merlynge, that *argent*
thus sayd: " a whyte knyght, syttynge on a whyte hors, berrynge *iij egles*
*dysplayed*
fowlis on his shelde, shal formyste assaylc vllystere." This Ihon *gules*
*crowned*
was a man ful whyte, and rode vpon a whyte hors, and bare in his *armed and*
shelde, ernys y-peyntyd. he went throw myth *and* throw Vriel thre *beaked*
*golde.*
dayes goynge; and the fourth day Erlych, come to doune, wythout
any lette of any enemy. Vn-wyttynge he come; In he wente.
Dunleue, the kynge, was schortlych agaste of so suddeyn comynge,
lefte the toun and flow; the mayny, that was myssaysid and
hungry, founde ther mette and drynke y-now, and Pylfre of
golde and Syluyr *and* clothis, *and* also wher-with thay wer wel
arrayed, and her herte wel confortid. In-to the toun was than
y-come a legate of Rome that was callid Vyuyen and was come *Romanae*
*sedis*
out of scotlonde. this legate was besy about, Pees to make *legatus.*
be-twen the kynge *and* Ihoñ. mych he spake, *and* mych he hym *multa*
*quidem*
proferid, *and* more he promysyd, *and* trewage to bere euery yere to *verba sua-*
Englyssh-men, So that he wolde the lond lewe, *and* turne agayn. *soria nec*
*persua-*
gretly her-of he spoke *and* be-soght; but noght he wolde hym hyre; *soria pro-*
For his thoght was al turned, the londe forto wynne, or his lyfe *ponebat.*
for-sake. Dounleue Saw that he, wyth fayre speche ne fayre [1] *se verbis*
promes, nothynge myght spede[1]. he send anoone aftyr his Pepill, *minime*
*profectu-*
and wyth-in viij^e dayes he gaddrid to-giddyr an hoste of x. M[1] *rum.*

I 2

<table>
<tr><td>Mac Don-<br>levy be-<br>sieges De<br>Courci in<br>Down.</td><td>to fyght, & besegete staluarthly the Cyte of doun þer Iohñ was In ;<br>for yn thys lond, as yn al otheꝛ, the northeren meñ ben stordyer &<br>smerteꝛ to fyght than other. Iohñ saw thay hostes comynge to<br>hym-ward : thegh he fewe weꝛ, natheles thay waꝛ al hardy & stal- 4<br>warth he chase ; & leuer hym was, out wend, & with streynth</td></tr>
</table>

De Courci      to assaye the aduenturs of battaylle, than yn the lytel feble fortelet
leaves his     that he yn & herne of the toun yn so lytel whyle hadde arerede,
corner of
the town,      amyd hys fomen, beseged & hungrod, deye.   He went hym out to 8
sallies out,   hard fyght : & whan thay hadde fyrste, from ferꝛ, I-suywed har
               arowes, thay smytten theꝛ aftyre hertelych to-gydder, sper ayeyne
fights         sper, swerd ayeyne sparth ; & many one the lyf ther forlese.   Bot
splendidly,    who hadde y-sey Iohnes dynttes with swerd, how he smote of þat man 12
               þe heed from the scholderes, that man the arme & þe shuldre from
[*Fol. 22      þe body, that man the heed I-clouen fer doun * ynto the body, he
b.]            myght wel sygge that hys myght & hys mayn oght wel be I-preysed.
backt well     Thegh many waꝛ yn thys fyght that stalwarthly dydden, natheles, 16
by Roger       Roger the power, that theꝛ-aftyr was of grete myght yn Osserye &
le Poer,       yn the Contrey of leghlyn, was the otheꝛ that best dydde.   Aftyr
and at last    grete fyght & lange, þat theꝛ was of wel vnlyche hostes, at þe laste
wins.          the Iresshe host was ouercome & I-scomfyte ; many I-slawe by the 20
               see strond whyder-ward they flowen : than was fulfylled a pro-
               phecye that Colmkylle seyde of thys fyght : he seyd, ' that so many
               meñ shold be I-slaw yn that place, that haꝛ fomen myght waden to
His men        the knees yn her blode.'  & so hyt was than ; ffor as thay flowen to-for 24
walk up        ham yn the slyme, thay folweden aftyr & slowen ham ; & as thay
to their
knees in       dyueden ̓adoun, the blode of ham that wareñ I-slawe, & fleted
Irish blood    abouen, toke to þe knee of ham that slowen ham.   The same
on the
slimy          prophete seyd also, 'that a pouere mane, & as thoght he weꝛ flow or 28
strand         banshed out of otheꝛ landes, with lytel folk shold come ynto doun [1],
[' ? dyn..]    & the toun wynne, wythout soccoure of any herrer '; & otheꝛ many
               fyghtes & aduentures of thynge that yn that contray shold betyde,
De Courci      whych al openly weꝛ fulfylled yn Iohn de Courcy.   That same 32
has his        boke, Ihon hadde an Iresshe I-wrytte, & was hym ther-aftyr as
Victory
written in     shewer of al hys dedys.   In the same boke was eke I-found, that
Irish.         a mañ with folke I-wepned shold, with strenynth, the walles of
               Waterford to-breken ; & with grette slaght of þe cytȝeynes, the toun 36

men, bolde to fyght / and besegyt boldely the Cite of doun ther
Ihon was In / For in this lond, as in al othyr, the nordryn men
ben sturdier *and* smyrtyr to fyght than othyr. Ihon Saw the
hostys comynge to-wardes hym, *and* chose; and lewyr was, out wende,
*and* wyth streynth to assay the aduentures of battayl, than in the
lytel feble fortelet, that he in *and* herne of the toun in so lytel
tyme hadd arrerid, amyd his enemys be be-segid, and to dey wit*h*
hungyr. he went out to hard fight. and when thay had fryste,
frome fer shote her arrowys, thay smytten aftyr hertely to-giddyr,
spere agaynys spere, Swerde agaynys Spare; *and* many there the
lyfe loste. But who had y-sey Ihonys strokys wyth Swerd, how
he smote Of that man the hede frome the sholdris, that man the
Arme and the shuldyr * frome the body, Hee myght wel Sey, that
His myght and His mayn oght Wel to be Praysid. Thegh many
wer in this fyght that boldely did, Natheles Rohere le Power, that
ther-aftyr was of gret myght in Ossory and in the contrey of
leghlyn, was the othyr that best did. Aftyr grete *and* lange
fyghtynge of wel vnlych hostis [1], at the last, the Irysh hoste was
ouercome *and* scomfited, *and* many slayne by the strondis syde
whedyr thay flowe / than was fulfillid a prophesy that colmekyl [2]
Sayde of this fyght. He sayde, 'that So many men sholde be slayn
in that Place, that har enemys myght wadyn to the knees in her
blode' / And so hit was than. For as thay fleddyn to-for ham in
the Slyme, thay folwedyn aftyr and kyllid ham; and as thay
dyuedyn done, the blode of ham that weryn slayne, *and* fletid
abow, toke to the knees of them that ham Slayne. The same
Prophet sayde also, 'that a pou*er*e man, and as thegh he were flow
or banshed but of othyr landys, wit*h* ly*t*el folke sholde come to
doune, and the toune wynne wyth-out Soccoure of any herrer'; and
othyr many fightes and aduentures of thynge that in that contray
sholde befalle, whych al opynly wer fulfillid in Iho̅n de Cursy.
That same boke, ther-aftyr had Ihon de Cursy on Irysh writte,
*and* was to hym ther-aftyr as merrowre of al his dedys. In þe
sayde boke is also fovnde, that a man wit*h* pepil wepenyd, sholde
wit*h* streynth the wallis of watyrford breke; *and* wit*h* grete slaght

[1] *nimis impari certamine.*
[2] *per mariuamglinim.* [2] *Hibernici Kolumbae. Prae glisis namque mollitie, dum ad ima penetraret humana ponderositas, terrae lubricie sanguis profluus superficiem tenens, genua cruraque de focili pertinge- bat.*

quam erili municipio, quod in urbis angulo tenuiter erexerat.

A.D. 1177. wyñ; & fro thennes, by Weysford, wend to dyuelyn without any
St. Colum-
ba's pro- letto; & þe cytè wyn: & al þis ys found fulfylled of the Erl: he
phecies seyd eke 'that the Cytè of lymeryke shold of Englysshe-men shold
fulfild by
De Courci. be twyes I-lefte, & at the thrydde tyme y-hold': & so hyt was, on 4
tyme of Reymond, another of phylepe de Bruse, as hyt openlyer shal
be I-shewed yn hys own place. Ther-of þe prophecye was thys
y-seyd, 'þe cytè thrise I-soght, at þe thryd tyme shal be I-hold.'

De Courci Twey grete fyghtes, Iohñ ther ledde & wan at doun; that oon aftyr 8
had Fights
1. and 2. at candelmase, as hyt ys I-told, þat other at mydsomyre, wher he, wyth
Down; fewe men, ouercome the battaylle of fyftene thousand, & slow of ham

3. at Fir- ful many. The þrydde was at ferly at a pray-takynge: thar thay
lee, where come throgh a narowe pas, and hadde so styf fyght, & so stronge, that 12
he was
beaten; hys meñ was, some y-slawe, & the oþer dele so dyscomfyte ynto
al þe woddes, that vnneth ther be-left hym wyth aleueth
thousandc; & he, as man wonderly stalwarth, with so fewe wyth
hym, whan thay hadde har hors I-loste, thay went a-fote al 16
y-wepned: a xxxti myl weye thay helden the fyght of har fomen; &
twey dayes & two nyght thay waŕ fastynge, tyl thay come to hys

4. at Uriel; castel. The ferth fyght was yn vryel; ther many of hys weren
5. at Newry I-sley, & the oþer descomfyte, & put ham to flyght: the fyfte at 20
Bridge. yueres brygge, as he come wyth fewe men out of England;
natheles, ther he ouercome, & slowe ful many, & come hol & sond to
hys owne. Thus yn thre grete fyghtes he wan the ouer-hand;
& yn twey, thegh he harme tholled, he dydde hys fomen mych 24

Jn. de more. Iohn was a man whyte & fayre; of lymmes bony & synowy;
Courci
described. mych of body; non hardyer than he, stalwarth, & fyghter stronge of
yought; yn euery fyght the fyrst, & the meste perrylle he wold

[*Fol. 23 * euer be In; he was so coueytouse of fyght, & so bernynge whan he 28
a.]
He loved hoste lad, & come to fyght, that he neuer wold hym hold as ledeŕ,
fighting, bot wyth the fyrst wold yn smyte, som whyle behynd, theŕ most
and often
attackt his perrylle was, that oft al the oste was the vnredyeŕ, and thoght that
foe in rear. thay wer ouercome, and al hadden forlore: & thegh he weŕ yn 32
wepne vnmetly stordy, & sterne, out of wepne natheles, he was
meke and sobre, & mych wyrshypped god & holy chyrche, & yn al
thynge he leuet god and hys seruyce; & al that hym betyd, he
thanked god that hym the grace sent. He spoused Godefreys 36

of the Citteseynes, the toun wyn : And al this fund fulfillid of the A. D. 1177.
Erle.   He sayde also that the Cite of lymeriko, of Englysh-men ab Anglo-
twyes sholde be lefte, and the thyrdo tymo sholde bo holde.   And *rum gente*
*bis dese-*
So hit was, on tymo of Reymonde, a-nothyr of Phylip de bruse, *rendam, et*
*tertio reti-*
as hit opynlyer shal be shewid in his owyn Place.   Therof the *nendam.*
prophesy was thus sayde : " The Cite thryse soght, at the thyrde
tymo shal bo holdo," Two greto fyghtis, Ihon ther abode, *and* ham
ouercomyd' at doun / that oone aftyr candylmasse, as hit is tolde /
that othyr, aftyr mydsomer, wher he, with few men, did ouercome (June 24.)
tho battail o xv. M$^t$, *and* Slayne of ham ful many.  The thyrd was
at ferly, at a pray takyn : thar thay come throw a narrow Paas, and *in praedae*
had so styfe fyght, that his men was, some slayne, *and* othyr Part so *captione.*
descomfite in-to al the woddys, that vnneth with hym was lefte M$^t$ ;
and he, as man woundyrly bolde, with so few with hym, Whan *Ipse vero,*
thay hadd har hors loste, thay went afoote al wepenyd : xxx$^{ti}$ myle *vir virtutis*
*invictae,*
wey thay heldyn the fyght of har ennemys; *and* two dayes and *cum tan-*
*tilla*
two nyghtes thay wer fastynge, til thay come to his castel. the *suorum*
iiij$^e$ fyght was in Vriel, ther many of his were slayn, and the othyr *paucitate.*
dyscomfite, and Put ham to flyght ; the v. fyght at yuores bryge, as *apud pon-*
*tem Ivori.*
he come with few men out of England.   natheles, ther he ouercome,
and slayne ful many, and come hole and Sounde to his owyn.
Thus in thre greto fyghtis he had the ouer-hande; *and* in two, *Descripcio*
*Iohann[is]*
thegh ho loste the ouer-hand, ho did his enemys mych more // *de Curcy.*
Ihon was a man whyte *and* fayre ; of lymmes, bony and * Synowy ; [*Fol. 22
b.]
myche of Body ; noone Hardier than Hee ; Bolde, and fyghter *vir fortis*
*et bellator*
*ab adoles-*
strongo of youth : in euery fyght the fryst, and the meste peril
he wolde euer be In / he was So covetouse of fyght, and So *centia.*
bernynge whan ho hoste ladd, *and* come to fyght, that he hym
neuer wolde holde as ledere, but with the fryste wolde smyte, *ducem*
*exuens, et*
Sumtyme be-hynnde, ther more Peril was, that ofte al the hoste *militem*
was the vnredyer, and thoght that thay wer ouercome, and al *induens.*
haddyn for-lore.   And thegh ho were in wepyn vnmetly sturdy *in armis*
*immode-*
and Sterne, Out of wepyn natheles ho was meke and sobyr, *and* *ratus.*
mych vyrchippid god and holy church, and in al thyng he lowid
god *and* his seruice ; and all that hym befel, he thankyd good that
hym the grace sende.   He Spousyd Godfredes doghtyr, the kyngo

A. D. 1177.

At last,
De Courci
overcame
all foes.

Not one of
the 4 great
Pillars of
the Con-
quest of
Ireland
had a child. doghter, the kynges of Mane; & aftyr many selcouth battaylles that
he dydde, nat wythout grete labour & perrylle of lyf & myche
myssayse, at the last he was all aboue, & clenlych hadde ouercomen.
He casteled the lond yn couenable places, & such pes made, that non 4
better ne myght be, ne stedfaster. Bot gret wonder ys, & nat bot
as god hyt wold, that thay four grete postès of the conquest of
Irland, namely, Robert steuenes-sone, heruy of Mountynorthy,
Reymon le Gros, and Ihon de Courcy, mythten neuer haue 8
chyldren of her spoused wyues. Thus mych we haue shortly I-told
of Ihon de Courcy; & the other parte of hys stalwarth gestes,
we leueth to wryte to other that ham wrytte wyllen, & turneth
ayeyne ther we afore lefte.    12

[CHAPTER XLVII.]

The Legate
Vivian
holds a
Synod at
Dublin,
March 13,
in Henry
II's favour, Wiuyen, that in-to Irlande was legat I-comen,
     come to dyuelyn; theder he made come to-for
hym al the bysshoppes & the clergye of Irland & held hys senne.
ther he shewed openly the kynges ryght of Engelond to Irland, 16
& the popes graunt, & hys confyrmacion; &, vp mansynge, forbed
lered & lewed, that non neuere so hardy to comen ayeyns the
kynges trouth. &, fore the Iresshe-men wer I-woned to don al
and gives
the English
leave to
take food
from
churches. har vytayllys yn chyrches, he yawe the Englysshe-men leue, that 20
whan me ladde hostes, & myghten nowher elles wytayll fynd,
that yn chyrch war I-found, me shold hardyly out take, & ycue
the kepers of the chyrch the worth, as ryght wer.

[CHAPTER XLVIII.]

Miles de
Cogan with
500 men,
invades
Con-
naught. Aftyr that, Miles de Cogan, that vnder Aldelinesse- 24
     sone was keper & conestable of dyuelyn, wyth fowrty
knyghtes, of whych Rolf, Robertes sone, fytz-esteuene, was one,
I-sette mayster ouer ham vnder Myles, & two hundret other
an hors, & thre hundret bowmen, passeden the water of shynnen, 28
& wentten ynto Connaght, whar Englesshe-men was neuere er
The Irish
take to
earth-
houses,
and burn
their
buildings. comen. The men of Connaght wer I-ware of har comes; thay
drowen ham ynto erth-hous many; & al the vytaylle that thay
ne myght nat take wyth ham, thay put yn chyrches; & tounnes & 32
chyrches thay setten al afyr & branten. & yn despyte of the Englesshe-men, & yn hope þat god shold take wrech of ham, thay toke

of man ; *and* aftyr many Selchouth battalys that he did, not A. D. 1177.
wyth-out grete laboure *and* Peril of lyfe *and* mych myssayse, And *tandem in*
at the last he was al abow, *and* clenly hadd ouercome. He *arce vic-*
*torine*
castelid the londe in behowabyll Placys; and Suche Pes made, *plene*
*constitutus.*
that noone bettyr ne myght be, ne stydfastyr. But hit is grete
wondyr, and not but as god hit wolde, that thay iiij⁰ grete Postes *hi grandes*
of the conqueste of Irland, Namely, Robert Stéuenes-sone, heruey *exjugmi-*
*lionis*
of Mountmorthy, Reymond le gras / and Ihon de Cursy, myghten *Hibernicae*
*postes.*
neuer haue childe of her Spousyd wyues / Thus mych we haue
Shortely tolde of Ihon de Curcy ; And the othyr Parte of his
bolde gestis, we lewyth to write to otheres that ham write wille,
And turnyth agayñe ther we afore lefte.

[CHAPTER XLVII.]

Vluyen, that into Irland was legate, come to deuelyn : *Capitulum*
*xlvij^m.*
thedyr he made come to-for hym al the bischopis and *conencata*
the clergy of Irland, *and* heldo his Senne. ther he Shewid opynly the *Dubliniae*
kyngis ryght of England to Irland, and the Popis gruunte and *episco-*
*porum*
his confirmacion ; *and*, vpon Payn of Cursynge chargid both lerrid *synodo.*
and lewyd, that noone neuer so hardy to come agaynys the kyngis
trouthe. And, for the Irysh-men wer wonyd to do al har vitalys *ad eclesi-*
in churchis, he yaue the Englysh-men leue, that whan thay ladd *arum*
*refugia*
hostis, *and* myght no vytalis ellys fynde, that that in church were *victualia*
founde, thay sholde hardely out-take, *and* yeue the keperes of the *transfer-*
*rentur.*
church the worthe, as ryght were.

*Capitulum*
*xlviij^m.*
[CHAPTER XLVIII.]

Aftyr that, Miles de Cogan, that vndyr aldelines-sone was *¹⁻¹ urbibus*
*undique et*
keper and constabil of Deuelyn, with xl. knyghtes, of wych *villis igne*
*proprio*
Rolfe, Robert-es sone, fitz-Steuen, was one, y-sette Maystyr ouer ham *combustis;*
vndyr Milis, and two C an hors, CCC bowmen, Passyd the watyr of *alimentis*
*quoque*
Shynnyñ, *and* went Into Connaght / wher englysh-men was neuer *cunctis,*
*quae*
therto-forne. The men of connaght wer y-ware of har comynge / *hypogeis*
¹ thay drew ham into Erthe-hous many; and al þ⁰ wytalis that thay *subter-*
*raneis*
ne myght take with ham, thay Put in churches; *and* touñes *and* *absconderе*
*non pote-*
churches thay sette afyre and brantyn ¹. and in dyspyte of the *rant, simul*
englysh-men, *and* in trust that god wold do vengeauce on ham, thay *cum eccle-*
*siis igne*
*consumptis.*

A.D. 1177. þe rodes crucyfyed, & ymages of halowen, & kesten to-for ham ynto

The English advance to Tuam, but find no food, and retreat safely to Dublin, beating King Roderic of Connaught on the way.

al the feldes.  The Englesshe meygne wentten tyl thay come to tuen, & ther thay abodde viij dayes yn bare lond & blote.  And whan thay myght no mane fynd, ne nothynge wher-by thay myght 4 lyue, thay turned ayeyne to the shynnen. ther thay found ayeyns ham, Oconghour yn a wodde, wyth thre grete hostes. the Engelesshe boldly smytten vpon ham, & slowe of ham ful many, passeden on, & come to dyuelyn al sound, out-tak þre men, that yn that fyght 8 weren I-lefte.

[CHAPTER XLIX.]

Fitz-Audeline goes back to England. He got Jesus's Crosier to Dublin.

[*Fol. 23 b.]

Hugh de Laci and Robert le Poer come to Ireland.

Miles de Cogan and Robert Fitz-Stephen get Cork. Philip de Bruse has Limerick.

They force peace on Dermot Mac-Carthy, and divide the town-lands near Cork.

Sone ther aftyr, Aldelinessone was I-sent aftir ynto Engelonde, that no good yn Irland dydde bot oon, that, by procurynge of hym, an holy baghell & of 12 grete vertue, that me cleped Ihesus baghel, was I-broght from Ardmagh to dyuelyn, & yet ys at the chyrch of the Try-nyte : & come * ynto Irland Hugh de Lacy, heye Seneshal of al the lond, & Robert de Power wyth hym, Conestable of Water- 16 ford.  Myles de Cogan & Robert steuenesson wentten also ouer the see ynto Engeland; bot thay comen sone ayeyne, & phylepe de Bruse wyth ham ; & hadde the kynge I-yeuen ham thre, al the lond of Desmond.  Robert & Myles hadden the south Con- 20 trey, that ys to wytten, from lysmore al aboute Corke vii Cantredes, saue the kynge the Cytè of Corke, wyth þe next cantrede.  Phylype de Bruse, the kynge yaf al the Controy of lymeryke, saue the Cytè & hys next cantred : these thre I-feffed 24 to-gedder, come ouer ynto Irland yn o felewshyppe, & arryueden at Waterford, & fro thennes thay wentten to Corke al harmles. Thay war thar fayr receyued of þe Cytteyns, & of a knyght that was keper of the Cytè, that hete Rychard of Londone.  Whan 28 thay hadde I-broght to pees Demot Mac charthy, prynco of desmone, & other many of the contrey of moche power, Robert and myles deled betwen ham the vij cantredes next the Cytè ; & felle by lot[1] to Robert, thre on the eeste syde ; Myles, four yn the weste ; 32 mo to the on than to the other, for the lond was wors ; the kepynge of the Cytè comune to ham bothe ; the renth & the trywage

¹ MS. bot.

toke tho roodys crucyfied, *and* ymagis of Sayntis, *and* kesten to-for  A. D. 1177.
ham into al the feldys.   The Englis-men wentyn tyl thay come to   ¹ *in hostili*
tuem, And ther abode viij dayes in bare * Londe ande Blote ¹.  And   *terra.*
                                                                      [*Fol. 23
When thay myght no man fynde, ne nothynge Wherby thay myght   *a.*]
lyue, thay turned agayn to the Shynnyn.  ther thay found agaynys  *terram*
                                                                  *alimentis*
ham / Oconghoure in a wodde, *with* thre grete hostis.  The  *vacuam*
englysh boldely smytten vpon ham, *and* Slow of ham ful many,  *inveniens.*
                                                               *tribus*
Passyd ou*er*, and come to Deuelyn al sounde, out-take thre men  *tantum*
                                                                 *arcuriis*
that in that fyght weryn lefte. /                                *amissis.*

### [CHAPTER XLIX.]

SOne theraftyr, aldelines Sone was sende aftyr in-to  *Capitulum*
    England, that no good in Irland didde but oone,  *xlix^m.*
                                                                   *baculum*
that, by procurynge of hym, an holy baghel and of grete Vertu, that  *virtuosissi-*
                                                                      *mum, quem*
is callid Iesu*s* ² baghel, was broght frome Ardmagh to Deuclȳu, and  *baculum*
                                                                      *Jesu*
yet is at the Trynyte church //  And come Into Irland' Hugh de  *vocant.*
lacy, hey Seneschal of al the londe ³, And Robert de Power with hym  ² *generalem*
                                                                       *Hiberniae*
Constable of watyrford, Miles de Cogan *and* Robert S[t]euenes-Sone  *procura-*
wentyn ou*er* the See also in-to England; but thay comyn Sone  *torem.*
agayn, and Philip de bruse *with* hame, and the kynge yaue ham
thre al the londe of Desmonde.  Robert and Miles haddyn tho
South contrey, that is to Say, from lysmore al aboute Corke, vij°
candredes, Saue the kynge the Cite of Corke, *with* the nexte
candrede; Philip de Bruse the kynge yaue al þe contrey of
lymerik, Saue the Cite and his nexte Candrede: thes thre, feffyd  *Trans-*
                                                                   *euntes*
to-giddyr, come ou*er* Into Irland in oo fellochipp, and londyn at  *igitur in*
                                                                     *Hiberniam*
Watyrford, and fro thens thay wenten to Corke al harmeles.  Thay  *meuse*
wer thar fayre rescewyd of the Cittescynys, and of a knyght that  *Novembri,*
                                                                   *cum tri-*
was keper of the citte, that was callid Richarde of london.  Whan  *plici fa-*
thay hadd broght to pees Dermot Maccarthy, Prince of Desmon, and  *milia, tres*
                                                                    *riri con-*
othyr many of the contrey of mych Powere, Robert and Miles delid  *feodati*
betwen ham the vij Candredes nexte the Cite; and fell by lotte to  *simul et*
                                                                    *confoe-*
Robert, thre on the Este syde ; Miles foure in the weste : mo to the  *derati.*
on than to the othyr, for the londe was wors ; the kepynge of the
Cite comȳn to ham both.  the rent and the triwage of the othyr

A Cantred is 100 townlands.

Robert Fitz-Stephen, Miles de Cogan, and Philip de Bruse go to Limerick.

Philip ought to attack Limerick, but funks it, and retreats: he has such a set of scamps in his force.

ofi the otheꝛ fouꝛ & xx cantredes, as hyt wold falle, euyn to dele betwen ham : & ys a cautrede to sygge, an hundret toꝛ lond. Whaꝛ thys was I-doꝛ, thay wentten wyth Phelype to lymeryke. Robert hadde wyth hym xxxᵗⁱ knyghtes & lxᵗⁱ sweynes; Myles, xxᵗⁱ 4 knyghtes & fyfty squyers; Phelype, xxᵗⁱ knyghtes & xlᵗⁱ squyers; & fotmen wyth euery of ham ful many: they came to the Cytè, & noght was betweꝛ ham bot the watyre of the shynneꝛ; & Robert & Myles baden Phylepe to wend ouer & assaylle the 8 toun; othyr, yf hym leuer weꝛ, to reꝛ hym a castele vpon the same watyre afor the toun. Phelepe, thegꝛ he knyght wer stalwarth & hardy yn hym selue, natheles, throgꝛ feble consaylle of ham that wyth hym, weꝛ he chase; & mych leuer hym was, leue 12 the Contrey, & harmles turne ayeyne to hys owꝛ, Than amonge so many fomeꝛ & so fer londes, yn so grete perrylle to abydde; & that no wondeꝛ nas, thegꝛ hym yn thyke vyage mys byfelle, that so many lyddeꝛ men, theues, & manslaghtres of the marche 16 of Wales—& thay to-fore al other—hadde I-chose & I-draw to hys felewshyppe. Noght lange ther-aftyr, Meredus, Robertes sone, yonge knyght & stalwarth, nat wyth-out myche wepynge & sorow

The Council of Lateran, March 1179, 3 eclipses in 3 years

ofi many, deyed yn the Cytè of Corke. That whylle, was I-hold 20 at Rome the consaylle ofi latran, that meꝛ so moche speketh of, vonder the pope Alyxsandyꝛ the thyrdde. & was wyth-yn thre yeꝛ, thre eclypses of the sone. ❡ Whaꝛ Robert steuenessoꝛ &

Miles de Cogan and his son-in-law go to Lismore,

Myles of Cogane, wel fyfe yeyr, al desmone yn good pees haddeꝛ 24 to-gyddyꝛ I-holde, Myles & hys Othome Rauf, Robertes soꝛ, that a lytyll ther-to-fore hadde hys doghteꝛ I-spoused, wentten to the contrey of lysmor, to hold parlement wyth ham of Waterford. & as thay sateꝛ yn the feldes abydynge aftyr ham, 28 Mactyr, that theder was wyth ham I-come, & wyth whom thay

and are treacherously slain, by Mac Tire.

sholdeꝛ that nyght[1] be I-herbrowed, vnwyttyngly smoꝛ vpon ham behynd, & ham both, wyth fyue otheꝛ knyghtes, theꝛ slowen wyth sparthes; & otheꝛ fewe that wer wyth ham vnneth escaped. 32

The Irish [* Fol. 24 a.] then rebel.

Throgꝛ that thynge, al the contrey forth theꝛ-aftyꝛ worth so I-storbet, that Demot Maccarthy & al the hegh men of * the contray, forth wyth Mactyre, ayeyne har trouth, wyth-droweꝛ ham

---

[1] MS. myght.

foure *and* xx<sup>ti</sup> candredes, as hit wolde fulle, euen to dele be-twen
ham // And a Candrede is as myche to Say as, an hundrid toun-
londe // Whan this was don, thay wentyn wit*h* Philip to Lymerike.
Robert had wyth hym xxx<sup>ti</sup> knyghtes and xl. Squyeres ; Miles, xx<sup>ti</sup>
knyghtes, l. Squyeres; and Philip, xx. knyghtys *and* xl. Squyeres; *and*
footmen wit*h* euery of ham ful many.  Thay came to the Cite, and
noght was betwen ham but the watyr of the Shynnyn.  And Robert
and Miles badyn Philip wende ou*er*, and assayle the toun ; Othyr,
yf hym leuer were, to rere hym a castel vpon the same watyr afor
the toun.  Philip, thegh he was knyght bolde and hardy in hym-Selfe,
natheles, 'throgh febil consail of them that wyth hym, were he chose ;
*and* myche leuer hym was, leue the contrey, *and* harmeles turne
agayn to his owyn, Then amonge so many enemys, *and* in so fere
londys, in So grete Peril to abyde ¹. and that no wondyr nas, thegh
hym in thylke vyage mys-be-felle, that 'So many wyckyd men, con-
dicon*es* and manequelleres of the marche of Walis (*and* thay to-for
al othir) hadd y-chose and y-draw to his fellochipp.  Not longe
theraftyr, Meredus, Rober[t]es-sone, yonge * Knyght *and* Bolde, not
wit*h*-out mych wepynge *and* Sorrow of many, Dyed in the Cite of
Corke.  That tyme, was holde at Rome ³ the consail of latran, that
men of mych Spekyth, vndyr the Pope Alysandyr the thyrde.  *and*
was wit*h*in iij<sup>e</sup> yere, iij<sup>e</sup> Eclipsis of the Sonne⁴.  Whan Robert
Steuenes-Sone and Miles de Cogan, wel v<sup>e</sup> yere al Desmond in good
pees hadden to-gaddyr holde, Miles, *and* his Sone-in-law, Raufe,
Robert-es Sone, that a lytel thertofore to his doghtyr had spousid,
wenten to the contrey of lysmore, to holde Parlement wit*h* ham of
watyrforde. and as thay Satyn in the feldys abydynge aftyr ham, Mactyre, that thedyr wit*h* hame was come, *and* wit*h* whome thay sholde
be that nyght logide, Vnwyttyngly Smote vpon ham ; and ham both,
wyth v. othyr knyghtes, thay Slayn wyth Sparres; *and* othyr few that
were wit*h* ham, vnneth escapid.  Throght that thynge, al the contrey
was in were, So that Dermot Maccarthy and al the hey men of the
Contrey forth wit*h* Mactyre, agayn*e* har trouth, wit*h*drowen al frome

*Margin notes (Latin):*

Quid est candreda. *tanta terrae portio, quanta centum villas continere solet.*

¹—¹ *pusillanimi tamen suorum consilio. potius indemnis ad sua reverti, quam in terra tum hostili tamque remota fortunae tentare pericula praecelegit.*

[* Fol. 23 b.]

² *viros homicidas, seditiosos ac flagitiosos.*

³ *sedit Romae.*

⁴ *non generales tamen, sed partiales.*

A. D. 1182.

*improvisis a tergo securium ictibus sunt interempti.*

A. D. 1182. al from the Englysshemeñ, & turned vpoñ Robert steuenes-sone,

Robert Fitz-Stephen is attackt by Irish rebels. (The North Irish are true, and fight; the South are false, and trick.) that oft hadde harde happes assayed; & neuer eft, tyl Reymond to hym come, and helpe hym for to wyn the londe & worth to herytage; ffor Robert ne myght nat pees haue, as he rather hadde. 4 As the northren me[n] loueth fyght, also the southren, falsness; thay trusteth to streynth, these to sleghtes; thay to staluarth-nesse, these to traysoune. Whan Reymond herd that Robert was so narow byladde yn the toun of Corke, wyth hys fomen al 8 about beseget, he put hym to shyppe yn the hauen of Watyrford,

Reimund Fitz-Gerald sails to Cork to help him. wyth xxti knyghtes & squyers, & bowmeñ, wel ccc; leftene the lond al oñ the ryght hond, & wentten about by the see, fort he come to Cork, to gaddre hele to hys frendes, & vnhele to hys 12 fomen. Aftyr many & selcouth camplynges, many of hañ fomeñ

They put down the rebellion. thay slow, & many out of contray thay dryueñ, & the moste parte & the beste come to pees; & so the grete tempeste of that weddyñ hupe, yn lytel whyle was I-queynt & I-stylled. 16

---

A. D. 1182-3.

[Chapter L.]

There come to Ireland, Richard de Cogan in 1182; and in 1183, Philip de Barry, and Giraldus Cambrensis, who wrote 3 books on Ireland.

Nat longe theñ aftyñ, come into Irland Richard de Cogan, Miles brother, wyth faiñ meygne from the kynge I-sent; & theñ-aftyñ, yn the begynnyge of Marce, come Phylype de barry, a mañ slegħ & staluarth, wyth moch 20 folk & fayñ, both for to help Robert & Reymond, & foñ to castely hys lond of Olethane, whych Robert hym hadde I-yeue; and yn the same flot come Maystyñ Geraud, that phelypees 24 brotheñ & Robertes neueu, ful good clerk, & a mañ that al the conqueste, & þe state, & þe wondres of Irland, & the kyndes of pepel from the begynnynge, ful Inly soght & oft greped, & thre bokes theñ-of maked wyth grete trauayl, sywo yeñ that he was

Hervey of Mountmaurice turns monk. theñ. about that tyme, heruy of Mountnorthy yeldet hym monke 28 at crystes chyrch yn cantyrbery, to whych he hadde thar-to-forne I-yeue hys chyrches of hys lond be Waterford & Weys-ford. Wold god that he hadde I-chaunget hys culuertnesse and he dydde hys knyghthode, and trecherye as he dydde hys 32 clothynge[1].

---

[1] Qui utinam sicut habitum, sic et animum, sicut militiam sic et malitiam deposuisset.—Gir. Camb. Op. v. 352.

the Englysh-men, and turned vpon Robert Steuenes-Sone, that ofte A. D. 1182.
had harde Aduenturis assayed ; and neuer efte, til Reymond to hym *donec Rei-*
*mundus, in*
come *and* helpyd hym forto wyn the londe *and* broght to heritage ; *heredi-*
*talem*
For Robert ne myght not pees haue, as he radyr hadd. As the *patruo Ste-*
northeryn men lowyth fyght, also the Southeryñ, falsnys : [1] thay *phanúlae*
*succedens,*
trustyth to Streynth, thes to sleghtes ; thay to boldnys, thes to *urbis*
*custodiam*
traysone [1] // When Reymonde herd that Robert was So narrow by- *solus*
ladde in the toun of corke, wyth his Ennemys al about besegid, he *obtinuit,*
*[nec tunc*
Put hym to shipp in the hawyn of watyrword' with xx. knyghtes and *plene] pris-*
*tinam*
Squyeris *and* bow-men wel CCC, leften the londe al on the ryght *pacem*
hande *and* wentyn aboute by the See, fort he come to corke, to *recupe-*
*ravit.*
gretto gladnys to his frendis, *and* Sorrow to his ennemys. Aftyr
many *and* selcouth Camplyngys, many of har enemys thay haue
Slayne, *and* many out of contray thay dryuen; and the meste Parte
*and* the beste come to Pees ; and Só the grete tempeste of that
weddyr hapid, in lytil whyle was broght to an [2] ende. /

[CHAPTER L.]                                                   A. D. 1182.

NOt longe ther-aftyr, come Into Irland Richard *Capitulum*
de Cogan, Miles-is brothyr, with fayre maynny *l.*
fromo the kynge y-Sende, and ther-aftyr, in the begynnynge of A. D. 1183.
Marce, come Philip do barry, a man sley and bolde, wyth mych
pepill *and* fayre, forto helpe both Robert *and* Reymond, and forto
castel his londe of olethane, whych Robert hym hade yeue. And *et alius*
*Stepha-*
in the same flytte come Maystyr Geraude, that Philippes brodyr *nidae*
*nepos*
and Robert-is Eme, ful good clerke, *and* a man that al the conquest *Philip-*
*pique*
*and* the state and the wondris of Irland, and the kynde of Pepill *frater,*
from the begynnynge, ful Inwardly soght, and thre bokys therof *tam avun-*
*culum*
makyd wyth grette trauayll, v. yere that he was ther-aboute // *quam*
*fratrem*
About that tyme, Heruey of Montmorthy yeldyd hym monke at *plurimum*
crystes church in cantyr-berry, to whych he had therto-forne yeue *consilio*
*juvans.*
his churchis of his lond betwen Watyrforde * And Weysforde. [*Fol. 24
Wolde god that he hadd y-chaunged His culuertnesse as he didd *a.]*
his knyghthode, and his trayson as he didd his clothynge //

---

[1]–[1] Illa laudis, haec fraudis cupida ; illa Martis, haec artis ope confisa ; illa
viribus nititur, hace versutiis ; illa praeliis, haec proditionibus.—*Op.* v. 350.
[2] and, MS.

A. D. 1177.
Hugh de
Laci castles
Leinster
and Meath,

and makes
such peace
that men
till their
land.

He so
attracts
the Irish,
that he is
suspected
of aiming
to be their
King.

A. D. 1181.

John,
Constable
of Chester,
and
Richard de
Pec arrive.
[* Fol. 42
b.]

Many
castles
are built.

Meiler
Fitz-Henry
gets Kil-
dare, but
changes it
for Leix.

The while that this was thus in Desmone I-done,
Hugh de Lassy, as man that queynth was &
staluarth, both leynester & meth [1] nobely casteled, & yn many
places ther other faylled to-for hym ; & fayn was about, to setten 4
yn har londes, Thay that wyth streynth & vnryghtly weren out
I-dryue, both englysshe & Iresshe ; so that, yn lytyll stond, was
so good pees that men arreden & tylleden har londes, and the
lond ynto al wel I-stored wyth corne. he drogh to hym 8
slegthlych, wyth wyrsshype doynge, & stydfaste forward makynge,
the heghest of the lond folk ; from place ·to place byled the
lond wyth castel ; & yn lytyll whyll, so good pees made, toke
of other, & auaunced hys owne ryuely, & rych ham maked. 12
The folk of Irland, wyth frenesse & sleghtes, drogh so, & allyed
to hym, that men hadden grete ortrow vpon hym, that he, ayeyne
the kynge & hys owne trouth, wold make hym self kynge I-crouned
of the lond. As thys was, & mych spech yn [         ][2] of thys 16
thynge, comon ynto Irland twey knyghtes from the kynge I-sent,—
that oon heet Ihon, the conestabel of chestre, & that other,
Rychard of the pek,—for to receyue the kepynge of Irland, & that
hugh shold wend ouer ynto Englond to the kynge ; both har[3] he 20
ouer went, by comyn red of ham al, thay arrereden yn that
somyr many castells yn leynester ; ffor ar that, Myth * was wel
castelled, & leynestre bot lytyl. Thar þay rereden a castel to
Reymond, yn forthred Onolan ; Another to Gryffyne hys brother; 24
the thyrde, yn Omurthy, to Water de rydlesford a kylka ; the ferth,
to Iohn the herford, at Tyllagh yn felmeth, & other many.
Meyller hadde that tyme kyldar of the erles yifte, & the contrey
about ; bot that me toke of hym for oo coste, & yaf hym þe 28
contray of leys as yn chaunge. for hyt was smert lond, woddy,
& of Marche, & ferr, me sette hym thar as man of marche,
that I-nowe couth theron.

---

[1] MS. moch.

[2] Space left for a word. A later hand has written something which is
illegible. The Latin has only 'fama': see opp. and Gir. Camb. Op. v. 355.

[3] but ere : Sed antequam.

[Chapter LI.]

The Whyle that this was thus dōne in desmond, Hugh de Lacy, as man that sly was *and* bolde, both leynyster and myth nobely he castelid, and in many Places ther othyr falid to-for hym; *and* fayne was aboute to Settyn in har londes, Thay that wyth Streynth *and* vnryght / were out-drywe, both Englysħ and Irysħ, So that, in lytel whyle, was So good Pees that men Erredyn *and* tilledyn har landys, *and* the lond Into al wel Storid wit*h* corñe. he drew to hym Slyly, wit*h* wyrchipp doynge and Stidfast forward makynge, the heghest of the lond-Pepyll; *and* frome Place to Place byled the lound wit*h* castelis; and in lytyll Whyle, so good Pees made, toke of othyr, *and* auaunced his owyn ryuely, *and* ryche ham made. The Pepill of Irland, wyth frenes *and* sleghtes, drow So, *and* allied to hym, that men haddyn grete exstymacion vpon hym, that he, agayn the kynge and his owyn trouth, wolde make hym-Selfe kynge y-crouned of the londe. As this was, *and* mych Spech in taale of thys thynge, comen Into Irland, two knyghtes from the kynge y-sende: that oone was callid Ihōn, the Constabill Of cestre, and that othyr, Richarde of the Peke, forto rescew the kepynge of Irland; and that hugh Sholde wend ouer Into Englande, to the kynge. but ar he ouer wente, by comyñ assente of ham all, thay arreredyn in that Somer many castelys in leynyster; For ar that, Mythe was well castelid, and leynyster but lytell. Thar thay reredyn a castell to Reymond in fothred o nolan [1]; Anothyr to gryffyn his brodyr; the thyrde in [2] Omurthy, to water de redelesford at kylka; the iiij^e. to Ihōn the herford, at Tillagh in felmeth, *and* othyr many. Meylere hadd that tyme kyldare of the Erlis yfte, and the contrey about; but that thay toke of hym for oo Purpos, *and* yaue hym the contray of leys in chaunge. for hit was wille londe *and* woddy, *and* of Marche, *and* ferre, thay sette hym there as man of Marche, þat y-now kouth theron.

*Capitulum lj^m. Hugo vero de Laci, summa solicitudine, victos ab aliis, et violenter a finibus ejectos, ad pacem revocans, eisdem olim deserta tam armentis pascua, quam ruricolis rura restituit. et praenotatae suspicionis fama crebrescente.*

[1 The O'Nolan's barony of Fothurtu, now Forth, in Carlow.]

*ex parte regis, tantoquam in excambium contulerunt.*

[2] MS to. Lat.: tertium in Omurethi, Gualtero de Ridenesfordia, apud Tristerdermoth; quartum Johanni de Clahulla super aquam Berubae, non procul a Lechlinia: quintum Johanni Herefordensi apud Collacht.—*Op.* v. 355.

[CHAPTER LII.]

Whan this was I-don, in the somyr Hugh wente
owt in-to Engelande.  Ayeyne the wyntter

Hugh de
Lacy is sent
back to
rule Ire-
land; and
John of
Salisbury
with him.
He builds
Castles.

the kynge toke of hym sykernesse, & sent hym sone ayeyne keper
of Irland, as he rather was sette ; wyth hym a clerk, Robert of 4
slepsbery[1], that shold hym be an help & consaylle, & wytnes
of hys deddes.  At thys comynge, hugh arered manye castells :
On to Meyller at tachmeho, & than he yaue hym hys nece to
wyue ; another that negh, yn Oboy, to Robert de Byga3 ; & 8
other many, both yn leynestre & yn Myth, that longe hyt wat
to namy al by name.

[CHAPTER LIII.]

Nota de
lupo con-
fitente.

A priest
is askt to
shrive a
sick
woman.

About that tyme, befel a wonder aduentur yn a
wodde of Myth, of a preste that yede by weyes ; 12
& as he come throgh that wodde, come a man ayeyns hym, &
badde hym, for goddys loue, that he shold wend wyth hym for
to shryue hys wyf, that lay seke þer negh.  The preste turned
wyth hym ; & whan he come somdel negh, he herd gronynge 16
and wonynge, as thegh hyt wer of a woman ; & whan he come

He finds
a sick
wolf,

ryght to, than was hyt a wolfi that lay ther & groned.  þe preste
that saw, & was wel sore aferd, & turned hym aweyward : the

who talks
to him :

man and the wolfi both spake to hym, & bad hym that he ne 20
shold nat be adredde, & that he shold turne to shryue hyr.  The
preste than toke herth to hym, & blessyt hym, & yede sytte besyde

he shrives
her.

hyr : & the wolf spake to hym, & shroue to þe preste.  & whan
thay hadde þat I-don, þe preste bethoght hym, and thoght that 24
thynge that was forshape, & hade gras to spek, that hyt myght also
wel haue grace & ynsyght of other thynge.  he sette to, & asked
of the out-comen men that ynto the lond wer comen, howe hyt

For the sins
of the
Irish, God
turnd her
into a
wolf.

shold be of ham.  The wolf answard & seyd, that 'for the syn 28
of þe lond-folke, almyghty gode tok wreche of ham, & sent that
folk for to brynge ham yn thraldome ; & so thay shold be
tyl the same folk war efte encombret whyth[2] syn ; & than thay
shold haue power for to done ham the same wrech, for har 32
synnes.'

[CHAPTER LII.]

WHan this was done, In the Somer Hugh went ouer Into England. agayn the Wyntyr, the kynge toke of hym Surle, *and* sende hym Sone agayn kepere of Irland, as he to-for was. Sende with hym a clerke, Robert of Slepsbery, that to hym sholde be helpe and consayl, *and* wytnes of his dedis. At this comynge, Hugh lette make many castelis. On to Meyler at tachmeho, and than he yaue hym his deth to rescew [!] Anothyr thar ney, in Oboy, to Robert de Bigaz ; *and* Othyr many, both in leynystere and in Myth, that longe hit were to reherse ham al by name.

*Capitulum lij*<sup>m</sup>.

A.D.
1181-2.

*Roberto ... Saloper- buriensi*

*cui et neptem suam tunc dedit uxorem.*

[CHAPTER LIII.] *

About that tyme, befel a merwelos aduenture in a wodd of Myth, of a Preste that went by weyes. And as he came throw that wodd, came a man agaynes hym [1], *and* Prayed hym for the lowe of god, that * He sholde go wyth Hym forto shrywe Hys wyfe, that Lay seke ther-By. The prest turned wyth hym ; *and* whan he came Somdel ney, he herde gronynge *and* con-Playnynge, as hit were of a woman ; *and* whan he came there wher she lay, than was hit a wolfe, that lay there and gronyd. the prest that Saw, *and* was sore aferde, *and* turnyd hym to goo / the man and the wolfe both spake wyth hym, *and* bade hym that he sholde not be afferde, *and* that he sholde turne to shryw hyre. The Prest toke herte to hym, and blessid hym, *and* wente *and* satte be-syde hyre. And the Wolfe spake to hym, *and* confeste hyr to the preste. *and* whan thay hadd that done, the preste bethoght hym, *and* thoght that thynge that was in myse-lyckenys, And hadd grace to speke, that hit mygh[t] also wel haue grace and Insyght in othyr thynge. He enquerid of the strangeres that were come Into londe, how hit sholde be of ham ? The wolfe answerid and sayde, that ' for the synne of the londe-pepil, almyghty god was displesyd wyth ham, *and* sende that Pepill to brynge ham in thraldome ; *and* So thay sholde be, thil the Same Pepill were aftyr encombrid wyth Synne [2]. And then thay sholde haue Power to do to ham the Same Wrechydnys, for har Synnes.'

*Capitulum liij*<sup>m</sup>.

*Nota de lupo con- fitente.*

[*Fol. 24 b.]

[See Gir. Camb.'s *Topo- graphia,* ch. 19, *Op.* v. 101 : it gives the story, with different details.]

[2] *Sin autem, quia pro- clivis est cursus ad voluptates, et imita- trix natura vitiorum, ad nostros ex conrictu mores forte descen- derint, dirimam in se quoque procul- dubio vindictam prorocca- bunt.*

[1] ecce lupus ad eos accedens. Gir. Camb. *Op.* v. 101.

K 2

[CHAPTER LIV.]

Nat longe ther-aftyr, þe yonge kynge henry, the
old kynge henryes sone, & his brother Geffrey, the
Erl of bretaynge, wyth-out many hegh men of thys half þe see, and
yen half that ham weren an help & consaylle, the thyrde tyme 4

Prince
Henry
dies,
11 June
1183:
Geoffrey
dies
19 Aug.
1186.

ayeyne hys fader began to aryse; bot sone ther-aftyr, as thegh
hyt wer throgh wrech of god, thay bothe deyeden, the on abóut
mydsomyr at Marcelle—& þat was the yonge kynge,—& þe erl
sone ther-aftyr deyed eke at parys: and thys þe kynges wer 8
ayeynes his[1] sones was y-endet.

[CHAPTER LV.]

WNder this, laurence, Erchebisshope of Dyuelyne,
(that at the consaylle of the latran hadde
I-be, & as me seyde, ther he hadde purchased ayenys the 12
kynge for loue of hys lond-folke, whar-of the kynge hadde grete
ortrow vp-on hym, wher-for he lete hym of hys passage ynto

Irland,) the xviij kalends of december, deyed at Oye yn normandye; a good mane and holy; & þat, gode almyghty sheweth, 16
by many myracles þat he openly doth for hym.   Me *rede
eke of hym, that he was seke thre dayes ar he thader come;
and whan he sawe our lady-chyrch, that ys the modyr-chyrch of

the toun, he seyd thys vers of the psauter, as prophecye, throgh 20
þe holy goste: 'Hec Requies mea in seculum seculi' et cetera:
& ys thus mych to sygge an-englysshe, 'Thys ys my reste, world
wyth-out end; her I wyll wonne, for I hyt haue I-chose.'

John
Comin is
next Arch-
bishop,
A.D. 1181.
He is con-
secrated at
Velletri,
A.D. 1182.

℄ Aftyr hym, was Erchebysshop of dyuelyne, Ihon comyn, a 24
man of England borne; & yn England, at euesham, of the clergye
of dyuelyn (by queyntyse and procurment of the kynge), by on
accorde I-chose; & of the pope lucye, at the Cyte of Wellet, ther-
aftyr I-hodet & I-sacred; a man, good clerke & ryghtful; & by 28
hys myght, mych ryght laked þe stat of holy chyrch yn Irland.

[CHAPTER LVI.]

The kynge henry, as he there-to-fore hadde
I-thoght, yaue the Lond of Irland to hys
yongeste sone, Iohn by name; & whan he hyt hadde hym I-yeue, 32

[1] overlined later.

[CHAPTER LIV.]

Not longe ther-aftyr, the yonge kynge henry, the *Capitulum liiij⁰.* olde kynge henryes Sone, and his brodyr Geffery, *A.D. 1180-6.* the Erle of brytayne, with othyr many hey men of this halfe the see, *prae-potentes* and yen half that ham weryn an helpe and consayl, the thyrde tyme *potentes* agayn his fadyr be-gan to arryse; but Sone ther-aftyr, as hit were *Pictaviae* throgh Sentence of god, thay both died, the one aboute Mid- *proceres, cum elcela* somyre at Marcelle, and that was the yonge kynge; and the Erle *Galliae militiae* Sone ther-aftyr diede also at Paris: and thus the kynges werre *juventute.* agaynes his Sonnes was Endyd.

[CHAPTER LV.]

Vndyr this laurance, Archebischope of Deuclyn, *Capitulum* (that at the consail of the Latran hadd I-be, and as *lv⁰.* thay Sayde, ther he had Purchasid agaynes the kynge for loue of his londe-Pepill, wharof the kynge had grette artrow vpon hym, Wherfor he lette hym of his passage in-to Irland,) the xviij kalendes 14 Nov. of Decembyr died at Oye in Normandy, a good man and holy, and ¹¹⁸⁰. that god almyghty Shewid many Mirrclis for / that he opynly doth for hym. We rede also of hym, that he was seke iij⁹ dayes ar he thadyr came; and whan he Saw our Ladyes churche, that is the modyr churche of the toun, he sayde this vers of the Sawter, as prophesy throw the holy goste: "Hec requies mea in seculum seculi: Hic habitabo ¹, quoniam elegi eam." And is thus mych to Say in Euglysh, "This is my reste, worlde wythout Ende. Her y wyl dwele, for y hit haue chose" // Aftyr hym, was Archebischope A. D. 1181. of Deuclyn, Ihon Comyn, a man of England borne; and in England, at euesham, of the clergi of deuelyn (by queyntyse and procurment of the kynge), by oone acorde chose; and of the Pope Lucie, at the *¹ ecclesiae* Cite of wellet, ther-aftyr y-hodet and y-Sacrid; a man, god clerke, *Hibernicae statum* and ryghtful, and by his myght / mych ryght lakyd the state of *egregie* holy churche In Irland². *subli-masset.*

[CHAPTER LVI.]

The kynge Henry, as he there-tofor hadd thoght, *Capitulum* yaue the londe of Irland to his yongest Sone, Ihon by *lvj⁰.* [Fol. 25 a.] Name. And whan he hit hadde hym yeue, he Sende tho Arche-

¹ habitobo, MS.

A. D. 1184. he sent þe Erchebysshope of dyuelyn ouer þe see, to ordeyn ayeyne

Archbp. Comin is sent to Ireland; Hugh de Lacy is recald, and Philip of Worcester takes his place. He took tallage of all, and curses with it.

hys sones comynge. & sone aftyr þat, hugh de lassy was I-sent
aftyr ynto Englond ; and come ynto Irland, Phelype of Wyrcestre,
procurato[ur] of þe lond, wyth fourty knyghtes ; a man that was 4
good knyght, curteys, & good mete-yeuer ; bot oþer good ne dydde
he noon, saue þat he went from contray to contray, & asked,
& wyth streynth toke, both of letred & of lewed, þe cursed
tallages of gold & of syluer. & I wnderstond that he neuer good 8
dydde þerwyth ; ne neuer mane shalle, that so catell gadereth ; for
many crystes curs, & trew mannys & womannes, pouer & ryche,
thay gadereth eke þer-wyth : & wel vnsyker may man be, to do
hys lyf yn aduentur wyth ham that catel so wynnethe.     12

[CHAPTER LVII.]

The fyrst comynge of kynge Iohn ynto Irland.

**W**han the kynges sone hadde arayed al dynge
that nede was, for to come yn-to Irland, he

He lands at Waterford

put hym to saylle at Melyford, a ferth estre day. he hadde
good wynd, & a-morow arryued at Waterford, wyth thre hun- 16
dret knyghtys, & other an-hors, & a-fote ful many. he arryued,

25 April,

the yer of hys old .xxij. ; of hys faderes comynge ynto Irland
.xiij. ; of the Erles comynge .xiiij. ; of Robertes comynge, fytz-

1185.

steuen .xv. ; the yeer of owr lordes Incarnacion .M. C. lxxxv. 20
Steuenes-sone was forman, & opened the wey to þe Erl ; the

Those who conquer the land before him deserve all praise.

Erl to þe kynge ; the kynge to hys sone ; & mych hyt ys to
preyse, & grete thynge he began, that fyrste ynto Irland so
boldly come, the thynge to begyn.   Moch also to preysene, he, that 24
aftyr the begynnynge, so nobely come for to eche thynge that
was begon ; & most of al to preysen, he that al thynge fulle

Nota the kyng his tytyle to Irland.

endet, & the lordshype clenlych wan ouer al other [Hy. II]. Her, men
mowen well vndrestond, that the Englesshy-men ne came nat 28
wyth so mych vnryght yn-to Irland as many folk weneth ; for

Fitz-Stephen and Striguil had good right to come to Ireland.

Robert, steuenes-sone, & þe Erl, wyth good ryght come to
Macmorgh ynto leynester ; the on, hys trouth for to hold, & hym
for to helpe ; that other, for loue of hys doghtre ; nathles, of 32
Waterford, ne of Myth, ne of Desmon, whych the Erl at the
begynnynge name to hym, & conquered out of leynestre, ne sey
I noght that he hadde al fully ryght ther-to.   Bot of the fyft

bischope of Deuelyn ouer tho see, to ordeyn agayñ his comynge. A.D. 1184.
And Sone aftyr that, hugh de Lacy was Sende[1] into England'; And
come Into Irland, Philipp of Wircestre, procuratour of the londe, [Philip,
with fourty knyghtes; a man that was good knyght / curteys, and in his expedition
goode mete-yeuer; but othyr good ne did he noone; Saue that he to
went from contray to contray, and askyd, and wyth streynth toke, Armagh,] a clero
both of lerid and lewid, the cursid tollagis of golde and Syluer. sacro auri tribulum
And I vndyrstonde that he neuer good did ther-with; ne neuer man execrabile
shall, that So good gadderid; for many crystis curs, and trew manys tam erigens
and womannys, Pouer and rych, thay gadderid also ther-wyth: and quam extorquens.
wel vnsure may a man to be, to do his lyfe in aduenture wyth them —Op. v.
that So goode doth gette. 360.

### [CHAPTER LVII.]

Whan the kynges Sone hadd arrayed al thynge Capitulum lvij<sup>m</sup>.
that nede was forto come Into Irland, he Putt hym
to Sayl at Milleford' the iiij° day aftyr Estyr. He had good wynde, The fryst
and amorrow londid at Watyrforde, wyth CCC knyghtes, and othyr comyng of kynge
an-hors and a-foote ful many. he londyd, the yere of his age xxij, Ihoñ Into Irlande.
Of his faderis comynge Into Irlande xiij, Of the Erlis comynge
xiiij, of Roberes comynge fitz Steuyñ xv, the yere of Oure lordys
Incarnacioñ M<sup>r</sup>. Clxxxv. Steuenes Sone was the fryst man, And [Op. v. 382]
oppenyd the wey to the Erle: the Erle to the kynge; the kynge to
his Sone; and gretly he is to Preyse, and grete thynge he began, that Multum
fryst in-to Irland So boldely come, the thynge to begyn; gretly also ergo contulit qui
he is to Preyse, that, aftyr the begynnynge, so nobely come forto ausu nobili princi-
execute the thynge that was begon; And moste of al he is to pium dedit.
Preyse, that al thynge full Endyd, and the lorchip clenly conquesyd
ouer al othyr // Here men mowen wel vndyrstond, that the Eng- Nota the
lysñ-men came not wyth so mych vnryght into Irland as many kyngys titil to
pepill wenyth. For Robert Steuenes-Sone and the Erle come to Irlande.
Macmurgh into leynystre; that oon, on his throuth forto holde, and
hym forto helpe, / that othyr, for loue of his doghtyr. Natheles, of
Watyrford, ne of Mythe, nethyr of Desmon, wych the Erle at the
begynnynge toke to hym and conquerid out of leynystre, I Sey not[2] quintae
that he hadd ful ryght therto. But of the fryst Parte of the londe[2] portionis insulae.

[1] Sende aftyr, MS.

Henry II's
fivefold
right to
Ireland:

1. All the
Irish
Princes
yielded to
him.
[*Fol. 25
b.]

2. The
Pope of
Rome
granted
Ireland to
him.

3. Gur-
guntius
won
Ireland.

4. Arthur
had truage
from
Ireland.

5. The
Irish came
from
Bayonne,
subject to
England.
English
kings are,
of right,
Lords of
Ireland.

Nota that
Ireshemen
bene false
of kynd.

parte of the lond that was the Erles throgh hys wyf, Tho
lordshype clenly þe erl yaf the kynge ; & al þe prynces of the
lond ther-aftyr, by har good wyll, yolden ham to the kynge, to
be euermor sugget to hym & to hys.   Vp*-on al thys, þe pope of 4
Rome, that ys heede of al crystendome, and that hath a specyall
ryght of al the Ilondes of crystendome as wyde as the world
ys, he yaf plenerly, and confermed to the kynge, the lordshyp
of the lond, as hyt ys to-fore I-told.  and of eldre ryght we 8
fyndeth eke I-wrytte, that the kynges of England haue to Irland
of Germon, Belynes sone, kynge of Brytaygne, that ys nowe
Englond, he come ynto Irland, & whan the lond ; & many yer
me bar hym truage, and other aftyr hym, ynto brytaygne. 12
Ther-aftyr the kynge Arthur hadde truage eke out of Irland ;
& Gylmory the kynge, that than was wyth other kynge of the
Ilondes, was wyth hym at the grete feste that he held at karlyon.
On other halue, the folk of Irland come formeste out of bastles 16
& out of Bayon, that longeth now to gascoyne, wherof the kynges
of england ben lordes.   And thys me may wel vnderstond, that
both by old ryght & by newe, the kynges of Englond owen wel
to haue the lordshyp of Irland.   And thegh the folk of the lond 20
neuer ne hadde be subyet ther-byfore, hyt oght be I-noght, þat
thay al by good wylle yold ham to kynge henry, by othes & by
ostages, & al sykernesse that hymself lyked ; & þe popes that
þer-aftyr hym graunted & confermed the lordshyp of the lond, 24
& accorsed al ham that yn any tyme thar-ayeyn come.   And
thegh thay, throgh kynd falsnesse & vnstablenesse that yn ham
ys, lytyl tel of othes & of mansynge, natheles, thay wer neuer,
throgh no man that power hadde, ther-of assoylled ne vnbound. 28
Bot man may bynd hymself wyth such thynge, bot nat so lyghly
vnbynd.

### [CHAPTER LVIII.]

Giraldus
says no
more of
the Con-
quest, but
explains
why it was
never com-
pletcd.

Maystir Geraud ne telleth no forther of the
conquest ; bot of þe lette where-through the lond 32
was [not] clenlych I-conquered, ne the folk fully I-broght yn thedone,
he telleth such resons :—Thay that fyrst comen, haddcn ful wel
I-speddo wyth-out any lette, yif þe kynge ne hadd so astyly

that was the Erlis by hys wyfe, The lorchipp clenly the Erle yauo
to the kynge; and al the Pryncys of the londe ther-aftyr, by har
good-will, yoldyn ham to the kynge to be euer-more subiecte to
hym and to hys. Vpon al this, the pope of Rome, that is hede of al
crystyndome, *and* that hath a Special ryght of al the Iloudys of *qui insulas omnes sibi speciali quodam jure re-*
crystyndome, as wid as the worldo is, he yauo Plenerly, *and* con-
fermyd to the kynge, the lorchipp of the lond, as hit is to-fore tolde.
And of eldyre ryght we fyndyth also y-writte, that the kynge *spiciunt.*
of Englande haue to Irlande * of Gormon, Belynes Soue, Kyng of [*Fol. 25 b.]
Brytaigne ¹, that is now England, he come Into Irland, and toke
the londe; *and* many a yere thay bare hym truage, *and* othyr aftyr ² *Hiber-niae reges Tribu-tarios habuisse.*
hym, Into brytaigne. Ther-aftyr also, kynge Artoure hadd truage
out of Irland ²; and Gylmory the kynge, that that tyme was wyth
othyre kynges of the Ilandis, was *with* hym at the grete feste that
ho helde at karliou. On othyr halue, the Pepil of Irlande como *Praeterea urbs Baonensis, quam hodie nostra continet Gasconia, Blasconiae caput est, unde Hiber-nenses pro-tenerant.*
fryste out of Bascles *and* out of Bayon, that longyth now to gas-
coyne, Wherof the kynges of Englande ben lordys. And thus ye
may wel vndyrstonde that, both by olde ryght and by new, the
kynges of England owen well to haue the lorchipp of Irland. And
thegh the folke of the londe neuer hadd be Subiecte ther-by-fore, hit
oght be y-now, that thay al, by good-will, yaue ham to the kynge
henry by othys and hostages, *and* by al maner Surte that he
desyrid³; and tho Popis that ther-aftyr hym graunted *and* confermyd
the lorchipp of tho londe, and acorsyd al them that in any tyme
ther-agayn come. ¶ And thegh thay, by kynde falsnes and *Nota that Iryss-men bene fals of kynde.*
vnstabilnes that in ham is, lytel tell of othys *and* of mansynge,
natheles, thay were neuer, by noo man that Power hadd, therof
assoilled ne vnbound. But a man may bynde hym-Selfe with Such
thynge, but noght So lyght vn-bynde.

[CHAPTER LVIII.]

Maister geraud ne tellyth no ferdyr the conquest; *Capitulum lviijm.*
but of the lette wherfor tho londe was [not] clenlych
I-conquerid, ne the Pepil fully y-broght in theudom, he tellyth
Such resonys:—Thay that fryst comen, haddyn full well y-Spedo

---

¹ Brytaytaigne, MS.          ³ firmis fidei sacramentique vinculis: v. 330.

1. Henry II's stopping the coming of the English.

I-sent, & forboden that no man ne shold to ham come; & thay that weP ynto þe lond I-come, shold the lond leue, & turne ayeyne, otheP forlese al that thay helden of the kynge yn otheP londes.    And whaꝫ the kynge was ynto the lond 4

2. His going home so soon after his Invasion of Ireland.

hymself I-come *wyth* so moch power, hyt had he wel ynoght, naP that he hadd so sone turned ayeyne, throgh the popes heste & þe cardynals, & eke the lyddernesse that hys sones hadden I-*pur*ueyed to do hym, the whyll that he was out of lond.  ffor 8 the folk that, at the begynnynge of so sodeyne comynge, was so

The Irish, at first frightend, learnt to fight and shoot,

swyth amayed, & aferd & agrysed of the wepned men stalwarth-nesse, and of the derne wondynge of arwes, throgh lange abydynge & sleuyth of Maystres that no stalwarthnesse ne sykernesse was 12 wyth, by lytyll & lytel lerned, wepne to berP, arwes to shote; & so wel woned ham ther-to, that oft ham byfelle wonderly goode

and often beat the English.

happes yn fyght vpoꝫ englysshe-meꝫ; & on thys maner, that at the begynnynge lyghly myght be I-shent & I-broght vnder fote, 16 wortheꝫ bold & staluarth to wythstond, & defend ham-self.  Me may rede & ouerseche the boke of kynges, þe prophetes, al the old rede fro end to otheP, & other tymes that afoor haue I-be;

War comes on folk only for their sins. The Irish sind, but God gave

me shal neu*er* fynd that werP & hate came vpoꝫ folk, bot for 20 haP synnes; & so hyt may wel be of the folk of Irland, that oft *ser*ued wel, for haP synnes, to haue werre & wrak of otheP out-londes men; natheles, god almyghty was nut ham so wengeable wrot, that he tholled ham fully, nether al to be vndone, ne fully 24

[*Fol. 26 a.]

I-broght yn-to theudome, nether * thay clenly forelore *grace*; ne the other clenlych hadden *grace*, the Maystrye to hawe, ham fully

no one grace to enslave them.

& preysebly yn theudome for to hold.  Me fynt that þe ·Iresshe-men haddeꝫ four prophetes, eu*er*y yn hys tyme, Patryk, Molynge, 28

The four chief Irish Prophets say that the

Braken, & Colmkylly, whos bokes ben wyth ham an Iresshe I-wrytte; eu*er*y of ham spekeꝫ of the fyght of thys conqueste, & seyno that ' lange stryf & oft fyghtynge shal be for thys lond; & oft the lond shal be I-horyed & I-steyned *wyth* grete slaght of 32

English shan't fully conquer Ireland till Doomsday;

men.'  Bot vnnethe thay beheteth the Englyssh peple fully þe maystrye a lytell nP domesday, & that the lond shal from see to see be I-castelled & fully I-won.  Bot the englysshe-meꝫ sholleꝫ, ar that, oft wel feble be, & myche desayse yn the lond so [? se].  Barcaꝫ 36

with-out any lette, yf the kynge ne hadd So hastely y-sende *and* *si non*
comandid that no man ne sholde to ham come ; and thay that were *primis praecur-*
Into the londe y-come, sholde the londe lewe, *and* turne ayeyn, *sorum adventibus*
othyr to lese al that thay heldyn of the kynge in othyre londys. *regio*
And whan the kynge was Into the land hym-Selfe y-come with So *fuisset elicto*
mych Power, hit hadd y-be wel y-now, ¹ nar that he hadd So Sone *praecisa sequela.*
turned agayn, throgh the Popis comandment and the cardynalis, ¹ *si ab*
And also the wickydnys that his Sones haddyn y-Purueyed to done *ausu nobili*
hym, the whyle that he was out of londe.   For the Pepil that, at *tum prae-mature*
the begynnynge of So Sodeyn comynge, was So gretly aferde *and* *intestina conspi-*
agrisid the wepynnyd-men boldenys, *and* of the cruel woundynge of *ratio non*
arowes, throw longe abydynge and Sleuth of Maysters, that no *revocasset.*
boldnys ne Sickyrnys was wyth, by lytell and lytell lernyd wepyn
to berre, Arrowes to shote ; *and* So wel vsyd ham therto, that
many tymys ham by-fell wondyrly good happys in fyght vpon
englysh-men ; and on this manere, that at the begynnynge lygh[t]ly *confundi*
myght be shente *and* broght vndyrfoote, Weryn bolde and hardy *poterul.*
to Wythstonde *and* defende ham-Selfe / We may rede and ouerseche the boke of kynges, the prophetis, al the olde rede fro ende to *totam . .*
oþer, *and* othyr tymys that to-for haue y-be, We shal neuer *Veteris Testamenti*
fynde that were ne hate came vpon Pepill, but for har Synnes. *seriem.*
And So hit may wel be of the Pepil of Irlnd, that ofte serued
wel, for har Synnes, to haue werre * and wrake of othyr strange [*Fol. 26
comen men.   Natheles, god almyghty was not ham so wengeabil a.]
wroth that he wolde fully ham Putte out of londe, nethyre al to be *vel omnino subjici*
vndone, ne fully broght Into traldome, nethyr thay clenly forlorne *meruit vel*
grace.   Nethyr ne othyr hadd not fully grace, the Maystry to haue, *deleri.*
and ham fully *and* Pesabilly in thraldome to holde /   ¶ We *Nota de*
fyndyth that the Irysh-men haddyn iiijᵉ prophetis euery in his *prophetis Hibernie.*
tyme, Patrike, Molynge, Brakan and Colmkylle, Whos bokis ben
wyth ham in Irysh writte.   Euery of ham Spekyth of the fyght of
this conqueste, And Sayne that ' lange stryfe *and* of fyghtynge shal
be for this londe ; *and* ofte the lond shal be defowlid *and* y-steynyd
wyth grete Slaght of men.'   But vnnethe thay grauntyth that the
Englysh pepil fully the maystry, a lytel ar the day of Dome, *and* that ² *ex toto subacta et*
the lond shal from See to See / be castelid *and* fully Enhabited ² / *incus-*
But þᵉ Englysh-men shal, ar that, ofte wel febil be, *and* mych *tellatu.*

but they
shall be
troubled
by a King
from St.
Patrick's
Moun-
tains.

scyth, that 'throgh a kynge that shal come out of the wyl mon-
tayngnes of seynt patrykes þat me cleppeth slesto (slesco?),
& on a soneday-nyght[1], a castel yn the wodd controys of Offalye
shal to-brek, most what al the Englysshe-men of Irland shullen 4
be 'I-stourbet' / /

I'll tell you
why Prince
John
didn't
succeed in
Ireland.

Now and for whych thynge hit was, that the
kynges sonnes trauaille, and har mochel costes,
at thys tyme ne sped nat as tham ogh, hyt ys non harme 8
thegh me her sette; for thegh of thynge that ys I-past ne be no
remedy, nathcles, of thynge that ys to come, me may be war

When he
landed,
rich men
welcomd
him, but
had their
beards
pulld by
his young
Normans.

by ensample of har dede. Whan the kynges sone was Icome
to lond at Waterford, theder come to hym Iresshe-men of the 12
contray, rych men, and of pees trew hym besoght, & made hym
grete gladnesshe as hare lord, & profred hym to kyssen. Thay
anoon ryght of tho new men, & namely of the Normannes, weren
shame-fully receyued, & lothly I-hokred, & by the berdes—whych, 16
yn the maner of the contrey, they hadden grete & long—some of
ham shamly weren I-shaken & I-draw. As sone as thay comen to

The Irish
went off
disgusted,
and told
their
country-
men.

har owne, wyth al that thay hadden thay wyth-drowen ham, & left
the contrey & wenten to the kynge of Thomon, and hym [told], & 20
also the kynge of desmon & the kynge of Connaght, what thay
hadd receyued & found wyth the kynges sone. ❡ A yonglynge al
wyth yonglynges gouerned ; & by yonge men rede, al he wroght ; no
wytte ne no staluarthnesse wyth hym was found ; no sekernese ne 24

The three
chiefs of
Ireland (of
Limerick,
Con-
naught,
and Cork,)

trouth to Iresshemen, thayr south nat behete. Whan tythynges
her-of was I-spronge, thay thre cheftayns of Irland that wer ther
redy to come to the kynges sone, & ham to hym, & do hym homage,
thay thogthten that, aftyr thay smal harmes, wolden come more ; & 28
whan me such thynge dydde to good men & meke, wel wors

swore
they'd fight
for their
freedom
to the
death.

me wold do the prouth & the vnbuxum. Thay toke ham to
rede, & sworr to-gedder that thay wolden vpon har lynes wythstond
the rygbtes of har old fredomes, & defende, for to be al to-hewen. 32
And for that thay shold [2] th[is] th[yng] the better to end brynge, thay

---

[1] MS. sone myght.     [2] From this line to the end of the page, the ends
of the lines are missing, the corner of the page being torn off.

myssayse haue in the londe.  So **Brakan Seyth,** that 'throgh [1] a kynge that shal come of the wylde Montaignes of Seynte Patrickes, that is callid Selfco, and on a soneday-nyght [2], a castel in the wode contreios of Ofelanye shal breke, most what al the Englysh-men of Irland shal be strobyd.'  *Slefto, alias Ofaley.*

**N**Ow and for wyche thynge hit was, that the kynges Sones travayll, *and* his grete costes, at this tyme sped noght as tham oght, Hit is none harme thegh I her rehorse.  Forto speke of thynge that is Paste, is no remedy ; Nevyrthelasse, of thynge that is to come, we may be-ware by ensampil of har dedes //  ¶ Whan the kynges Sone was come to londe at Watyrforde, thedyr come to hym Irysh-men of the contray, rych men [3], and of trew Pees hym be-soght / and made hym grete gladnys as har lorde, *and* proferid to kysse hym.  Than anoone ryght / of two new men, **'and** namely of the Normanes, waryn shamefully rescewid, *and* lewidly Pullid ham by the Berdys, whych, in the maner of the contrey, thay haddyn grete *and* longe.  Some of them wer Shamefully shaken *and* ydrawen.  As Sone as thay comen to har owyn, wyth all that thay hadde, thay wythdrowen ham *and* lefte the contrey, *and* wente to the kynge of Thomonde, *and* tolde hym, *and* also the kynge of Desmonde and the kynge of Connaght, what thay hadd rescewyd *and* found with the kynges sone.  ¶ A yonglynge al wyth yonglynges gouernyd, *and* by yonge men consayl al didd; And no witte ne boldnys wyth hym was founde; ne Surte, ne trouth, to yrysh-men thay couth not promyse [5].  ¶ Whan tythyngys herof was sprouge, thay iije captaynys of Irland [6] that was that tyme redy to come to the kynges sone, *and* yelde ham to hym, *and* to do hym homage, thay thoghten, that aftyr thay smale harmys, wolde come more ; and whan thay Such thynge did to good men *and* meke, Wel wors thay wolde do to the Prute *and* the vnbuxum.  Thay toke hame to * consail, and Sware to-gadderes that thay woldyn vpon Har Lywes wythstond the ryghtes of har olde fredomys, *and* defende til thay were al hewyde.  And for thay sholde this thynge the bettyr brynge to

*Capitulum lixᵐ.*
*[3] viri non infirmi, fuleles haetenus Anglis, et pacifici, tanquam domino congratulantes, et eum in osculo pacis suscipientes.*
*[4] a noxis nostris et Normannis.*
*[5] nullam Hibernicis securitatem promittentes.*
*[6] tres principales tunc temporis Hiberniae postea, Limericensis, Connactensis, et Corgagiensis. Ihesus.*
*[*Fol. 26 b.]*
*antiquae libertatis sub capitum discrimine jura tuendum.*

[1] per quemdam regem, de desertis Patricii montibus venturum, et nocte Dominica, castrum quoddam in nemorosis Ophelanie partibus irrupturum, omnes fere Anglici ab Hibernia turbabuntur.—*Op.* v. 385.

[2] MS. sone myght (the same mistake, as before, in both MSS.).

senttcñ about ynto al the lond, & allycd h . . . & maden frendes of
ham that weꝰ byfore fome[n], & thus throgh ham that th . . -nyge
putte (þrogh pryde) from ham, both thaye & al other most dele
were . . . . þys folke, as euery otheꝰ wyld folk, thegh thay no 4
wyrshype ne couthe . . . . me shold do ham wyrshype &
manshype.    And thegh thay nat be . . . . . . wyth falsnesse,
nathcles thay shonneth that otheꝰ do ham [any falshede;] & thus
the good that thay loueth yn otheꝰ, thay rech. . . . . . . . ham 8
to-gydder thay . . . . . . . . . . *Euery wysman vnderstond hym
by Roboam, Salomones sone, how mych harme falleth of pryde &
oueꝛtrowshype. whañ he, aftyꝰ hys fadyꝰ, was made kynge of Israel,
þe folk come to hym, & bysoght hym that he shold ham somwhat 12
allegge of þe seruyces that thay weꝰ I-woned to do hys fadyr.    He
was yonge ; and by yonge meñ consaylle, answard & seyd, 'My
fyngyꝰ ys gretteꝰ thañ was my faders ryggebone; & yf he yow
bette wyth yardes, y wyl yow bette wyth breres.'    ⟪ Throgh that 16
answaꝰ, the ten kynredes hym lefteñ, & maden ham kynge of
Ieroboam, & neuer aftyꝰ weren vnder hym ne nooñ of hys: of al
þe folk of Israel, non wyth hym abode, bot twey kynredes.    Vpon
thys, þe Iresshe-men londes, that, fro the tyme that Robert steuenes- 20
sone fyrst come ynto þe lond, trewly wyth englysshe-men haddeñ
I-be, weꝰ I-take fro ham, & yeuen to the newe meñ.    And thay
anooñ turned to the Iresshe-men, & aspyed al the harme that thay
myght do to þe Englysshe ; & werꝰ, so mych the more harme dydde, 24
that thay so pryue werꝰ wyth ham ther-byfore

[CHAPTER LX.]

The tounes vp-on the see, and the castels, wyth
the londes that to ham belonget, & the truages
& the rentes that shold be I-spende yn comyn nede of the 28
lond, & to ham, of rebelles thay waꝰ I-sette to such that wel
fayne gadered gold & syluer wyth-yn wowes, eten wel & drynkeñ,
and laddeñ Idel lyf, & al thynge vnprofytably wastedeñ, to harme
of pees-meñ, & nat of fomeñ.    Amonge otheꝰ harmes betydde yit 32
more, that yn lond so smert & so kene, & folk so weyward & so
vnredy, & so mych harme doynge, The kepynge & the maystry toke

Ende, thay Sende about into al the londe, and allied ham togad- *Quia*
deris, *and* madyn frendys of tham that were enemys. And thus throw *primos a nolhe insolham*,
ham, that thay at the begynnynge Putte (throw Pryde) from them, *leuter re-*
both thay and al otheres for the more parte was fro them stirrid. *pulimus... tam illos*
¶ This Pepyll, as euery othyr wylde Pepill, thegh thay no wyrchipp *quam*
kowth not, Natheles thay wolde that hy sholde do ham wyrchippe *majores uniuersos*
*and* manshipe. And thegh thay be not aferde ne ashamyd to be *eo exemplo*
founde wyth falsnesse, Natheles, thay Shonnyth that any othyr *procul abslerrui-*
sholde do ham any falshede : and thay lowyth trouth ; and thus *mus bonum*
good that thay lowyth in otheres, thay thynke no fors whow lytill *quod in aliis*
be found in ham-Selfe therof. Euery vysman vndyrstond hym by *diligunt,*
Roboam, Salomones Sone, how mych harym fallyth of Pryde. *minus in se reperiri*
Whan he, aftyr his fadyr, was made kynge of Israel, the Pepil *non erubescunt.*
come to hym, *and* besoght hym that he sholde ham Somewhate
allegge of the Servyces that thay were wonyd to do to his fadyr. *ego vos*
He was yonge ; aud, by yonge men consayl, answerid and Sayde, *caedam scorpio-*
¶ "My fyngyr is more *and* grettyr then was my Fadyris bake-bone; *nibus.*
And yf he bette yow wyth yardes, y will bette you with breris" / [1] *nouis nostris,*
¶ And for that answere, al the tene kynredes lefte hym / *and* *contra*
made ham a kynge of Ieroboam ; *and* neuer aftyr weryn vndyr *promissa contu-*
hym, ne noone of his. Of al the Pepil of Israel, none with hym *limus.*
abode, but two kynredis. Vpon this, the Irysh-men londes that [2] *tanto*
fro the tyme that Robert Steuenes Sone fryste come Into the londe, *quidem ad nocendum*
trewely wyth englysh-men haddyn, wer take fro ham, *and* yewyn *efficaciores,*
to two new men [1]. And thay anoone turnyd to the Irysh-men, *and* *quanto prius*
aspied al the harme that thay myght do to þe Englysh ; and *fuerant fami-*
werre, so mych the more harme didde, that thay were so Pryue *liariores.*
wyth ham therto-fore [2]. [3] *talibus est*

[CHAPTER LX.] *assignata, qui aurum*

The tounes vpon the See, *and* the castelis, wyth *Capitulum lx.*
the londys that to ham Partenyd, and the truages *assidue*
and the rentes that sholde be I-Spend in the comyn Profite of the *intra*
londe, *and* ynue hit to Rebellys [3], *and* to suche that well fayne *muros aucupantes*
gaderid golde and Syluer wyth-In wowes, etten wel, and drounken, *... cum*
*and* laddyn ydill lyfe, and al thynge vnprofytably wastyne, to grete *cirium, non hostium*
harme of Pees men, *and* noght to enemys. Amonge al othyr harmys *damno*
befell yit more, that in the londe So Smyrte *and* So kene, *and* *cuncta inutilitercon-*
Pepil So weywarde and So vnredy, *and* So mych harme doynge, *sumebant.*

The English Governors were cowards, and liked women better than war.

an hand, that leu*er*¹ hadde har rych robes, than ham to wepne;
leu*er* to sytte at borde, þan hoste to lede; redye*r* to fle þan to
fyght; leu*er* to hold a fayr mayd by the womb, than sper & sheld
to ber an hand; nethe*r* trewe to har vnderlynges, ne dredful to har 4
enemyes.   Thay had nat that good herte, ne of ky[nde] yt com to
ham, for to spar the meke, & wreke ham on the prout; bot al ayeyne
that, thay sp[arid & ²] lykled w*yth* the sterne, & pulled & strope

The Irish now burnt, slew, and stole.
The English of the coast stuck to wine and women.
The inland was plunderd by the Irish.

ham that noñ harme dydde.  Vnder whych gouernours, the 8
Iresshe-meñ begoñ to pryde & take ouer-hand of the englysshe,
branten and slowen, robbedeñ And stelleñ; for the maystres wyth
har meygne, heldeñ ham alwey yn the cytees vpoñ the see, þer
plente was of wyñ & of womeñ, to whych they weren al clenlych 12
I-yeue to. Bot the lond w*yth*-In, & the marches next har enemyes,
& the castles & the tounes that weren amyd, weren I-lefte &
I-brant, the men I-robbed & I-sleyn, w*yth*-out any lette.  The
good knyghtes & the eldre folk of the lond, as meñ that me 16
noght told-by that whyle, w*yth*-drow ham al sleghtly, & held ham
al stylle, for to awayty al soft, what endynge such hyddous stormes

Everywhere was wailing;

wold ham.   That whyle, þe state of the lond was such, In al places
was weylynge & wonynge, yollynge & crynge; Al þe weyes forlete; 20

every day fresh news of fire and slaughter.

no mañ ne trust to mete wyth other; euery day come newe
tythynges of bernynge & sleynge, robbynge & revyng ³ yn the out
londes: vnneth a lytel shadow of pees was yn þe bourgh tounes, þer
the wyn quenched al þe sorowe; the gold & the sylu*er*, al oþer 24
harmes; thar me shold yn so lydd*er* world wend from contray to

Judges

contray wyth folk I-wepned, and chasty ham that mysdeden.   Thay
setten Iustyces of bench yn har robes of scarlet & menyu*er*: meñ

ruind good men and true,
[*Fol. 27 a.]
worse than Irish foes did.

wyth swerdes & battes ham for to kepe, ther no nede was.  Than 28
was þe motynge, the pledynge and reynnynge of good men and
trewe that * non harme dydden: wors ham dydde the harme & the
ten that þay ther-throgh haddeñ, þañ the robbynge & reuynge that
thar enemyes ham dydde.  ❡ Another thynge that mych was to 32

---

¹ MS. lou*er*.                              ² Torn out.
³ The corner of p. 26 b was torn off before being written upon, so that there
are no words missing, and the lines follow each other as usual.

The kepynge[1], *and* the men that was Maysteres to kepe the lande, he ᴀ. ᴅ. 1185.
had lewer his rych clothis to were, than wepyn to berre; *and* lowid
bettyr to sitte at borde, than hoste to lede; and more redyer to fle
than to fyght; leuer to holde a fayre mayde by the wombe, than
spere and Shelde to ber an honde. And also they wer not trewe
to har Subiectis, ne dredfull to har enemys. Thay had not that
* good Herte, ne of good Kynde Hit come to Ham, forto Spare the
meke, *and* wreke Ham on the Prowte; but al the contrary thay did.
Thay Sparid *and* fikyllid wyth the sterne, and toke *and* Pullid the
meke, *and* them that noone harme did // Vndyr whych gouernors,
the Irysh-men begon to be Prowde, and to haue the Maystry of the
Englysh-men, *and* branten, *and* Slayne, *and* Stellen / For thay
Maysteris, wyth har meny, heldyn[2] ham at al tymys in the Citteis
vpon the see-syde, ther Plente was of wyne and of women, to the
wyche thay yaue ham clenly to. But the lond wyth-In, and the
marchis nexte har enemys, and the castelis *and* the tounes that
weryn a-myde, weryn lefte and brante, the men robyd and Slayn,
wyth-out any resistence. The good knyghtes *and* the eldyr Pepill
of the londe, as men that noght is tolde by, that tyme wythdrow
ham al Slyly, *and* held ham al stylle, for-to witte al Softe what
Ende Suche grete Stormys sholde haue. That tyme, the state of
the londe was Suche, In al Placis was wepynge and cryenge, and
myche Sorrow. Aff the weyes was lefte, that no man trustid not
to mete with anothyr; euery day come newe tythyngis of brennynge
and Sleynge, robbynge and rewynge in the out-landis. Vnneth a
lytyll Sadow of Pees was in the burgage tounes[3], ther the wyne
quenchid al the Sorrow; the golde and the syluere, al the harmys.
Thar thay Sholde, in so wyckyd a tyme, goo from contray to
contray wyth Pepill y-wepenyd, *and* correcte ham that did amys;
Thay Syttyn Iustices of benche in hare Roobis of Scarlete *and*
menywere; men with Swerdis *and* battis forto kepe ham, ther
no nede was. Than was the motynge, the pledynge, *and* reyuynge
of goode men and trew, that noone harme didde. Wors hame didd
the harme and the angyr that thay ther throgh haddyn / than the
robbynge and reuynge that har enemys ham dide // Anothyr
thynge that gretly is to mowrne, be-felle also, wher-of god was

[1] *Stipendiaria quippe familia, suos imitata magistros, suisque majoribus morem gerens.*
[*Fol. 27 a.]
[2] [ heldym MS.]
*vino veneri-que data, maritimis in urbibus moram assidue faciebat. Antiqua vero militia novorum ingruente malitia, tanquam vilis et reprobata, latuit interim et siluit.*
[3] *sed solum in urbibus pacis ut cumque servari umbra videbatur.*
[See the Latin below, P. 152.]

L

A.D. 1185. rewe byfelle also, whař-of gode was worste I-quemed : Ther
prince cometh newly to londe hyt becometh welle that he wyrshype
god & holy chyrch, mayntenynge the ryghtes, & yeue more there-to.

**Prince John spoild the Irish Church.** Bot þe newe prynce nat only held hym from that for to eche the 4
good of holy chyrch, bot londes & rentes & pryuyleges that thay of
old world hadde & vsed, at hys fyrst comynge yn many places he
bename al clene ; yñ otheř places he chaunged, & yaue wors & lasse
thař foř ; & hyt may wel be, þat hys spede yn othere thynges was 8

**The Irish began to rebel.** euer the wors & noght þe bettyř.  On thys maner the englysshe
wereñ both argh & woke to assayllen and to fyght, þe Iresshe
stronge & bold to wythstonde, tyl that þe new prynce saue openly
that al thynge vndeř hys newe meñ yede to loste ; he chaunget 12
ham & renued, as meñ that nothynge couth, & drogħ to hym the

**So John de Courci was made Ruler, and at once mended matters.** old knyghtes & the good meñ that wareñ ther-to-foř Ivsed to
fyght yn the maner of þe lond, & sette Ioħn de Curcy maystre &
chefteyne of al thynge that was to done ; vnder whoñ þe state & 16
þe pees of the lond, by as mych began anooñ ryght to amend, as
Ioħn, of hert & of staluarthnesshe, passed al otheř, passynge &
throgh sechynge the Inlondes, as Desmone, Thomone, Mounesteř,
Connaght ; & let nat the meygne vndo hamself wyth oft harme & 20
lostes, doynge to hys fomen, & oft to hym-self & to hys, as he that
noght was adredde to assaye þe vnsykeř aduentures of fyght & of
baret.

[CHAPTER LXI.]

**Prince John had three sets of men : 1. Normans, the worst, whom he trusted most ; 2. the English he brought with him ; 3. the English in Ireland, the best, whom he trusted least.** ¹The yonge prynce at the begynnynge hadde wyth 24
hym thre manere of meygne, Normannes,
Englysshe, & þe Englysshe that he found yn the lond.  In wyrshype, gret frenshype, & loue, he hold the fyrst & the worst ; In
lasse, the mydmest & the better ; In allerleste, the latest & þe 28
beste.  The fyrst ne myght nat lyue wyth-out wyn, yn whyche thay
wereñ fostred ; & for-thy thay forsokeñ on al wyse to beñ yn
marches & yn castels feř from the see I-sette ; no-wheř bot about
the kynges sone & hys body, kepe thay myght nat be, & hym folwen, 32
& negh hym be, wyth-out any departynge.  feř from the weste &

¹ The usual large initial letter is omitted here, a space being left for it in
which a small t is put.

moste dysplesyd.   Ther Prynce comyth newely to londe, hit  *A. D. 1185.*
becomyth that he wirchippe god and holy churche, mayntenynge  *nihil de*
the ryghtes, *and* yeue more therto.   But the new Prynce, not oonly  *noro con-*
*ferentes . .*
helde hym frome that, forto eche the good of hooly church ; but  *quinimmo*
londis and rentis *and* Pryuylegis that thay of olde Worlde hadde  *terria*
*statim sub-*
*and* vsyd / At his fryst comynge, in many Placis he toke al clene,  *latis et*
and in othyr Placis he chaungid, *and* yaue Wors and lasse therfor.  *possessioni-*
*bus . .*
And hit may wel be, that his Spede in othyr thyngis was euer the
wors, *and* noght the bettyr.   On this maner the Englysh-men wer
both febill and feynte to assaylen and to fyght, and the Irysh-men  *hostibus*
bolde *and* stronge to wythstonde, till that the new Prynce opynly  *autem ad*
*rebellan-*
Saw that al thynge vndyr his new men yede to loste.   he chaunged  *dum auda-*
ham, *and* remewid as men that nothynge kowth, *and* drewe to hym  *cissimis.*
the olde knyghtes, and the good men that weryn therto-for y-vsyd  *summam*
*rerum*
to fyght in the maner of the londe, And Sette Ihōn de Curcy,  *geren-*
Maystyr and captayn of al thynge that was to doun, Vndyr Whom  *darum*
*curam*
the State and the Pees of the londe, by as-mych began anoone  *commisit.*
ryght to amende, as Ihōn, of herte * and of Boldnys, Passid all  [*Fol. 27
othyr, Passynge *and* throw shechynge the In-Londys, As Des-  b.]
*penitimas*
monde, Thomon, Mownyster, Connaght, *and* lette not the meny  *terrae*
Vndo ham-Selfe wyth ofte harme *and* lostis, doynge to his ennemys  *partes.*
*and* ofte to hym-Selfe *and* to his, as he that noght was adrede  *incertam*
to assay the vnsure aduentures of fyght And of battaylle.  *bellici*
*certaminis*
*aleam.*

[CHAPTER LXI.]

The yonge Prynce at the begynnynge hadd *with*  Cap*itulum*
hym thre maner of menny, Normanes, Englyssh,  lxj*m.*
and the Englyssh that he founde in the londe / In grete wyrchipp,  *In summa*
frendshipp and loue, he helde the fryste and the worste.   In lasse,  *familiari-*
*tate primos*
the Secounde and the bettyr.   And in alltherleste, the latyste and  *habuimus.*
the beste.   The fryste myght not lyue wyth-out wyn, in whych they  *;  solum*
weryn fosterid ; And therfor thay forsoke to be in marchis and in  *filii regis*
*latera*
castelis ferre frome the See ysette[1] / *and*[2] myght not be in no  *stipare,*
Place but aboute the kyngis Sone, (*and* [from] his body, kepe thay  *solum filio*
*regis in-*
myght not be,) and hym followyn, *and* ney to hym be, wi*th*-out any  *separa-*
departynge. fer*re* from the Weste, and ney to the Eeste ; Fer from  *biliter*
*assistere.*

[1] Primi vino, quo nutriti fuerant, carere non volentes, in remotis marchiis,
et castris procul a mari constructis, moram facere modis omnibus recusabant.—
*Op.* v. 394-5.

A.D. 1185. negh al eeste ; ser from myssayse, & negh ayse, thay wyllet euer to
John's  be sette.  ⁋ Ianglers & bosters, & of grette othes, and stronge
young men
were  lyers, foderes, whybelers, Moch told by ham-self throgh pryde, &
boasters,  lytel by other ; yiftes & wyrshype to receyue, thay wer the fyrst ; 4
liars, bribe-
takers.  dout & perrylle to receyue, thay war euer the laste.  The lytel good
that thay dydde that *wyth* hym comen, that was throgh the
englysshe that he *wyth* hym broght ; bot thay was no thynge
derward *wyth* hym ayeyns the other, that no good ne couth do. 8
He forsook  And for the good knyghtes & the men throgh whych the wey ynto
the good
old Eng-  the lond was fyrst I-opened, wer *wyth* ham bot as forsaken &
lishmen,  forlete ; non I-cleppeth to conssaylle bot the newe ; to non trusted
he bot to the newe ; to non was wyrshype I-do bot to the newe. 12
Hyt byfelle, that whan thay other wythdrowe ham for such thynge,
& lete ham I-worth, yn al thynge that thay dydde, lytel or noght
thay sp[ed]de.  Such gyltes & so many, thegh thay both wer myche
the wise  to wite, yong old & yonge rede, natheles þe yonge lydder rede was 16
whom the
rebels  more gylty ; ffore boustyous lond and vnredy, hadde al nede to be
needed.  Irotet and I-kept throgh wyse men & redy.

### [CHAPTER LXII.]

John  ¹ Aftyr that the kynges sone hadde the lordshype
builds three
Castles, at     of Irland, & ynto the lond was y-come, Aduentures byfelle 20
Ardfinan,
Lismore,  that maystyr Gerot shortly toucheth.  Of thre castels that he
Tibragh.  anon ryght lete rere, on at Ardfynan, another at lysmore, the
[*Fol. 7  thyrd at Tybraghnych.  Of thre staluarth * knyghtes that throgh
b.]  grete mesaduentur weren I-slawe, Robert de Barry at Lysmore ; 24
Three
Knights  Reymond, hughes sone, at Olethan ; Reymon of Canteton yn
are slain.  Osserye.  Of a partye of the meygne of Ardfynan that the kynge
R. Fitz-
Hugh, &c.  of Thomon descomfyted yn a wod þer negh on a mydsomyr day,
Men of  And four knyghtes that ther wer y-slaw ; & thay of Tothmon the 28
Thomond,
or Lim-  sam day wer dyscomfyt to-for Tybragh ; & a grete Iresshe-man,
erick,  Ograde, was ther I-slawe, wyth many other of the meygne of
slain ; and
O'Grady (?)  Ardfynan, that sone aftyr, yn a prey-takynge toward lymeryke
Dermot,  weyes dyscomfyte, & xix knyghtes I-slawe.  Of the prynce Of 32
King of
Desmond  Desmon, Dermot Maccarthy, that *with* many other yn a parlement
dies.

¹ The usual large initial letter is omitted, space being left for it.

myssayse, *and* nygh to ayse, thay wolde *euer* to be sette. // Iangleris, A. D. 1185. bosteris, and of grete othis, stronge lyeris, lycheres, Why-beleres, *verbosi, jaclutores,* Moche sette by ham-selfe for Pride, *and* lytill by othere*s*: yiftis *enormium* and wyrchipp to rescewe, thay were the fryst; Dowte and Peril *juramentorum* to rescewe, thay wer *euer* the laste.   The lytill good that thay *auctores.* didd' that wyth hym comyn, that was throgh the Englyssh that ¹ *solum* he wyth hym broght.   But thay was nothynge Derward wyth hym *novis fidem habentes,* agaynys the othyr, that no good ne couth do / And for the *solum* good knyghtes and the men, throw whych the wey into the lond *novos dignos* was fryste oppenyd, wer wyth ham but as forsakyn *and* forlete / *honore putacimus.* non callid to consaill, but the newe ; to noone trustid he ¹, but to the new ; to noone was wirchipp dou͞e, but to the newe.   ² Hit ² *effectum est ut illis* befel that, whan thay othyr wythdrow hame for Suche thynge, *se retrahentibus, et* and lette ham alone, wyth al thynge that thay did, Lytell or *invilis* noght thay Spede.   Such gyltes and So many, thegh thay both *operas non ingerentibus, in* wer mych to witte, yonge elde *and* yonge rede, natheles the yonge *bus, in* lewid consaylle was mor gylty ; For bostious, loude *and* vnredy, *cunctis agendis* hadd grete nede to be y-rotid and y-kepete throgh wysmen and *parum isti* redy. *proficissent.*

[CHAPTER LXII.]

Aftyr that tyme that the kynges Sone hadde the *Capitulum* lordshipp of Irland', and into the londe was come, ad- *lxijͫ.* uentures befell that Maystyr gernude Sortely touchyth.   Of th[r]e castelis that he anoone ryght lette rere, oone at ardfynan, anothyr at lysmore, the thyrde at Tybraght.   Of thre bolde and hardy knyghtes, that throw gret mysaduenture weryn slayne, Robert *fulls adversis et* de Barry at lysmore, Reymond Hughes-sone at Olethan, Reymond *arersis.* of Canteton in Ossory.   Of a party of the meny of ardfynan, that *De parte quadam* the kynge of Thomo͠n descomfited in a wodde ther neygh, On a *Archphinensis* Mydsomer day, And four knyghtes that were Slayn ; and thay of *familia.* Thomonde the same day wer discomfite to-² for tybraght ; and a [*Fol. 28 grete Irysh-man, Odrade, Was ther Slayn, wyth many othyr Of the *a.*] *De . .* meny of ardfynan, that Sone aftyr in a pray-takynge toward *Oggravi* lymerike weies Discomfite ², and xix knyghtes wer Slayn.   Of the *interemptione.* Prynce of Desmonde, Dermot Maccarthy, that *with* many othyr in

² in praedae captione versus Limericum confectis.—*Op.* v. 386.

A.D. 1185. besyde Corke, throgh Tybaud wauter & the mcygne of Corke, was

Ulstermen slain. I-slawe.  Of the meñ of kenalayne, that to boldely wentteñ ynto Mythe to preyciñ, & ther wereñ I-slawe throgh Wyllyam le petyt,

Saints' bodies found. & an hundert heedes of ham I-broght to dyuelyñ.  Of otheř holy [4] bodyes, patryke, Bryde, &, Colmekyl, at douñ I-found, & by Iohn de

Hugh de Laci slain, A. D. 1186. Courcy weř translated; of hugh de lacy, that to trysty was vpon hys Iresshe-meñ, & by traysoñ of ham was I-heded at dernagh.

℃ Of thretteñ knyghtes, that vndeř Ihon de Courcy weren I-slawe [8] at a comynge out of Connaght.  Of the staluarth yonge knyght

Roger le Poer slain. The Irish silently conspire, destroy castles, and kill men. Roger the poweř, that wyth many of hys, throgh traysone, yn Osscrye was I-slawe; & throgh that thynge, al the Iresshe of the lond stylly sworne ham to-gyddyř ayeyns the Englysshe; wheř [12] throgh that, [1] castels yn many places wereñ I-cast adoun, many meñ I-slawe, to grete perrylle to al the lond; & of many otheř aduentures that betyddeñ aftyr that the kynges sone was lord of Irland, of whyche maystyř Geraud, ham & hař gestes leueth to [16] other that ham wrytte wold, & lust haddeñ theř-to [1].   And as thys An end maked of thys boke.

[1-1] destructis castris pluribus, gravi insulae universae perturbatione : non indigna memoratu singula, translato in filium regis jam regni dominio, sua suorumque gesta suis assignando scriptoribus, ad ulteriora simul et utiliora festinamus.—*Op.* v. 387-8.

## The unenglisht last Chapters.

Thus ends Ch. 35 of Giraldus's 2nd Book of his *Expugnacio.* His Ch. 36 is our 60, pp. 142-7, with an added Vision of ' Prince John marking out the foundations of a church, with a large nave and a very small chancel.'  His Ch. 37 is our 61, pp. 146-9. In his Ch. 38, he states how the Irish are to be conquerd : in Ch. 39, how they are to be governd.  Mr. Dimock's side-notes to these two Chapters are :

Ch. 38.  " In every expedition, the counsel of those ought to be followed, who are best acquainted with the country and manners

a *parlement* besyde Corko, throgh Tybaud **Wau***ter and* the meny A. D. 1185.
of Corke, was y-Slayñ. Of the men of kynnaleȳñ, that So boldely *in colloquio prope Cor-*
wentyn Into Myth, ther to take a pray, *and* ther weryn Slaȳñ *cagiam, a*
throgh Willam le Petyte, and an C. hedys of ham broght to *Corcagien- sibus*
Deuelyn // Of othyr hooly bodies, Patrike, Bryde, and Colmckil / *et Theo- baldi*
at doun y-found, *and* by Ihoñ de Curcy were translated. Of *Gualteri*
Hugh de lacy, that to trysty was vpon his Irysh-men, And by *familia ferro*
traysone of ham was hedid at Dernagh // Of xiij° knyghtes, *peremptis.*
that vndyr Ihōū de Curcy weryn Slayn at a comynge out of *Dernagh in fereall.*
connaght; of the bolde yonge knyght, Roger the Powere, that
wyth many of his, throw trayson, in Ossory was Slayñ; And *et ejusdem*
Throw that thynge, aït the Irysh-men of the londe Pryuely Sworne *causa occa- sione,*
ham to-giddyr ayeyñes the Englyssh-men; Wherthrow that, *castellis clandestina*
in many Places weryn caste dovne, *and* many men Slaȳñ, in Peril *quoque totius*
of al the londe. And of many othyr aduentures that by chanse *Hibernici populi in*
fell, aftyr that the kynges sonne was lorde of Irlande, the whych *Anglos con-*
Maystyr Geraud, ham and har gestis lewyth to othyr that ham *juratione.*
write wille, *and* luste haw therto ; And as thus an endo makyth of
this boke.

Et Sic finis est istius Libri.
Laus deo clementissimo.

---

of the people. The great difference between French warfare, and
that of Ireland and Wales [is]: In these countries, light-armed
troops [are] more especially necessary. In any expedition into
Ireland or Wales, the troops of the Welsh Marches [are] by far
the best. In Irish warfare, archers [ought] to be united with the
cavalry. The three parts of the island on this side the Shannon
[ought] to be well incastellated ; the other part won by degrees.

Ch. 39. The necessity of firm, severe, but moderate rulers.
In time of peace, castles [ought] to be built, and roads to be

improved. The Irish, once fully subjected, [ought] to be forbidden the use of arms; [and] meanwhile not to be allowed to bear the axe. [They ought] to pay an annual tribute in gold or birds."

Giraldus's Third Book tells how he found and translated the Prophecies of Merlin of Celidon.

When John became King of England, Giraldus sent him a copy of his *Topographia* and *Expugnacio*, with a Proem or Dedicatory Letter printed in the Rolls edition, v. 405-411. It reminds John of Ireland, exhorts him not to forget *it*, the Golden Isle, in favour of England, the Silver one; says it will form a kingdom for one of his sons; warns him that he must leave no danger behind him in Ireland when he goes to recover the foreign possessions he has lost; calls on him to fulfil Henry II's pledges to Pope Adrian, that is, to exalt the Church in Ireland and pay Peter's pence; instances God's vengeance on the non-keeping of these pledges; says how miserable the state of the Irish Church is; and advises John to take an annual tribute of gold, birds, or trees, from the Irish in token of subjection. Lastly, Giraldus asks that a scholar may translate his books into French; gives Walter Map's opinion on his own talk and Giraldus's writings; and says that he (Giraldus) is now old, and 'desires only God's favour and the appreciation of his labours by posterity.'

---

pp. 144-5, lines 9-2 from foot. The side-note and Latin in the Rolls edition, v. 392, are:

Prevalence of law-suits.    Praeterea, quamquam hostilitatis instante procella, armatae militiae tempus ingruerit, non togatae, tanta tamen civilium causarum urgebat importunitas, ut miles veteranus non tam hoste foris, quam intus foro vexaretur.

---

As to the state of Ireland in 1515, see the document printed in my *Ballads from MSS.* (Ballad Soc.), p. 38-40.

# GLOSSARY

(MAINLY)

BY THOMAS AUSTIN.

———◆———

& (and), an, a, 2/3, 116/7 ; & noon, anon, 72/18.

A, *prep.* on, 12/17, 16/35 ; in, 44/8 ; by, 66/2.

Abate, *vb.* flutter the wings, 56/32. Used like *Bate.*

Aboue, *adv.* above, he was all a., had the upper hand, 120/3 ; abouen, 116/27 ; abow, 117/26, 121/3.

Abydynge, *sb.* expectation, 111/33.

Abydynge, *vb.* a. aftyr ham, waiting for them, 124/28.

Adde, *vb.* had, 68/2.

A-fryght, *pp.* frightened, afraid, 114/22.

Agryse, *pp.* terrified, 100/2.

Agylte, *vb.* sin, 88/1.

Aleueth, *num. adj.* eleven, 118/14. See opposite page.

Allerformest, foremost of all, 50/24 ; alther-formyst, 51/24.

Allerleaste, least of all, 146/28 ; all-therleste, 147/28.

Aller-next, next of all, 12/33 ; alther-nexte, 13/34.

Allience, *sb.* alliance, allies, 73/27, 87/8.

Allyees, *sb.* allies, 72/27. Fr. *alliés.*

Alonge, *adv.* always, 54/29.

Alout, *adv.* all out, or ? aloud, 104/12.

Althyr, 101/3, ? either.

Aly, *adj.* holy, 42/36.

Amaied, *pp.* amayed, dismayed, 12/16 ; amayed, 16/31, 20/33, 56/5.

Amonneschyd, *vb.* admonished, warned, 57/13 ; amonessed, 93/10 ; amonested, 56/13, 92/10.

An, *prep.* on: an-heghe, on high, 112/34, an-hey, 113/34 ; an-hond, in hand, 74/17 ; an-hors, on horseback, 58/25, 100/28 ; an Iresshe, in Irish, 116/33.

Anguysshes, *sb.* anguishes, anxieties, 96/13 ; augwysshis, 97/13.

Anguysshous, *adj.* anxious, 104/8. O.Fr. *anguissous.*

Anone ryght, *adv.* strnightway, 148/22 ; anoone-ryght, 82/2.

Aplesid, *pp.* a. of, pleased with, 37/35.

Ar, *pron.* their, 8/17. See *Har.*

Ar, *conj.* ere, 8/9, 22/23, 74/34 ; are, before, 9/10 ; before, 58/10.

Ared, *vb.* tell, declare, 97/25 ; arede, 96/26.

Arere, *vb.* lift up, stir up, 22/1 ; set right, heal, restore, 44/5 ; restore, rebuild, 106/9 ; areren, raise, 44/15 ; arered, raised, 30/16 ; arere, 23/1.

Arew, arow, in a row, 71/13 ; a rewo, 70/13.

Argh, *adj.* timid, cowardly, 16/30, 114/6 (feinte, 115/6) [1].

Argly, *adv.* timidly, in a cowardly way, 16/23 (fently, 17/23) [1].

Arreden, *vb.* eared, ploughed, cultivated, 128/7 ; Erredyn, 129/7.

Artrow, *sb.* overtrow, mistrust, suspicion, 133/13 ; ortrow, 132/14.

[1] In all old words like *argh, arghly,* the reader should look on the opposite page for the Rawlinson MS. equivalent, which is generally later, tho' for the Dublin ar[y]red, 24/34, the Rawlinson has *londide.*

**Aryse,** *vb.* arise, rebel, 132/5; arryse, 133.

**Aryued,** *vb.* arrived, landed, 24/34.

**As,** *conj.* for *ae*, but, 4/2.

**Asquynt,** *adv.* asquint, aslant, obliquely, 94/20.

**Assemble,** *vb.* join battle, 24/15, 30/26.

**Assembly,** *vb.* assemble, 64/5.

**Asseth,** *sb.* satisfaction, penance, 86/23.

**Astage,** *sb.* hostage, 24/23.

**Astryf,** *adv.* astrife, emulously, with rivalry, 50/26.

**Atene,** *vb.* vex, irritate, 38/24.

**Ather,** *conj.* either, or, 100/3. Note pronunciation.

**A thre,** in three parts, 104/26; at thre, 67/19.

**Attyre,** *sb.* venom, 20/23, 102/27, 114/2.

**Auctorice,** *vb.* legalise, set in authority, 107/27 (avaunce, 106/27).

**Aurel,** *sb.* April, 77/28; auril, 76/28.

**A-waitede,** *vb.* watcht, expected, 2/19.

**Aweyward,** *adv.* awayward, off the land, *i. e.* westwardly, 66/33; away, 130/19.

**Awreke,** *vb.* a. hym, awreak himself, avenge himself, 4/5.

**A yere,** *adv.* yearly, 66/2.

**Ayeyne,** *prep.* against, on the approach of, 130/2; *adv.* again, 130/3.

**Ayeyns,** *prep.* against, to meet, 54/13.

**Ayse,** *sb.* ease, 148/1.

**Bad,** *vb.* prayed, 28/11.

**Baghel,** *sb.* bagle, crosier, 122/13, 123/12; baghell, 122/12. L. *baculum.*

**Bale,** *sb.* sorrow, evil, 20/24.

**Baret,** *sb.* barrat, strife, battle, 146/23.

**Barnen,** *vb.* burnt, 54/4.

**Battes,** *sb.* bats, sticks, staves, 144/28; battis, 145/31.

**Becomlyche,** *adj.* becoming, comely, 76/14; becomly, 102/20; becumliche, 54/24.

**Becryed,** *vb.* cryed to, called on, 30/32, 46/20.

**Begetes,** *sb.* begets, gains, 81/15; beyetes, 80/15.

**Begynnyge,** *vb.* begin, 54/21.

**Be-heght,** *pp.* promised, 40/9; be-het,

*vb.* promised, 18/34; behete, 28/19, 114/29.

**Behoud,** *sb.* behoof, benefit, 112/30.

**Behowaybyll,** *adj.* behovable, needful, suitable, 121/4; covenable, D.

**Belad,** *pp.* narrow b., treated them straitly or hardly, 40/21; bilad' hym, led him, lived, 2/9; hard' biladde, *vb.* treated hardly, 2/6; bylad, 41/22; by-ladde, conducted, bore, 54/12.

**Beleft,** *vb.* remained, 118/14; *pp.* remaining, left, 58/10.

**Belokene,** *pp.* shut in, 50/12; belokken, 51/12. See *Belouke*, N. E. D.

**Belyggynge,** *vb.* beleaguing, beleaguering, 104/5.

**Be-name,** *vb.* forbad, 31/9; be-nomen, *pp.* taken away, 60/34; byname, deprive of, 100/9.

**Berewid,** *vb.* bereft of, 45/5; berewys, bereave, *imper.*, 35/10.

**Berre,** *vb.* bear, 145/2.

**Besech,** *vb.* beseek, try to get, cast at, show to, 110/30 (malyngne agaynys, 111/30).

**Besete,** *vb.* beset, blockade, 48/16: *pp.* set, possest, 102/19; besette, 103/19.

**Be-taght,** *vb.* betook, gave, committed, entrusted, 86/14.

**Be-tak,** *vb.* accompanyed, 20/18; betake, 21/18; betaken, settled, arranged, 72/31; betoke, entrusted to, 108/27.

**Betheght,** *vb.* betook, gave to, 92/11; betoke, 93/11.

**Bethwene,** *prep.* between, 10/12.

**Blote,** *adj.* soft, marshy, wet, 122/3.

**Blywe,** *adv.* belive, quickly, 29/30.

**Bolnys,** *sb.* boldness, 111/35.

**Bolthenys,** *sb.* boldness, 75/15.

**Bostious,** *adj.* rough, boisterous, 149/17; boustyous, 148/17.

**Bot,** *adj.* both, 106/12.

**Bot,** *conj.* but, unless, 68/13, 106/12; bot yf, unless, 78/30.

**Both,** *conj.* but, 14/34, 22/7, 82/25, 50/4; bott, 22/32; bot, 106/12.

**Boxome,** *adj.* obedient, loyal, non-rebellious, 32/29.

**Boxom-fastines,** *sb.* buxomfastness

firm obedience, 62/18; buxumfast-
nys, 63/18.
Branden, *vb.* burnt, 14/24; brandyn,
15; branten, 120/33.
Brouken, *vb.* brook, enjoy, hold, 34/13.
Buryles, *sb.* buryels, burials, graves,
37/21; (pute, pits, 36/18).
Buttellerie, *sb.* butlery, buttery, 62/27.
O. Fr. *bouteillerie.*
By, *vb.* be, 106/15.
By, *prep.* about, near, 15/6; by so, on
these terms, 24/23; by forward, by
agreement, 74/9; by-halues, besides,
aside, 74/24; by so that, on the
terms that, 24/23.
Bygger, *sb.* buyer, 40/2, 7.
Byled, *vb.* built, 128/10.
Bynyn, *vb.* benime, take away, 68/22.
Bysay, *adj.* busy, 99/18.
Byth, *vb.* beeth, are, 33/26.

Cabilys, *sb.* cables, 13/12.
Calange, *sb.* challenge, claim, 21/1.
O. Fr. *Calanger.*
Campled, *vb.* wrangled, contended,
fought, 74/33; camplid, 75/33.
Camplynges, *sb.* wranglings, contests,
battles, 126/13.
Candrede, *sb.* cantred, hundred, 56/21;
cantred, 8/19, 12/33; a Cantrede is
'an hundret toun lond' (100 town-
lands or townships), 124/2.
Castel, *vb.* castle, fortify, 127/22;
castely, 126/22; casteled, 128/3.
Cee, *sb.* see: Cce churche, Cathedral,
37/31.
Chamfaste, *adj.* shamefast, 76/13.
Chase, *pp.* chosen, 124/12.
Cheffar, *sb.* trade, 12/7.
Chek-toth, *sb.* cheek-tooth, grinder,
double tooth, 108/8.
Chepmen, *sb.* chapmen, 38/33.
Cheuetayn, *sb.* chieftain, 26/11.
Chippe, *sb.* ship, 13/13; chippis, ships,
13/6.
Chippmen, *sb.* shipmen, 13/10.
Churchey, *sb.* churchyard, 71/26;
church-hay, 63/32.
Clene, *adv.* clean, quite, entirely, 146/7.
Clenly, *adv.* cleanly, quite, wholly,
121/3, 145/15; clenlych, 120/3.
Clepynge, *sb.* calling, call, 76/2.

Clewe, *vb.* cleft, clave, 31/34, 71/32.
Clos, *sb.* close, enclosed land, 10/5.
Come, *sb.* arrival, coming, 108/15,
120/30; comys, 109/15.
Comerous, *adj.* cumbrous, difficult to
pass, 54/8.
Comynly, *adv.* in common, together,
34/33, 38/30.
Condicones, *sb.* 125/15; theves, 124/15.
Conquestre, *sb.* conquest, 56/22. O. Fr.
Constytucions, *sb.* constitutions, laws,
64/26.
Cornelis, *sb.* crenelles, battlements,
16/31.
Corpus domini, *sb.* mass-wafer, 52/23.
Coste, *sb.* purpose (It.), 68/4, 74/17.
Costes, *sb.* coasting-vessels?, 80/5.
Croice, *sb.* cross, 36/29; cros, 37/29.
O. Fr. *crois.*
Croun, *sb.* crown of the head, 42/27;
croune, 42/24.
Culuertnesse, *sb.* falseness, villainy,
126/31.
Cytteyns, *sb.* citizens, 122/27. O. Fr.
*citeien; citayn.*

Dawes, *sb.* days, out of d. = out of
life, 34/10, 76/4.
Defended, *vb.* = defendeth, let us de-
fend, *imper.*, 20/28.
Defeuly, *vb.* defoul, tread under foot,
35/29; defouly, 34/29.
Dele, *sb.* deal, part, 62/21.
Deled, *vb.* dealt, divided, 104/25.
Delycion, ? *sb.* daintiness, 98/13.
Delycious, *adj.* delicate, dainty, 99/14.
Demyd, *pp.* deemed, doomed, sen-
tenced, 35/15.
Dennysh, 46/17; Danish.
Derne, *adj.* hidden, 18/30, 114/22.
Dernely, *adv.* secretly, privily, 78/8.
Derward, *adj.* dearworth, precious,
110/34; derwarthest, most valuable,
36/25.
Destrued, *pp.* destroyed, 106/10.
Deue, *adj.* deaf, 44/13.
Deynously, *adv.* disdainfully, 72/3.
Didden, dydde, *vb.* See *Do.*
Do, *vb.* put, 30/6, 38/34, 94/16; turn,
76/6; done hym on, set him on,
100/3; didde, *past t.* turned, 16/31;
didden, set, 10/1; dydde, set, 70/7.

Dobbe, *vb.* dub, 94/13.

Dome, *sb.* judgment, 34/14.

Dotous, *adj.* doubtful, uncertain, 86/17; doutos, 87/17; doutouse, 24/13.

Doute, *vb.* fear, 24/15.

Drawen, *vb.* protract, lead, 50/4.

Dredlyche, *adj.* dreadly, dreadful, terrible, 114/9.

Drent, *vb.* drowned, 32/5.

Durke, *adj.* dark, 50/9.

Durknesse, *sb.* darkness, 50/10.

Durre, *sb.* door, 42/22.

Dyd, *vb.* set, placed, 74/29. See *Do.*

Dynt, *sb.* dint, stroke, 46/17.

Dysheryted, *vb.* 40/20; disinherited. D for th, 16/34.

Day, *pron.* they, 10/19, 12/21, 24/10.

Droġn, *prep.* through, 12/24, 14/8, 18/9, 22/7.

I-Drow, *pp.* thrown, 18/1.

Dynge, *sb.* thing, 88/27.

Eche, *vb.* increase, 146/4.

Edwyte, *vb.* reproved, twitted, rebuked, 60/9.

Eft, *adv.* after, 82/13, 88/26, 90/1 efte, 108/29.

Elde, *sb.* eld, age, 58/30.

Eldren, (*adj.*) ? *sb.* forefathers' (or ancestral), 38/17; eldryn, 39/17.

Eldrene, *sb.* ancestors, 28/6, 7; eldryn, 29/6, 7.

Elf (fare), 17/13; helf (fare), 16/14; elves' doings.

Eme, *sb.* eam, nephew, 31/14, 73/35; emys, 15/33, 101/15.

Enchesoun, *sb.* occasion, cause, 88/2, 20/16.

Encombrement, *sb.* encumberment, obstruction, annoyance, harm, 22/13.

Eneche, *vb.* (? increase) ineche, implant, 92/1.

Engyn, *sb.* art, contrivance, 18/28.

Ense, *sb.* ends, 80/29.

Entre, *sb.* entry, 54/6; entreat, 55/7.

Entredyte, *vb.* interdict, lay under interdict, 68/15.

Enuy, *sb.* envy, 20/19.

Enuyouse, *adj.* envyous, 114/6; envyouse, emulous, 100/2.

Er, *adv.* ere, before, 120/29.

Erne, *vb.* earn, mourn, 34/28.

Erne, *sb.* eagle, 114/18.

Ers, *sb.* ears, 15/24.

Erthe-weyes, *sb.* ways under ground, 19/30.

Erth-hous, *sb.* underground dwelling, 120/31.

Estren, *adj.* eastern, east, 28/27.

Ette, *vb.* ate, 89/22.

Eunynge, *sb.* evening, equal, peer, 54/19.

Evyncrystyñ, *sb.* fellow - christian, 39/11, 67/14.

Exstymacioun, *sb.* suspicion, 129/14. O. Fr. *exstimation.*

Eygne, *sb.* eyes, 97/17.

Facon, *sb.* falcon, 58/4; faucoun gentel, 56/30.

Fale, *adj.* fele, many, 74/10, 86/4.

Falthyr, *sb.* fautors, favorers, partisans, 79/7. Fr. *fauteur.*

Fantstones, *sb.* fontstones, stone fonts, 64/33; fantstonys, 65.

Farcostes, *sb.* far-coasters?, 80/5, 81/5.

Fawes, *sb.* falls?, heavy, things dropt, 96/2; fawis, 97/2.

Febelier, *adj.* more feeble, 69/5.

Fele, *adj.* many, 16/10.

Felony, *sb.* villany, 102/3.

ffer, *adv.* f. with*in*-yn nyght, far into the night, 16/9.

Ferd, *sb.* host, army, 14/5.

Ferde, *sb.* fear, 17/14.

Ferdnesse, *sb.* fear, fright, 20/29, 38/27.

Ferly, *adj.* strange, 16/29.

Ferly, *adv.* wonderfully?, 16/12.

Fersly, *adv.* fiercely, 17/11.

Ferth, *num. adj.* fourth, 118/19.

Festnen, *vb.* make firm, restore, 44/14.

Feynte, *adj.* faint, idle, 115/6.

Feyre, *adv.* far, 50/34.

Fikyllid, *vb.* temporised, 145/9.

Fleted, *vb.* floated, 116/26.

Fletes, *sb.* fleets, 80/9; flittes, 81/9; flot, 126/23; flytte, 127/23.

Fleysly, *adj.* fleshly, fleshy, 100/1.

Flittes, *sb.* See *Fletes.*

Flote, *sb.* fleet, herd of swine, 74/1.

Flowen, *vb.* fled, 96/21.

Fobler, *adj.* feebler, 68/6.

Foderes, *sb.* deceivers, 148/3.

Folk, *adj.* ? for foble, feeble, 50/15.

Folke-mele, indiscriminately, 36/3.

Foolrede, *sb.* fool's counsel, foolery, folly, 68/20; fooly, 69.

Foot-falle, *vb.* prostrate oneself, 62/18.

For, *conj.* in order that, 104/24.

Foroleue, *vb.* cleft, 58/2; for-clew, 59/2.

Fore-lete, *vb.* let go, 68/29.

For-hold, *pp.* withheld, kept unburied, 108/14.

Forlese, *vb.* forelost, lost, 54/11.

Formane, *sb.* leader, 36/1; formene, front ranks, 30/33.

Forme, *adj.* first, 64/15; formost, *super.*, 50/28; formyst, 51.

Forshape, *pp.* misshapen, 130/25.

Forsoke, *vb.* renounce, refuse, decline, 4/13, 78/17; for-sok, 72/16.

Forsoken, *vb.* declined, 104/12.

Forswely, *vb.* swallow up, 58/27.

Fort, *conj.* till, 84/27, 126/11.

Fortelet, *sb.* fortlet, 116/6.

Forth, (before 'with ') *adv.* forthwith, 20/5, 90/20, 104/32.

For-pane, *conj.* Nat f. notwithstanding, 4/1.

For-they, *conj.* therefore, 73/22; ffor-thy, 72/23.

Forthmost, *adj.* foremost, 16/4.

Forume, *sb.* form, 39/12.

Forwarde, *sb.* bargain, 10/12; agreement, 74/9, 108/30; forward-makynge, m. of agreements, 128/9.

Fourdyr, *adv.* further, 15/25.

Franchise, *sb.* freedom, 20/15.

Fresly, *adv.* fiercely, 14/12, 35/34; fressely, 81/9.

Frightnes, *sb.* fright, 16/15, 26.

Fryst, *num.* first, 17/4, 31/33.

Fyf, *num. adj.* five, 62/21; fywe, 63/21.

Fylthed(e), *sb.* filthhead, filthiness, 64/6, 65/6.

Fyne, *sb.* fine, 66/10.

Galosis, *sb.* gallows, 35/16.

Galyots, *sb.* pirates ?, 22/32.

Garnesyd, *pp.* garnished, fortified, 51/1. Fr. *garnir.*

Gentil, *sb.* gentry, set, 101/17.

Gentryce, *sb.* set, clan, 112/2.

Gentrye, *sb.* gentry, 100/18.

Gestes, *sb.* deeds, 120/10.

Gettynges, *sb.* gettings, gain, plunder, 26/34.

Girsliche, *adv.* terribly, 14/22 (? *adj.*).

Good, *sb.* goods, 54/5.

Grad, *vb.* cried out, 4/1.

Greped, *vb.* griped, gripped, 126/26.

Grewid, *vb.* grieved, pained, 109/9; grewid, *pp.* 39/25.

Grymly, *adj.* dreadful, terrible, 59/13.

Gylte, *sb.* fault, 40/8.

Gyued, *vb.* gyved, fettered, 60/10; gywid, 61/10.

Half, *sb.* side; ethere h., either side, 8/19; euerich h., every side, 4/16; euche h., each side, 5/18; hys h., his side, 24/32; oon h., one side, 22/25; a south h., on the south side, 30/16; on his moþer half, on his mother's side, 8/15; halue, *pl.* 100/21.

Halte, *vb.* held, 64/10; holte, hold, 64/11.

Halowene, *sb.* saints, 122/1; halwene, 44/11.

Hame, *pron.* them, 4/12.

Hamlynge, *adj.* ambling, 89/21.

Hand, *sb.* other h., second hand, 78/17.

Har, *pron.* their, 9/17, 10/20, 74/31, 120/30; hare, 31/14; theirs, 32/15.

Har, *adv.* ere, sooner.

Hard, *pp.* heard, 29/32.

Hardynes, *sb.* hardiness, boldness, 110/35.

Haris, *pron.* theirs, 49/33; hars, 48/34.

Hauteyne, *adj.* haughty, 76/16. O. Fr. *hautain.*

Haw, *vb.* have, 34/7; hawydyn, had, 27/7.

Haye, *sb.* hay, haw, churchyard, 63/32; 62/32.

Hedid, *pp.* headed, beheaded, 151/8.

Heed, *sb.* ? head, 78/33; heeddes, heads, princes ?, 34/28.

Heere, *sb.* hair, hair-cloth, 42/5; here, 43/5.

Hegh, *vb.* hight ('was callid'), 92/23.

Hegheste, *adj.* highest ('host' 12/33), 13/33.

Heghlygh, *adv.* highly, 90/25.

Helf far, 16/14, *sb.* elves' doing.

Helle, *vb.* helde, 2/24.

Hellen, *vb.* conceal, hide, 78/1.

Hent, *vb.* received, 10/35; henten, grasp, seize, 56/33, 80/26.

Herbrowe, *vb.* harbour, seek shelter, 66/6.

Here, *pron.* their, 18/29.

Here, *adv.* here, 32/10.

Herly, *adv.* early, 70/7.

Herne, *sb.* nook, corner, 116/7.

Herrer, *sb.* herre, lord, 116/30.

Herth, *sb.* heart, 2/8, 22/28, 50/20.

Herthly, *adj.* earthly, 66/4.

Hertly, *adv.* heartily, courageously, 52/2; hertely, 53/2.

Het, *vb.* was named, 2/3.

Heudes, *sb.* heads, 14/17.

Hey, *adj.* high, 57/29.

Heye, *sb.* 70/27. See *Church-hey.*

Heyth, *adj.* high, noble, 22/32.

Hite, *pron.* it, 25/20.

Hoft-sithes, *adv.* oftentimes, 16/14.

Hold, *adj.* whole, faithful, 60/14; holde, whole, healthy, 59/24.

Homward, *adv.* take h., go home, 86/3.

Hoped, *vb.* looked to, trusted in, had confidence in, 70/22.

Horynesse, *sb.* filthiness, 66/27. Comp. *horowe,* foul, used by Chaucer, pronounced *horry* in Devon. H.

Host, *sb.* army, 16/10, 11, 104/26, 144/2.

Host, *adj.?* heat, hext, highest, largest, 12/32.

Hostyngis, *sb.* expeditions, armies, 17/14.

Hungrod, *adj.* hungered, hungry, 116/8.

Hurtyng, *sb.* hurting, hurt, 16/34.

Hym, *pron.* him; hym þriddesom, comp. Gr. αὐτὸς τρίτος, 14/1, 32/20.

Hyrynge, *adj.* hireling, waged, 22/31.

Iappynge, *sb.* japing, jesting, 54/26; Iaypynge, 55/27.

I-bansheth, *pp.* banished, 24/1; y-banshet, 25/1.

I-bydde, *pp.* abided, stayd, 62/8.

I-corne, *pp.* chosen, 22/18.

I-deleth, *pp.* dealt, divided, 66/19.

I-destrued, *pp.* destroyed, 84/32.

I-dobbed, *pp.* dubbed, 94/13.

I-drow, *pp.* thrown, d=th, 18/1.

I-dyght, *pp.* prepared, 58/19.

I-endeth, *pp.* ended, 22/16.

I-flow, *pp.* fled, 46/27.

I-fulled, *pp.* baptized, 64/33; yfullid, 65/33.

I-garnset, *pp.* garnished, fortified, 50/1.

I-hard, *pp.* heard, 28/32.

I-heded, *pp.* beheaded, 150/7.

I-helled, *pp.* iheled, covered, 10/21.

I-herberged, *pp.* filled, stowed, 108/34; I-herbergide, 109/34.

I-herberowide, *pp.* harboured, sheltered, 63/31; I-horberowed, 62/31.

I-hodet, *pp.* hooded, 132/28.

I-hokred, *pp.* insulted, 140/16.

I-horied, *pp.* defiled, 138/32.

I-hosted, *pp.* hosted, quartered, 16/9.

I-lacet, *pp.* laced, 10/17.

Illy, *adv.* in an ill way, 78/7.

Ilyche, *adv.* alike, 66/19.

I-meygnet, *pp.* mingled, 102/27.

Inamliche, *adv.* namely, especially, 16/28.

In-leyde, *pp.* laid in, 37/21.

I-primseined, *pp.* catechized, 64/32, 65/32.

I-quenyted, *pp.* pleased, 36/35.

I-retted, *pp.* charged with, 68/26.

I-roted, *pp.* rooted, 20/27, 112/3, 148/18.

I-sacred, *pp.* sacred, consecrated, 132/28.

I-scomfyte, *pp.* discomfited, 116/20.

I-shent, *pp.* ruined, 68/28, 38/16.

I-shwerne, *pp.* sworn, 24/26.

I-slawe, *pp.* slain, 80/13.

I-stablet, *pp.* established, 64/27.

I-storbet, *pp.* disturbed, 124/34.

I-suywed, *pp.* issued, shot, 116/9.

I-swewed, *pp.* showed, 64/12.

I-told, *pp.* reckoned, 2/4.

I-wepned, *pp.* armed, 80/11.

I-worth, *pp.* become, 102/6, 148/14.

I-wyted, *pp.* blamed, 8/13.

Kappe, *sb.* 46/17; lappe, R. 47/17.

Karue, *vb.* k. of, cut off, 14/23.

Kene, *adj.* keen, fierce, sharp, 112/33.

Kepynge, *sb.* keeping, watch, guard, 53/10; kypynge, 52/9.

**Kernel,** *sb.* battlement, 10/28.

**Knyghten,** *sb.* knights', 92/15.

**Kynde,** *sb.* kind, nature; of k., by nature, naturally, 18/27; Throgh k. of Troy, Through our Trojan origin, 22/26.

**Kynde,** *adj.* natural, own, 6/27.

**Kyndly,** *adj.* kindly, natural, 76/16.

**Kyndly,** *adv.* kindly, naturally, by birth, 22/28 ; kyndlych, 22/24.

**Kynly,** *adv.* by kin, by birth, 23/24. See *Kyndly.*

**Laked,** *vb.* enjoyd, 132/29 ; lakyd, 133/29.

**Large,** *adj.* bounteous, generous, 25/2; largh, 24/1.

**Laser,** *sb.* lazar, leper, 44/13.

**Lastes,** *sb.* faults, deceits, 102/21.

**Latest,** *adj.* last in place, 52/1.

**Lede,** *adj.* folk, 4/24; leed, 64/18.

**Lef,** *adj.* dear, 108/8 ; lefe, 111/34.

**Lered,** *adj.* learned, 42/2 ; lerid, 43/2.

**Leth,** *vb.* let, hindered, 52/7 ; leth, allowed, causd, 64/5.

**Lette,** *sb.* let, hindrance, 94/5.

**Leue,** *adj.* dear, 108/6.

**Leue,** *vb.* leave, omit, 108/10.

**Leuet,** *vb.* loved, 118/35.

**Lewed,** *adj.* lewd, uneducated, vulgar, 42/2 ; lewid, 43/2.

**Lewidly,** *adv.* lewdly, wickedly, 47/30.

**Leyden,** *vb.* leyden on, laid on, attacked, 96/2 ; leydyn, 97/2.

**Lif,** *adj.* lief, pleasing, 8/22.

**Lodderly,** *adv.* wickedly, 22/33.

**Lodesmane,** *sb.* pilot, leader, 22/21 ; 36/28.

**Loge,** *sb.* lodge, wattled hut, 10/3.

**Loghe,** *adj.* low, short, 88/10.

**Loly,** *adj.* grim, terrible, 40/8, 58/12.

**Lolych,** *adj.* lovely, affable, 103/18; louelyche, 102/18.

**Lome,** *adv.* often, frequently, 44/36.

**Lost,** *sb.* loss, 112/23 ; loste, 146/12 ; lostes, 8/2 ; lostis, 97/24; Lostys, 9/2.

**Loth,** *adj.* hateful, unpleasant, 14/6, 30/19.

**Lotles,** *adj.* buxom, obedient, 114/4.

**Lout,** *vb.* l. ham, lout themselves, do obeisance, 44/26.

**Lowe,** *sb.* love, 131/14.

**Lych,** *sb.* like, body, 88/26 ; lyche, 89.

**Lyddere,** *adj.* lither, bad, wicked, 44/6, 68/7 ; lyder, 32/14.

**Lyddyrly,** *adv.* litherly, wickedly, 46/30.

**Lyddernysse,** *sb.* litherness, wickedness, 76/29.

**Lygne,** *adj.* gentle ?, 102/17.

**Lyket,** *vb.* was liked, pleasd, 34/14.

**Lyme,** *sb.* limit, bond ?, 62/18.

**Lyuo,** *sb.* life, 82/32.

**Manequelleres,** *sb.* mankillers, 125/16.

**Maner,** *sb.* manner; many m. metes, many kind of meats, 62/28; manners, politeness, 22/10.

**Mane-shipe,** *sb.* manship, courtesy, 4/33; manshype, 70/12.

**Manly,** *adv.* in a manly way, 24/6.

**Manred,** *sb.* homage, 56/20.

**Man-shyply,** *adv.* worshipfully, reverently, 66/22.

**Manslaghtres,** *sb.* manslaughterers, 124/16.

**Mansynge,** *sb.* cursing, excommunication, 120/17.

**Marche,** *sb.* march, border, 72/18 ; 146/31.

**Mayny,** *sb.* 115/22. See *Meigne.*

**Me,** *pron.* men (comp. German man), one, they, 16/5, 24/14, 32/27, 42/10, 70/33.

**Meet-yeuer,** *sb.* meat-giver, 54/25 ; met-yeuer, 112/36. Comp. *mete-gavel.*

**Meigne,** *sb.* household troops, 22/18 ; menny, 79/28 ; mennye, 79/13 ; meny, 115/10 ; meygnees, 66/5 ; meyne, 26/8 ; meynne, 39/5 ; meyngne, 27/9. O. Fr. *meignee, meyne.*

**Mekely,** *adv.* humbly, kindly, 48/2.

**Membres,** *sb.* manly m., manly members, privy parts, 44/18.

**Merres,** *sb.* meres, boundaries, 38/17.

**Meste,** *adv.* most, 42/7.

**Mesury,** *sb.* misery, 43/15.

**Meteful,** *adj.* moderate, 113/24. See *Methefull.*

**Methe,** *sb.* moderation, 98/12.

**Methefull,** *adj.* moderate, 112/24.

**Methelyche,** *adj.* moderate, 70/18 ;

methlych, 98/28; metlych, 76/15; metlyche, 98/10; middle-sized.

Mich, *adj.* much, large, 34/27; mich yuell, much or great evil, leprosy, 32/7.

Modelyng, *sb.* meddling, 56/18.

Mone, *sb.* moan, complaint, 28/23.

Morowenynge, *sb.* morning, 82/21.

Most, *vb.* must, could, 40/22.

Mostdele, *adv.* mostdeal, mostly, 16/1.

Mostwhat, *adv.* mostly, for the most part, 88/17.

Mother-church, *sb.* cathedral, 36/29.

Motynge, *sb.* mooting, pleading, disputing, 144/29.

Mych, *adj.* large, 56/29, 74/1; myche, 74/2.

Myght & mayn, might & main, 116/15.

Mynyed, *vb.* reminded, warned, 74/29, 84/25.

Mys-byfelle, *vb.* misbefell, fell amiss, 124/15; mys-be-felle, 125/16.

Mysdone, *vb.* misdo, 101/32.

Myse-lyckenys, *sb.* mislikeness, strange shape (a wolf-woman), 131/25.

Myssayse, *sb.* misease, 40/5. O. Fr. *mesaise.*

Myssayse, *adj.* miseased, 114/23; mysaaysid, 115/22.

Na, *adv.* not, 112/2.

Name, *sb.* name, 6/33.

Name, *vb.* took, 6/12; name, 2/22, 23; n. an hand, 72/24; namen, 80/4; n. sekernesse, took surety, 74/8.

Namely, *adv.* especially, 52/17, 66/4.

Namy, *vb.* name, 130/10.

Narow, *adv.* narrowly, closely, 40/21; narowe, 4/19; narrow, 41/22, 97/10.

Naroweis, narrow ways, 81/26.

Nas, *vb.* ne was, was not, 16/21, 26/21, 72/16, 114/8.

Nat forthy, *conj.* notwithstanding, nevertheless, 76/20, 77/22.

Nathales, *conj.* nevertheless, 78/10.

Neb, *sb.* (? nose), face, *vultus*, 98/11.

Neght, *adv.* nigh, nearly, 26/13.

Nembre, *sb.* number, 101/22; nenbre, 100/23.

Ner, *vb.* ne were, were not, 30/31, 100/8.

Neue, *sb.* nephew, 14/33. See *eme.*

Neuer (ne were), *vb.* should never be, 121/18; neuere, 120/18.

Never no more, 48/31.

Neyght, *adv.* nigh, near, 74/16.

Nobelych, noblych, *adv.* nobly, 35/29, 34/29.

Noon-dayes, *sb.* noonday, 50/32.

North, by n., to the north of, 70/26.

Nuy, *sb.* noy, vexation, affliction, 90/7. Comp. *noxia.*

Nyst, ne wist, knew not, 4/29.

Nythe, *sb.* a nythe = at night, 72/33.

O, *num.* one, 106/12; oo, 89/26, 106/12.

O, *prep.* of, 108/34.

Of, *adv.* off, 12/11, 14/23, 32/4, 74/32.

Oftere, *adv.* oftener, 54/22.

Oke, *vb.* ached, paind, 108/9.

Omost, omyste, *adv.* overmost, uppermost, 106/1, 107/1.

Ond, *sb.* hatred, malice, 110/30; onde, 111/30.

Onful, *adj.* ondfull, malicious, 102/24; onfull, 103/24.

Onþer, *prep.* under, 6/31.

Opyn, *adj.* open, uncovered, 42/22.

Ordeynly, *adv.* well o. = in good order, 46/12.

Ortrow, *sb.* overtrow, mistrust, suspicion, 128/14, 132/14; artrow, 133.

Ost, *adj.* burnt ?, 50/2.

Ostmen, *sb.* hostmen, soldiers, 82/23.

Ostynge, *sb.* hosting, expedition, 16/14; see *Hostyngis.*

Oper, *conj.* other, or, 24/6.

Other, *adj.* second, 50/29, 76/12, 88/8.

Ouerd[r]ede, *vb.* ouerdrede, overdreaded, 14/20.

Ouergoste, *vb.* goest beyond, 38/17.

Ouer-hand, *sb.* upperhand, superiority, 34/6, 50/11, 106/3, 118/23.

Ouersaille, *vb.* sail over, upset ?, 16/12.

Ouerthrowen, *vb. pass.* be prostrated, 62/21.

Ouer-truste, *sb.* overboldness, presumption, 22/10. Comp. *Overhope.*

Oure, *pron.* ours, 24/7, 96/15.

Out-chese, *vb.* choose out, 34/8.

Out-commyn, *adj.* come from foreign parts, 12/29; out-comen, 18/5.

Out-tak, *pp.* outtaken, except, 122/8.

Owne, *adj.* = own house, tent, 62/31.
Owre, *prep.* over, 130/2.
Ows, *pron.* us, 22/3, 30.

Paas, *sb.* pass, 104/22 ; pas, 104/25 ; paace, 55/9.
Panetrye, *sb.* pantry, 62/27. Fr. *paneterie.*
Pany, *sb.* penny, 92/5.
Paralys, *adj.* paralysed folk, 44/14.
Parlement, *sb.* conference, 6/21, 18/11, 72/31. O. Fr. *parlement.*
Party, *sb.* part, side, 110/1.
Party arms, arms vertically divided, 10/4.
Pelfre, *sb.* pilfer, plunder, 52/8. O. Fr. *pelfrer.*
Pledynge, *sb.* suing, 112/20.
Plenary, *adv.* fully, openly, 31/27.
Pleneden, *vb.* sported, 74/18 ; pleydyn, 75.
Plente, *sb.* generosity, 102/31.
Plete, *sb.* plate, 46/10.
Poere, *sb.* power, O. Fr. 48/11.
Postes, *sb.* pillars, supports, 120/6.
• Powere, *sb.* forces, 2/22, 4/17.
Prayes, *sb.* preys, booty, 80/1.
Prayes-takynge, *sb.* taking of booty, 78/27 ; pray-takynge, 118/11.
Praye, *vb.* prey, plunder, 80/3, 23 ; preedyn, plundered, 81/3.
Presons, *sb.* prisoners, 54/5, 15.
Primseine, *vb.* 'sign with the cross, make a catechumen,' 64/32.
Priuisant, *adj.* foreseeing ?, 80/28.
Prout, prowt, *adj.* proud, 22/5, 38/20.
Prow, *vb.* prove, 85/5.
Prutter, *adj.* prouder, 56/7.
Pullid, *vb.* plundered, robbed, 145/9.
Pullynge, *sb.* pilling, plundering, 112/21.
Purueynge, *adj.* provident, prudent, 98/21.
Pute, *sb.* pit, 36/18.
Pylfre, *sb.* pilfer, plunder, pillage, 80/4, 114/24. O. Fr. *pelfrer.*
Pynsynge, *sb.* affliction, 88/6.

Queller, *sb.* killer, 44/5.
Queme, *vb.* please, satisfy, 54/30, 98/15.
Quenyntyse, queyntyse, *sb.* cunning, craft, 98/22, 99/22. O. Fr. *quointise.*

Quethens, *vb.* overcome R., 44/15.
Queynt, *adj.* cunning, sly, wily, 26/1, 98/21 ; quent, 27/1 ; queynth, 128/2.
Quyte, *adj.* quit, clear, free, 96/20.
Quytten, *pp.* free, clean away, 80/27.

Raas, *sb.* race, rush, 16/12.
Radyr, *adv.* rather, more willingly, 7/13 ; earlier, before, 91/20.
Raght, *vb.* raught, recked, 32/9.
Ran, *vb.* r. to harme, 112/26.
Rascayll, *sb.* rascal, rabble, 50/21. O. Fr. *rascayle.*
Rathe, *adv.* soon, 24/29, 84/1 ; rather, sooner, 28/23, 68/14 ; before, 90/20, 130/4.
Rather, *adj.* earlier, previous, original, 86/4, 88/2.
Raunceoun, *sb.* ransom, 46/29.
Rebuked, *vb.* repulsed, checked, 34/34.
Recet, *sb.* refuge, harbour, 18/29, 30/28, 56/5 ; recette, 19/29, 31/28.
Recheste, *vb.* reckest, 108/9.
Rede, *sb.* counsel, 10/18, 68/33.
Remewid, *vb.* removed, 147/13.
Rere, *vb.* rear, raise, exalt, 46/2 ; rerid, took, captured, lifted, 107/30.
Rescewyd, *vb.* received, 123/27.
Reue, *vb.* rob, 114/3 ; rew, 115/3.
Reuer, *sb.* riever, robber, 112/21.
Reut, *sb.* ruth, pity, 8/1 ; reuth, 22/34, 54/18.
Reuthful, *adj.* ruthful, 32/23.
Reuynge, *sb.* rieving, plundering, 144/31 ; rewynge, 145/25 ; reyuynge, 145/32.
Rewe, *vb.* rue, regret, 146/1.
Robbed, *vb.* plundered, 80/23.
Rodes, *sb.* r. crucyfyed, crucifixes, 122/1.
Roghly, *adv.* r. lokynge, rough looking, 88/9.
Row, *adv.* r. lokynge, rough looking, 89/9. A. S. *ráw.*
Ruthlynge, *sb.* rattling, 16/13.
Rychesshe, *sb.* riches, 96/24. Fr. *richesse.*
Rygge, *sb.* back, 58/2.
Ryght, *vb.* r. vp, raise up, 44/3 ; set up again, restore, 86/4.
Ryuely, *adv.* especially ?, 128/12.

M

**Salletis,** *sb.* sallets, light helmets, 11/24.

**Sam-crysp,** *adj.* somewhat curled, 98/11; **sam-roed,** *adj.* somewhat ruddy, 54/27; same rede, 89/8; saunrede, 88/8. A. S. *sam,* half.

**Saue,** *vb.* saw, 49/6, 146/11.

**Sawe,** *prep.* save, except, 18/21, 54/10.

**Sawe,** *vb.* save, 73/6; sawit, saved, 4/23.

**Schavnge,** *sb.* change, 51/6.

**Scomfited,** *pp.* discomfited, 117/19.

**Screwid,** *adj.* shrewd, cursed, bad, evil, 69/6.

**See way,** seaway (comp. highway, roadway), 80/3.

**Seke,** *adj.* sick, 66/13.

**Sekernesse,** *sb.* security, 74/8; syke[r]nesse, 50/7.

**Sekiritesse,** *sb.* securities, bonds, 6/22.

**Selcouth,** *adj.* various, 28/33; wonderful, 44/11, 120/1, 126/13.

**Selth,** *sb.* happiness, benefit, 50/8, 92/18; success, 98/23.

**Selue,** *adj.* same, 100/18.

**Selyly,** *adv.* happily, 42/32.

**Semblant,** glad s., 98/12; sterne s., 98/27; fayr s., 102/18; semblant, 112/36; look, countenance.

**Senne,** *sb.* synod, 120/15.

**Senthe,** *adj.* seventh, 58/30; Senfte, 59/29.

**Seysyne,** *sb.* seisin, possession, 82/12.

**Sheldrun,** *sb.* shields, 31/29.

**Shendshype,** *sb.* injury, harm, 114/3; shenshipp, 115/3.

**Sho,** *pron.* she, 4/1.

**Shorthlych,** *adv.* shortly, presently, 114/22.

**Shroue,** *vb. int.* confessed, 130/23.

**Shyrth,** *sb.* shirt, 42/5.

**Sill,** *vb.* sell, 39/34. See *Syllene.*

**Sitè,** *sb.* city, 32/17, 18.

**Sithe,** *sb.* times, 26/6.

**Skyer,** *sb.* squire, 8/32, 33.

**Slaght,** *sb.* slaughter, 14/16, 20/28, 116/36, 138/32.

**Slaked,** *vb.* slacked, failed, 48/24.

**Sleghly,** *adv.* slily, 68/3.

**Sleghtes,** *sb.* contrivances, 128/13.

**Sleghtlych,** *adv.* craftily, 128/9; sleghtly, 144/17.

**Slouedyne,** *vb.* slow, 39/8.

**Smert,** *adj.* smart, sharp, rough; smert lond, rough wild land, 128/29.

**Smertly,** *adv.* smartly, vigorously, 104/33; smyrtly, 105/33.

**Smyth,** *vb.* smite, 24/12; *pt.* smote, 106/35.

**Snel,** *adj.* quick, active, 74/27.

**Snellych,** *adv.* quickly, 82/3.

**Soine,** *adv.* soon, 60/11.

**Soldrys,** *sb.* shoulders, 89/11.

**Solempnelych,** *adv.* solemnly, 90/25.

**Soth,** *adj.* sooth, true, 54/1.

**Sortelych,** *adv.* shortly, 93/14; Sortely, *adv.* shortly, 149/22.

**Sorynesse,** *sb.* sorriness, soreness, sorrow, 110/1, 112/23.

**Spares,** *sb.* battle-axe, 83/7; sparris, 17/12. See *Sparth.*

**Sparth,** *sb.* battle-axe, 74/11, 26, 33; sparthes, 16/13.

**Spendynge,** *sb.* spending, money, 78/27.

**Spourges,** *sb.* spurge, thing to get rid of, scourge, 112/3. Comp. O. Fr. *espourger.*

**Spousbrych,** *sb.* spousebreach, adultery, 102/23.

**Spousehede,** spoushode, *sb.* wedded state, 64/30.

**Sproty,** *adj.* thin, small, 54/28. Comp. *Sprot,* sprout, splinter.

**Stabil,** *vb.* establish, confirm, 69/29; stable, 68/30.

**Staluarthly,** *adv.* stalwartly, sturdily, 116/1.

**Stalwardnesse,** *sb.* stalwartness, strength, sturdiness, 52/2; stalwarthnesse, 54/20.

**Sted,** *sb.* stead, place, state, 22/35; 'state,' 23/35.

**Stordy,** *adj.* sturdy, 118/33; stordyer, 116/2.

**Storkes,** *sb.* storks, 28/24.

**Strange,** *adj.* strong, 54/8.

**Streynth,** *vb.* strength, strengthen, 68/30.

**Streynth,** *sb.* strength, force, meaning, 90/29, 96/14.

**Streyntnesse,** *sb.* strongness, strength, 94/24; streyntnys, 95/24.

**Stronge,** *adj.* strong, stormy, 66/33.

Stronge, *adv.* strongly, greatly, 4/3.

Stryffly, *adv.* strivingly (? for 'styffly'), 26/29. See *Styfly.*

Styd, *sb.* stead, place, 42/5; stydde, 42/6; styddes, places, 50/11.

Styfly, *adv.* strongly, valiantly, 80/8, 104/31.

Stylly, *adv.* stilly, in secret, 46/19, 150/12.

Stynte, *vb.* stopped, 111/30; stynt, 112/30.

Suget, *adj.* subject, 24/21; subyect, 26/33; subyett, 26/21. O. Fr. *Suget.*

Surnesse, *sb.* sureness, security, 51/7.

Surtey, swrte, *sb.* surety, 75/9. Fr. *Sûreté.*

Sybbe, *sb.* relation, 64/29.

Syblynges, *adv.* kinwise, with relatives, 102/23.

Sybrede, *sb.* relationship, 42/11.

Sydlynge, *adv.* sidling, obliquely, 94/19.

Sygge, *vb.* say, 54/18, 98/20.

Sykernesse, *sb.* security, 50/7. See *Sekernesse.*

Sykyrlychest, *adv.* most securely, 68/34.

Syllene, *vb.* sell, 38/32, 40/5.

Syller, *sb.* seller, 40/1.

Talent, *sb.* desire, wish, 6/25.

Tanked, *pp.* thanked, 14/19.

Tene, *sb.* tene, hatred, 4/12.

Tened, *pp.* grieved, vexed, 4/3.

Tethynges, *sb.* tithings, tithes, 66/1.

Thare, *conj.* there = where, 82/18.

Tharmes, *sb.* entrails, intestines, 88/4.

That, *adv.* ? read *thar*, 2/24, 65/5.

Thay, *dem.* those, 80/12, 14, 90/26, 116/3; they, the, 97/14.

Theghe, *conj.* though, 18/27, 32/9.

Ther, *conj.* where, 32/8, 57/30, 128/4; ther-to-for, *adv.* before, 63/29.

Thewes, *sb.* qualities, 16/28, 90/34.

Thewis, *sb.* thieves, 81/30.

Thedynge, *sb.* tiding, 10/7; thythyngis, 11/7, 35/31; tythynge, 6/15.

this, *adj.* these, 21/29.

Tho, *conj.* when, 4/9.

Tho, *prep.* to, 62/19.

Thoght, *conj.* though, 15/31, 32/7.

Tholie, *vb.* thole, endure, suffer, 4/20; polled, 42/3, 118/24; tholleth, sufferd, 38/15; tholy, *infin.* 40/5.

Tholmode, *adj.* forbearing, 98/15.

Thondred, *sb.* thunder, 58/28.

þorwe, ? go through with it, 28/12.

Thre, *num.* a thre, in three parts, 66/20; at thre, 67/20; tre, 14/5.

Thretynge, *sb.* threatening, 60/9; tretynge, 70/9.

þriddesum, *adj.* third, 14/1; thrydsome, 32/20; thyrdesum, 15/2.

þurleth, *vb.* thirleth, pierceth, 112/5.

Thus, from t. = from this, thence, 60/15.

Thwey, *num.* two, 12/35.

To, *adv.* too, 54/26, 82/3.

To, *art.* the, 10/27.

Toght, *vb.* thought, 16/25, 18/7.

To-hakked, *vb.* hackt to pieces, 82/2.

Toke, *vb.* reacht (to the knee), 116/27.

Told, *sb.* reckoned, 60/8; Moch told by ham-self, thought much of themselves, 148/3; tolde, thought, 94/1, 96/25, 97/24.

Tollid, *pp.* sufferd, 89/15.

Ton, *sb.* town, 12/33; ton land, townland, division of parish, 124/2.

Toun londe, *sb.* townland, township, division of parish, 125/2.

Tre, *adj.* three, 14/5.

Trewage, *sb.* tribute, 114/29; truage, 60/15. O. Fr. *treuage.*

Trogh, *prep.* through, 22/6, 26/1, 62/18; troghe, 20/24; troght, 28/29.

Trukked, *vb.* trucked, was bartered ?, 48/9.

Trywly, *adv.* truly, 12/27.

Turnet to, *vb.* turn to, 78/32.

Turues, *sb.* turves, turfs, 30/17.

Twonty, *num.* twenty, 50/28.

Tynge, *sb.* things, 24/14; thing, 28/8; notynge, nothing, 16/5, 20/9.

Tynke, *vb.* think, 6/26; tynken, 22/4.

Tywesday, tywesdaye, tyvysday, tywysday, *sb.* Tuesday, 98/1, 99/1, 2.

Vanhope, *sb.* wanhope, despair, 57/5.

Vend, *vb.* wend, 54/15.

Vepne, *sb.* weapon, 110/24.

Viokydly, *adv.* wickedly, 53/35.

Vncharged, *vb.* unloaded, 10/2.

**Vndedde,** *vb.* undid, ruined, 114/4; vndid, 115/4. See *Vndo.*

**Vnderfonge,** *vb.* receive, 62/19; vndrefynge, 4/32, 8/1; vndyrfonge, received, 9/1.

**Vndo,** *vb.* destroy, ruin, 20/6, 22/4, 84/11, 94/32.

**Vndrestondeth,** *vb.* understand ye, *imper.* 20/15.

**Vneuenly,** *adj.* uneven, unequal, inferior, 30/25.

**Vnhap,** *sb.* mishap, 56/5.

**Vnhele,** *sb.* misfortune, 126/12.

**Vnkede,** *adj.* strange, 20/20, 24/28; vnkyde, 31/6, 35/2.

**Vnkyndely,** *adv.* unnaturally, 87/18.

**Vnmercyably,** *adv.* unmerciably, mercilessly, 55/1. Comp. O. Fr. *merciable.*

**Vnmesurable,** *adv.* unmeasurably, beyond measure, 54/26; vnmeasurably, 55/26.

**Vnmetly,** *adv.* unmeetly, immoderately, 118/33.

**Vnnowmmerabill,** *adj.* innumerable, 19/15.

**Vnryght,** *sb.* wrong, injustice, 86/18; vnryght, 112/32.

**Vnsikere,** *adj.* unsure, 10/2.

**Vnsurnes,** *sb.* unsureness, insecurity, 51/8.

**Vnwardly,** *adj.* unwary, ignorant, 52/14.

**Vnwarly,** *adv.* unwarely, unexpectedly, 78/9.

**Vnwemmed,** *pp.* unstained, undefiled, 44/7, 92/4; vnwemyd, 93/3.

**Vpon,** *prep.* from, against, 106/32.

**Vp-rerid,** *pp.* raisd up, 13/2.

**Vptake,** *vb.* succour, help, support, 92/3.

**Vreke,** *vb.* wreak, avenge, 145/8.

**Vs-self,** ourselves, 22/1.

**Vyrchip,** *vb.* worship, 43/20.

**Vyrchipp,** *sb.* worship, 5/32.

**Wanhope,** *sb.* despair, 17/29, 32/12.

**Wanhoply,** *adj.* desperate, 88/6.

**Warliere,** *adv.* more warily, 12/19.

**Waryr,** *adv.* more cautiously, 13/19.

**Warytres,** *sb.* cursed trees, gallows, 34/16; 'galoais,' 35/16.

**Wax,** *vb.* grew, turnd, became, 2/7; arose, grew up, 26/22.

**Wayte,** *sb.* wait, expectation, 110/33.

**Wecchene,** *vb.* move, take, 36/31. A.S. *weecgan*: comp. weigh anchor.

**Wel,** *adv.* well, quite, 52/13; frankly, 78/30; much, 78/32; very, 2/11.

**Wenttene,** *vb.* think, say!, 106/8.

**Wenynge,** *sb.* whining, mourning, 54/17.

**Wepne,** *sb.* weapon, out of w. = out of harness, when not fighting, 54/31; wepyn, 55/31.

**Wepne,** *vb.* weapon, arm, 50/27; weppen, 16/32; wepyn, 17/30.

**Wer,** *vb.* war, 'wer the fight,' 10/27; were, 11/28; weren, *inf.* 82/16; werret, 3/6; werry, *inf.* 8/11; werryn, 83/16.

**Were,** *sb.* war, 125/32.

**Weued,** *sb.* altar, 42/26. A.S.

**Whan,** *vb.* won, 136/11.

**Whan-hopefully,** *adv.* unhopefully, despairingly, 16/30.

**What for,** on account of, 108/21.

**Whodyreso,** *adv.* whithersoever, 40/11.

**Whybelers,** *sb.* quibblers?, 148/3.

**Whyle,** *sb.* the w. = at that time?, 82/13; = *conj.* while, 82/15; That whylle = at that time, 124/20.

**Whyth,** *prep.* with, 130/31.

**Wille,** *adj.* wild, rough, 129/29.

**Willych,** *adv.* vilely, 54/1.

**Wndre,** *prep.* under, 28/7.

**Wnneth,** *conj.* unneth, scarcely, 88/15.

**Wnselth,** *sb.* disadvantage, 50/8.

**Wo,** *adj.* sorry, 4/35.

**Wode,** *adv.* wildly, madly, 94/34.

**Wodere,** *adj.* wilder, madder, 42/27.

**Woke,** *adj.* weak, 146/10.

**Wolf,** woman turned into a, 130.

**Wombe,** *sb.* belly, 88/4.

**Wonder,** *adj.* wonderful, 130/11.

**Wone,** *sb.* custom, usage, 34/15.

**Wonet,** *pp.* wont, accustomed, 38/33.

**Wonne,** *sb.* custom, 66/29. See *Wone.*

**Wood,** *adj.* mad, wild, 42/27.

**Worth,** *vb.* happened, existed, was, 38/26; became, 124/33.

**Worthly,** (worthy, R.) *vb.* honor, 92/3.

**Worthy,** *vb.* honor, 93/2.

Wrech, *sb.* wreak, vengeance, 120/34 ; wreche, 130/29.

Wrechydnys, *sb.* vengeance, 131/33.

Wrethe, *sb.* wrath, 74/22.

Wreyer, *sb.* wrayer, betrayer, 102/24.

Wryttes, *sb.* writs, writings, letters, 56/13 ; yne wrytte, in writing, 64/7.

Wryynge, *sb.* distorting, falsifying, 102/11.

Wayd, *pp.* used, accustomed, practist, skilful, 23/27.

Wyage, *sb.* voyage, 62/7.

Wylle, *sb.* at w. = as he wished, 58/22.

Wynd abydynge, wind-bound, waiting for wind, 50/6.

Wyrchiply, *adv.* worshiply, worshipfully, 67/22.

Wyssed, *vb.* directed, guided, 94/19 ; wissede, 95/19.

Wyt, *prep.* with, 50/15.

Wytht, *prep.* with, 46/17.

Wyttaylle, *sb.* victual, 104/6.

Wyttynge, *sb.* witting, knowledge, 27/3.

-y, *infin.* : See—assembly, castely, de-

fouly, forswely, namy, tholy, werry, 8/11.

Yardes, *sb.* boughs, sticks, 30/17.

Yarne, *vb.* rushed, ran, 82/3.

Y-cast, *pp.* purposed, 68/30.

Y-douted hym, was afraid, 86/1.

Y-dene, *pp.* done, 28/29.

Y-dropesie, *sb.* dropsy, 44/14.

Yern, *vb.* rush, hasten, 74/1, 76/2.

Yernynge, *vb.* running, rushing, 94/34.

Yew, *vb.* yeve, give, 55/32 ; yewyn, *pp.* 51/9.

Y-lacet, *pp.* laced, 52/11.

Y-leued, *pp.* believed, 102/10.

Ymeuyd, *pp.* moved, 101/4.

Yold, *sb.* yule, Christmas, 42/34 ; yolde, 43/34.

Yolowe, *adj.* yellow, 98/10.

Yorne, *adv.* gerne, eagerly, 92/21 ; yonre, 104/10.

Yought, *sb.* youth, 68/20, 118/27.

Youre, *adj.* yare, active, 114/27.

Yoy, *sb.* joy, 100/29.

Yroked, *pp.* rocked, 42/9.

Y-rotid, *pp.* rooted, 149/17.

Yuel, mich, much evil, leprosy, 32/7.

Yurne, *sb.* eagerness ?, 112/1.

# INDEX